The Award in Education and Training

Ann Gravells

 SAGE | LearningMatters

Los Angeles | London | New Delhi
Singapore | Washington DC

Learning Matters
An imprint of SAGE Publications Ltd
1 Oliver's Yard
55 City Road
London EC1Y 1SP

SAGE Publications Inc.
2455 Teller Road
Thousand Oaks, California 91320

SAGE Publications India Pvt Ltd 150
B 1/I 1 Mohan Cooperative Industrial Area
Mathura Road
New Delhi 110 044

SAGE Publications Asia-Pacific Pte Ltd
3 Chuch Street
#10–04 Samsung Hub
Singapore 049483

Editor: Amy Thornton
Development editor: Jennifer Clark
Production controller: Chris Marke
Project management: Deer Park Productions, Tavistock
Marketing manager: Catherine Slinn
Cover design: Wendy Scott
Typeset by: C&M Digitals (P) Ltd, Chennai, India
Printed and bound by Henry Ling Limited,
at the Dorset Press, Dorchester, DT1 1HD

Library of Congress Control Number: 2013940922

British Library Cataloguing in Publication Data

A catalogue record for this book is available from the British Library

MIX
Paper from
responsible sources
FSC
www.fsc.org   FSC® C013985

ISBN: 978 1 44627 434 7
ISBN: 978 1 44627 434 4 (pbk)

CONTENTS

Acknowledgements   vii
Author statement   viii
Preface   ix

Introduction   xi
- The structure of the book and how to use it   xi
- Teaching in the Further Education and Skills Sector   xii
- The Award in Education and Training   xiv
- Progression   xvii
- Educational abbreviations and acronyms   xviii

1 Teaching and learning   1
- Roles, responsibilities and boundaries   1
- Working with other professionals   7
- Quality assurance   9
- Record keeping   13
- Legislation, regulatory requirements and codes of practice   15

2 Factors contributing to learning   21
- The teaching, learning and assessment environment   21
- Motivation   29
- Learner age ranges and locations   33
- Learning preferences   38
- Theories of learning   42

3 Identifying needs   51
- Identifying needs of the organisation, teachers and learners   51
- Initial and diagnostic assessment   55
- Potential needs of learners and points of referral   56
- Inclusive learning   58
- Equality and diversity   60

4 Planning learning   67
- Teaching and learning plans   67
- Differentiation   80
- Resources   81
- Opportunities for English, maths and wider skills   85
- Using information and communication technology   89

5 Facilitating learning   97

- Induction, icebreakers and ground rules   97
- Teaching and learning approaches   102
- Communication, behaviour and respect   125
- Working with groups and individuals   130
- Maintaining a safe and supportive learning environment   137

6 Assessing learning   143

- Assessment in education and training   143
- Assessment types and methods   152
- Involving learners and others, peer and self-assessment   170
- Making decisions and giving constructive feedback   174
- Assessment records   176

7 Evaluating learning   181

- Evaluation in education and training   181
- Obtaining and responding to feedback   183
- Reviewing own progress and using learning journals   185
- Continuing professional development   189
- Using a checklist for teaching, learning and assessment   191

8 Micro-teaching   197

- The micro-teach session   197
- Planning to deliver your session   200
- Facilitating your session   201
- Assessing learning   203
- Evaluating your session   204

Award units

Appendix 1 Understanding roles, responsibilities and relationships in education and training   207
Appendix 2 Understanding and using inclusive approaches in education and training   208
Appendix 3 Understanding assessment in education and training   209

Learning and Development units

Appendix 4 Facilitate learning and development for individuals   210
Appendix 5 Facilitate learning and development in groups   211
Appendix 6 Understanding the principles and practices of assessment   212

Appendix 7 Qualification structure for the level 3 Award in Education and Training   214

Index   215

ACKNOWLEDGEMENTS

I would like to give a special thanks to the following people who have helped me with this edition of the book. They have freely given their time, knowledge and advice which has resulted in some excellent contributions.

Angela Faulkener
Dawn Upton
Gill Payne
Susan Simpson
Vic Grayson
Warwick Andrews

I would also like to thank the following people who have supported me with previous editions of this book.

Peter Adeney
John Fewings
Peter Frankish
Jacklyn Williams

Special thanks also go to my father Bob Gravells who is so good at proof reading and pointing out my typing errors.

I would like to thank my editor Jennifer Clark for her continued support and excellent guidance, Belbin Associates for permission to reproduce copyright material, and the Learning and Skills Information Service for the content of the units in the Appendices.

I would especially like to thank Amy Thornton from Learning Matters (which is now part of SAGE Publications Ltd) for her advice, encouragement and tremendous patience with all my questions, e-mails and telephone calls.

Particular thanks go to readers of previous editions of this book who have taken the time to give valuable feedback, which has greatly assisted me when preparing this edition.

I would like to dedicate this book to Gaynor Mount, who sadly died in May 2013. She was an extremely knowledgeable teacher educator and helped many people qualify into the profession. She was also a great inspiration to me, both personally and professionally.

Every effort has been made to trace the copyright holders and to obtain their permission for the use of copyright material. The publisher and author will gladly receive any information enabling them to rectify any error or omission in subsequent editions.

Ann Gravells
www.anngravells.co.uk

AUTHOR STATEMENT

Ann is a director of her own company *Ann Gravells Ltd*, an educational consultancy based in East Yorkshire. She specialises in teaching, training and quality assurance for the Further Education and Skills Sector.

Ann creates resources for teachers and learners such as PowerPoints and handouts for the Award in Education and Training, as well as other qualifications. These are available via her resource website www.anngravells.co.uk/resources

Ann is a consultant to The University of Cambridge's Institute of Continuing Education. She has worked for several Awarding Organisations producing qualification guidance, policies and procedures, and carrying out quality assurance of teacher training qualifications. She has been teaching in further education colleges since 1983.

Ann holds a Masters in Educational Management, a PGCE, a Degree in Education, and a City & Guilds Medal of Excellence for teaching. Ann is a Fellow of the Institute for Learning and holds QTLS status.

She is the author of:

- *Achieving your TAQA Assessor and Internal Quality Assurance Awards*
- *Delivering Employability Skills in the Lifelong Learning Sector*
- *Passing Assessments for the Award in Education and Training*
- *Passing PTLLS Assessments*
- *Preparing to Teach in the Lifelong Learning Sector*
- *Principles and Practice of Assessment in the Lifelong Learning Sector*
- *The Award in Education and Training*
- *What is Teaching in the Lifelong Learning Sector?*

She is co-author of:

- *Equality and Diversity in the Lifelong Learning Sector*
- *Passing CTLLS Assessments*
- *Planning and Enabling Learning in the Lifelong Learning Sector*

She has edited:

- *Study Skills for PTLLS*

The author welcomes any comments from readers; please contact her via her website. www.anngravells.co.uk

PREFACE

Teaching qualifications in post-compulsory education seem to change regularly. This is not only because of government regulations, but also to reflect different approaches to teaching, learning and assessment, and to keep pace with the influence of new technology.

This book was first published in 2006 and was called *Delivering Adult Learning* to reflect the level 3 qualifications at that time. It was successful due to its plain English approach and ability to put complex theories into language new teachers could understand. It was then revised and became *Preparing to Teach in the Lifelong Learning Sector* to complement the PTLLS qualifications introduced in 2007 which were offered at both level 3 and level 4. It has since been revised a further four times, and this edition is to support those working towards the *Award in Education and Training* which is now offered at level 3. The book is also appropriate to anyone taking relevant units from the Learning and Development qualification, or anyone just wanting to know what it's like to become a teacher.

This edition of the book has been fully updated and contains new bullet lists, tables and checklists. It follows a revised version of the teaching and learning cycle which is now referred to as the teaching, learning and assessment cycle. This has quality assurance at its centre but all aspects focus upon the learner.

The appendices contain all the learning outcomes and assessment criteria for the units which can be taken to achieve the Award.

Learners taking the *Award in Education and Training* would also benefit from reading the companion book *Passing Assessments for the Award in Education and Training*. This book, also by Ann Gravells, gives key advice on completing written and practical assessments to help achieve the qualification.

INTRODUCTION

In this chapter you will learn about:

- the structure of the book and how to use it
- teaching in the Further Education and Skills Sector
- the Award in Education and Training
- progression
- educational abbreviations and acronyms

The structure of the book and how to use it

This book will help you if you are working towards a teaching qualification; for example, the introductory *Award in Education and Training*, or if you just want to find out what it's like to be a teacher or trainer. The book has been written with new teachers in mind, in an accessible language and without too much educational jargon. It will also prove useful for staff working in human resources, administrators, technicians or in staff development and train the trainer roles.

The Further Education and Skills Sector, previously known as the Lifelong Learning Sector, includes those aged 14 and upwards who are in:

- adult education
- armed, emergency and uniformed services
- charitable organisations
- community education
- further education colleges
- higher education institutions and universities
- immigration and detention centres
- on site learning centres
- prisoner and offender centres
- private sector learning
- probation services
- public sector learning
- schools and academies
- sixth form colleges
- voluntary sector learning
- work-based learning

At the end of this chapter you will find a useful table listing many of the educational abbreviations and acronyms you might come across when teaching. At the end of all chapters is a *theory focus* which lists additional texts and websites to help inform your learning further.

The chapters relate to the full process of teaching, learning and assessment and cover the content of all the units which contribute towards the Award in Education and Training. The book is also applicable to anyone working towards units of other qualifications such as those known as *Learning and Development*. Throughout the book, the term *Award* will be used to denote the Award in Education and Training.

If you wish to know how the content of the book relates to the *Professional Standards for Teachers, Tutors and Trainers in the Lifelong Learning Sector (2006)* as well as the individual units of the *Award in Education and Training*, you will see a cross-referenced grid at the end of each chapter.

Throughout the book, the terms of *teacher* and *trainer* are used, even though you might carry out a different role: for example, *assessor, coach, counsellor, facilitator, instructor, learning co-ordinator, lecturer, mentor, presenter, supervisor* or *tutor*. The term *learner* is also used in the book and refers to other terms such as *apprentice, candidate, delegate, employee, participant, pupil, student* and *trainee*. The term *programme* is used to refer to courses and events which do or do not lead to qualifications.

You can work logically through the book by starting with Chapter 1, or you can just look up appropriate topics in the index (at the back) to access aspects relevant to your current area of study or interest. There are *activities* to enable you to think about how you will teach and assess, and *examples* to help you understand the process of teaching, learning and assessing. At the end of each chapter section are *extension activities* to develop, stretch and challenge your learning further. These are aimed at helping you work towards the requirements of the Award.

While this book covers the theory required for the Award, the companion book *Passing the Award in Education and Training* by Ann Gravells will help you put theory into practice and structure your work to meet the qualification's requirements.

If you are teaching nationally or internationally, some of the regulations and organisations referred to in this book might only be relevant in England. You are therefore advised to check what is current and applicable to the nation or country in which you work.

The appendices contain the learning outcomes and assessment criteria of each of the units which make up the Award.

Teaching in the Further Education and Skills Sector

Teaching is about helping someone reach their full potential, whether this is for personal or professional reasons. The Further Education and Skills Sector can include learners from age 14 upwards, therefore you have the opportunity to help make a difference to someone's life and career, which can be very rewarding.

If you are new to teaching, this could be because you are contemplating a change of profession, or you are required to take a particular teaching qualification because of your job role. Perhaps you have a hobby or a trade you would like to teach others; you know you are good at it and feel you have the skills and knowledge which you could pass on to others. While this book will guide you through the process of teaching, learning and assessing, it is up to you to ensure you are current with your subject knowledge. Depending upon where and what you are going to teach, you may not need to be qualified in your particular subject, but be able to demonstrate appropriate skills and knowledge at a particular level. Some subjects require you to have a level above that which you will teach, for example, holding a level 3 qualification to teach it at level 2. Others might not require you to hold a subject qualification at all, but just have the necessary skills and knowledge. If you are teaching towards qualifications, there will be a *Sector Skills Council* or *Standards Setting Body* responsible for your subject. They, along with the awarding organisation who accredit and certify the qualification, will decide what is required to deliver and assess in your subject area.

Not all programmes, courses and events will lead to qualifications: some are for leisure, for example, pottery, or learning a language; some are for work, for example, to help employees improve their knowledge and skills; and others are to help people improve their confidence or health and wellbeing. There are many programmes available for different reasons or to fulfil certain needs, for example, those aimed at reaching vulnerable people and deprived communities. Programmes are often known as *vocational* (work or employment related), *non-vocational* (leisure or interest related) and *academic* (theory related). Records of achievement or attendance might be issued to learners who are taking programmes which are not certificated by an awarding organisation.

The most important aspect of teaching is to ensure that learning is taking place. If you are currently teaching, your delivery methods might be based on experiences of how you were taught in the past. However, there are many different approaches you could use and this book will hopefully give you new ideas to use in a more engaging and motivating way. Teaching isn't just about delivering to groups in a classroom; it can take place in many different environments such as training in the workplace, public, private or voluntary settings, delivering sessions indoors, outdoors, or online. It can also be on a one-to-one basis or remotely via the internet or other means.

Professional teaching standards

In 2006, Professional Standards were produced for all new teachers in the Lifelong Learning Sector (now known as the Further Education and Skills Sector) who taught on government funded programmes in England. There are different requirements for teachers in Northern Ireland, Scotland and Wales.

The standards state that *the key purpose of the teacher is to create effective and stimulating opportunities for learning through high-quality teaching that enables the development and progression of all learners* (LLUK, 2006, page 2). Teachers in the Further Education and Skills Sector should value all learners individually and equally. They should be committed to lifelong learning and their own professional development, and strive for continuous improvement through reflective practice.

The full standards are based on six domains (A-F):

A Professional values and practice

B Learning and teaching

C Specialist learning and teaching

D Planning for learning

E Assessment for learning

F Access and progression

At the end of each chapter in this book, there is a grid showing which areas of the domains are covered. The standards might be revised in the future; however, you might wish to have a look at the domains to see the values and commitments which should be demonstrated by teachers. A shortcut weblink to the document is available at: http://tinyurl.com/b3k2r4o

The Award in Education and Training

The Award in Education and Training is an introductory teaching qualification achievable at level 3 on the Qualifications and Credit Framework (QCF) which roughly equates to Advanced (A level) study. You will find more information on the QCF in the next section of this chapter. As it's an introductory qualification it will not fully qualify you as a teacher, but it will give you a good idea of what it's like to teach. You can then take a further teaching qualification if required. The Award is ideal if you are not yet in a teaching role, have just started teaching, or just want to know what's involved.

The qualification is made up of different units to the value of 12 credits. Think of one credit as approximately 10 hours of learning, therefore 12 credits equates to 120 hours of learning. This will consist of a certain amount of *contact time* with a teacher such as attending sessions and being assessed. It also consists of your own time, known as *non-contact time* which can be used for reading, research, completing assignments and gathering evidence of work towards meeting the requirements of the qualification.

The Level 3 Award is made up of the following three units (which total 12 credits):

- Understanding roles, responsibilities and relationships in education and training (3 credits)

- Understanding and using inclusive approaches in education and training (6 credits)

- Understanding assessment in education and training (3 credits)

However, it is possible to achieve part of the Award by taking units from the Learning and Development qualification. These units are known as *accepted equivalents*, but they are only for those who are currently in a teaching and assessing role with learners of their own.

Everyone must take the first unit of *Understanding roles, responsibilities and relationships in education and training*, which is classed as a mandatory unit.

You could substitute the unit *Understanding and using inclusive approaches in education and training* with one of the following units from the Level 3 Learning and Development qualification:

- Facilitate learning and development for individuals (6 credits) OR

- Facilitate learning and development in groups (6 credits)

You could also substitute the unit *Understanding assessment in education and training* with the following unit from the Level 3 Learning and Development qualification:

- Understanding the principles and practices of assessment (3 credits)

If you wish to substitute any units, you will need to discuss this with the organisation you are taking the Award with, as they might only offer the three main units of the Award and not the Learning and Development units.

This book covers all the requirements of all the units which can be used to make up the Award, you can see the units' content in the appendices. However, you are responsible for keeping up to date with the subject that you wish to teach. While the book will help you with ideas for teaching and assessing in general, you will need to adapt these to suit your subject and the environment within which you will teach. You also need to ensure that your English, maths and information and communication technology (ICT) skills are of a good quality. You won't want to be making mistakes in front of your learners as this will give a bad impression.

As part of the Award, you will need to deliver a short *micro-teach* session to your peers (usually 15 or 30 minutes), or be observed with your current learners. Chapter 8 will give you lots of information to help with this.

The Award can be delivered in different ways depending upon where you choose to take it. For example, a series of evening classes, daytime classes or an online course.

How you are assessed towards achievement of the Award will differ depending upon who you are registered with. The organisation you are taking the qualification with will register you with an awarding organisation (AO). Each AO will specify how you will be assessed, for example, assignments, case studies, written work and projects. Some might have a more academic focus, i.e. require formal writing and the use of research and referencing. You will need to find out how you will be assessed before you commence, to ensure you can meet the requirements. While the delivery and assessment methods might differ, the content of the qualification will be the same no matter who you are registered with.

If you haven't applied to take the Award yet, you might like to find out where it is offered, how it is delivered and how it is assessed before you apply.

If you are currently teaching, this is known as *in-service*, and if you are not yet teaching, this is known as *pre-service*. Throughout your career, you might be known as a *dual professional,* i.e. a professional in the *subject* you will teach, as well as a professional *teacher.*

Qualifications and Credit Framework

The Qualifications and Credit Framework (QCF) is a system for recognising skills and qualifications by awarding credit values to units of qualifications in England and Northern Ireland. The equivalent for Scotland is the Scottish Credit and Qualifications Framework (SCQF), and for Wales the Credit and Qualifications Framework for Wales (CQFW).

These credit values enable you to see how long it would take an average learner to achieve a unit. For example, the *Understanding roles, responsibilities and relationships in education and training* unit of the Award is 3 credits which equates to 30 hours. These hours include *contact time* with a teacher and assessor, and *non-contact time* for individual study and assignment work.

There are three sizes of qualifications on the QCF, each with a title and associated credit values:

- Award (1 to 12 credits)
- Certificate (13 to 36 credits)
- Diploma (37 credits or more)

All qualifications on the QCF use one of the above words in their title, for example, the *Level 2 Certificate in Women's Hairdressing*, the *Level 3 Award in Education and Training*, or the *Level 4 Diploma in Accounting*. The level of the qualification defines how difficult it is to achieve and the credit value defines how long it will take to achieve.

You don't have to start with an Award, progress to a Certificate and then to a Diploma as all subjects are different. The terms Award, Certificate and Diploma relate to how *big* the qualification is (i.e. its size), which is based on the total number of credits. For example, a Diploma with 37 credits would equate to 370 hours of learning and is therefore a bigger qualification than an Award with 12 credits and 120 hours of learning. The bigger the qualification, the longer it will take to achieve.

The QCF in England and Northern Ireland has 9 levels; ranging from entry level through levels 1 to 8, for example, level 3 would be easier to achieve than level 5.

A rough comparison of the levels to other qualifications is:

1. GCSEs (grades D–G)
2. GCSEs (grade A*–C), Intermediate Apprenticeship
3. Advanced level (A level), Advanced Apprenticeship
4. Vocational Qualification level 4, Higher Apprenticeship
5. Vocational Qualification level 5, Foundation Degree
6. Bachelors Degree

7. Masters Degree, Postgraduate Certificate and Diploma

8. Doctor of Philosophy (DPhil or PhD)

Progression

While working towards your Award, it would be extremely beneficial for you to have a mentor, someone who can help and support you, not only with teaching skills, but also with your specialist subject knowledge. If you are currently teaching or training, your mentor could observe you and give you developmental feedback as to how you could improve your interaction with your learners. Conversely, you could observe them to gain useful ideas and tips for delivering your subject.

When you are nearing completion of your Award, you may find it useful to summarise your learning and create an action plan for your future development. This could be a list of your strengths and achievements so far, aspects you would like to develop or improve, and how you aim to work towards accomplishing them.

After achieving the Award at level 3, you might wish to progress further and work towards a higher level teaching qualification such as the:

- Certificate in Education and Training at level 4 or the

- Diploma in Education and Training at level 5

It is possible to progress to the Diploma without taking the Certificate first, but this would depend upon how skilled and knowledgeable you are at the time, and your job role requirements.

The Diploma has the same content as the Certificate in Education or Professional or Post Graduate Certificate in Education (PGCE for anyone holding a degree). However, these qualifications are usually accredited via universities rather than an awarding organisation.

The Institute for Learning (IfL) is currently the voluntary professional body for teachers, trainers, tutors and trainee teachers in the Further Education and Skills Sector. You can register at any time with the IfL and benefit from the information and activities they offer.

The IfL has a *Code of Professional Practice* (2008), which defines the conduct of their members into seven behaviours:

1. professional integrity

2. respect

3. reasonable care

4. professional practice

5. criminal offence disclosure

6. responsibility during Institute investigations

7. responsibility

There are other professional bodies such as the Education and Training Foundation, the Association of Teachers and Lecturers (ATL), the Association of Colleges, the Association of Employment and Learning Providers (AELP) and the University and College Union (UCU) which you might like to join or research further.

Obtaining a teaching or training position

It can be overwhelming making a career move from your current profession into teaching, or indeed continuing working while training others in the workplace. Once you have made the decision, you need to research what jobs are available for the amount of time you are able to commit. For example, you might like to give up your current career and teach full time, you might like to teach evening classes while continuing working, or train others in your place of work. Positions will differ depending upon the demand for your particular subject. You could be:

- full time (permanent or termly contract)

- part time (permanent or temporary contract)

- peripatetic (working for several organisations)

- self-employed freelance (invoicing for work done, without the benefits of being an employee)

- sessional (hourly paid)

- supply (providing temporary cover for absent staff through an agency)

- voluntary (unpaid)

- workplace based (training others in your place of work)

You will need to be prepared to put in time of your own, particularly if you are part time or sessional. Even though you might feel you get a good hourly rate of pay, you have to take into account that this covers you for all the work you do which is outside of these hours. Most organisations now work throughout the year, therefore don't expect to have long breaks like schools do if you are employed full time as a teacher or trainer.

Educational abbreviations and acronyms

All working environments use jargon such as abbreviations and acronyms at some point. Education is no different and the ones used seem to be continually updated and added to. Throughout this book, the first occurrence of any acronym in each chapter will always be written in full, followed by the acronym in brackets. The following table lists most of those you will come across as a new teacher or trainer.

Table 1 Educational abbreviations and acronyms

ACL	Adult and Community Learning
ADD	Attention Deficit Disorder
ADHD	Attention Deficit and Hyperactivity Disorder
ADS	Adult Dyslexia Support
AELP	Association of Employment and Learning Providers
AI	Awarding Institution
AO	Awarding Organisation
AoC	Association of Colleges
ASD	Autism Spectrum Disorder
ATL	Association of Teachers and Lecturers
ATLS	Associate Teacher Learning and Skills
BEd	Bachelor of Education
BIS	Department for Business, Innovation and Skills
BME	Black and Minority Ethnic
CCEA	Council for the Curriculum, Examinations and Assessment (Northern Ireland)
CETT	Centre for Excellence in Teacher Training
Cert Ed	Certificate in Education
CL	Community Learning
CLA	Copyright Licensing Authority
COSHH	Control of Substances Hazardous to Health
CPD	Continuing Professional Development
CQFW	Credit and Qualification Framework for Wales
CRB	Criminal Records Bureau
DCELLS	Department for Children, Education, Lifelong Learning and Skills (Wales)
DSO	Designated Safeguarding Officer
E&D	Equality and Diversity
EBD	Emotional and Behavioural Difficulties
ECDL	European Computer Driving Licence
EDAR	Experience, Describe, Analyse and Revise
EDIP	Explain, Demonstrate, Imitate and Practice
EI	Emotional Intelligence
EHRC	Equality and Human Rights Commission
ESOL	English for Speakers of Other Languages
EQA	External Quality Assurance
FAQ	Frequently Asked Questions
FE	Further Education
FHE	Further and Higher Education
GCSE	General Certificate of Secondary Education
GLH	Guided Learning Hours
H&S	Health and Safety
HEA	Higher Education Academy
HEI	Higher Education Institution
IAG	Information, Advice and Guidance
IAP	Individual Action Plan
ICT	Information and Communication Technology
IfL	Institute for Learning
IIP	Investors in People
ILA	Individual Learning Account
ILP	Individual Learning Plan
ILT	Information and Learning Technology
IT	Information Technology
ITE	Initial Teacher Education
ITP	Independent Training Provider
ISA	Independent Safeguarding Authority
ITT	Initial Teacher/Trainer Training

(Continued)

Table I (Continued)

IQ	Intelligence Quotient
IQA	Internal Quality Assurance
IWB	Interactive Whiteboard
LA	Local Authority
LAR	Learner Achievement Record
LDD	Learning Difficulties and/or Disabilities
LLUK	Lifelong Learning UK (no longer operational)
LSA	Learner Support Assistant
LSIS	Learning and Skills Improvement Service (no longer operational)
LSCB	Local Safeguarding Children Board
MLD	Moderate Learning Difficulties
NEET	Not in Education, Employment or Training
NIACE	National Institute of Adult Continuing Education
NLH	Notional Learning Hours
NOS	National Occupational Standards
NQT	Newly Qualified Teacher
NRDC	National Research and Development Centre for adult literacy and numeracy
NTA	Non-teaching Assistant
NVQ	National Vocational Qualification
Ofqual	Office of Qualifications and Examinations Regulation
Ofsted	Office for Standards in Education, Children's Services and Skills
PAT	Portable Appliance Testing
PCET	Post Compulsory Education and Training
PLTS	Personal Learning and Thinking Skills
PGCE	Post Graduate Certificate in Education
PLTS	Personal Learning and Thinking Skills
POCA	Protection of Children Act (1999)
PPP	Pose, Pause, Pick
PSHE	Personal, Social and Health Education
QCF	Qualifications and Credit Framework
QTLS	Qualified Teacher Learning and Skills
QTS	Qualified Teacher Status (schools)
RLJ	Reflective Learning Journal
RPL	Recognition of Prior Learning
RWE	Realistic Working Environment
SEAL	Social and Emotional Aspects of Learning
SCN	Scottish Candidate Number
SCQF	Scottish Credit and Qualifications Framework
SFA	Skills Funding Agency
SL	Student Loan
SLC	Subject Learning Coach
SMART	Specific, Measurable, Achievable, Relevant and Timebound
SoW	Scheme of Work
SP	Session Plan
SSB	Standard Setting Body
SSC	Sector Skills Council
SWOT	Strengths, Weaknesses, Opportunities and Threats
T&L	Teaching and Learning
TAQA	Training, Assessment and Quality Assurance
UCU	University and College Union
ULN	Unique Learner Number
VACSR	Valid, Authentic, Current, Sufficient and Reliable
VARK	Visual, Aural, Read/write and Kinaesthetic
VB	Vetting and Barring
VLE	Virtual Learning Environment
WBL	Work Based Learning
WEA	Workers' Educational Association
WWWWWH	Who, What, When, Where, Why and How

Summary

In this chapter you have learnt about:

- the structure of the book and how to use it
- teaching in the Further Education and Skills Sector
- the Award in Education and Training
- progression
- educational abbreviations and acronyms

Theory focus

References and further information

Castle, P and Buckler, S (2009) *How to be a Successful Teacher*. London: SAGE Publications Ltd.

Gravells, A (2012) *What is Teaching in the Lifelong Learning Sector?* London: Learning Matters.

Gravells, A (2013) *Passing Assessments for the Award in Education and Training*. London: Learning Matters.

IfL (2008) *Code of Professional Practice: Raising concerns about IfL members*. London: Institute for Learning.

LLUK (2006) *New Overarching Professional Standards for Teachers, Tutors and Trainers in the Lifelong Learning Sector*. London: LLUK. Available online at: http://tinyurl.com/b3k2r4o

Reece, I and Walker, S (2007) *Teaching, Training and Learning: A practical guide* (6th Edn). Tyne & Wear: Business Education Publishers.

Wallace, S (2011) *Teaching, Tutoring and Training in the Lifelong Learning Sector* (4th Edn). Exeter: Learning Matters.

Websites

Ann Gravells (information and resources) – www.anngravells.co.uk

Association of Colleges – www.aoc.co.uk

Association of Employment and Learning Providers (AELP) – www.aelp.org.uk

Association of Teachers and Lecturers – www.atl.org.uk

Centres for Excellence in Teacher Training (CETT) – http://cett.excellencegateway.org.uk/

Credit and Qualification Framework for Wales (CQFW) – www.cqfw.org

Department for Business, Innovation and Skills – www.bis.gov.uk

FE Advice – www.feadvice.org.uk/next-steps

Institute for Learning – www.ifl.ac.uk

National Institute of Adult Continuing Education – www.niace.org.uk

Post Compulsory Education and Training Network – www.pcet.net

Qualifications and Credit Framework (QCF) – http://www.ofqual.gov.uk/qualifications-and-assessments/qualification-frameworks/

Scottish Credit and Qualifications Framework (SCQF) – www.scqf.org.uk

Sector Skills Councils – www.sscalliance.org

Teaching and training job sites:

www.eatjobs.co.uk

www.fecareers.co.uk

www.fejobs.com

www.jobs.ac.uk

www.tes.co.uk/jobs

University and College Union – www.ucu.org.uk

1 TEACHING AND LEARNING

In this chapter you will learn about:

- roles, responsibilities and boundaries
- working with other professionals
- quality assurance
- record keeping
- legislation, regulatory requirements and codes of practice

There are activities and examples to help you reflect on the above which will assist your understanding of the process of teaching and learning. At the end of each section within the chapter are extension activities to stretch and challenge your learning should you wish to carry them out. A list of useful references, further information and website links can be found at the end in case you would like to research the topics further.

At the end of the chapter is a cross-referencing grid showing how the chapter's contents relate towards the units of the Award in Education and Training and the Professional Teaching Standards.

Roles, responsibilities and boundaries

Your main role should be to teach or train your subject in a way which actively involves and engages your learners during every session, whether this is in the workplace, in a college or other training environment. However, it's not just about *teaching and training*, it's about the *learning* that takes place as a result. You can teach as much as you wish, but if learning is not taking place then your teaching has not been successful. Most careers are quite challenging and demanding, the role of a teacher or trainer is no exception to this. The role can be very rewarding, particularly when you see your learners' achievements and success, which is a direct result of your contribution and support.

This book will give you lots of ideas of how to deliver your subject, i.e. pass on your skills and knowledge to others, and assess that learning has taken place. Assessment can be formal by asking questions to confirm knowledge and/or observing practice to confirm skills. It can also be informal by using discussions, quizzes and tasks. If you don't assess you won't know what has been learnt.

When you are with your learners, you should always use clear language at an appropriate level and in terms they will understand. Although you know what you are talking about, this might be the first time your learners have heard it, therefore never be afraid of repeating yourself or going over aspects again. Think back to when you learnt something for the first time, perhaps you didn't take it all in at once and you need to know this will be the same for your own learners.

You need to involve your learners by making your sessions interesting, therefore engaging them in the subject, keeping them motivated and leaving them wanting to learn more. Ideally, you should be involved with all aspects from when your learners apply to when they achieve. Your job role as a teacher or trainer will depend upon the subject you are delivering, i.e. whether it is a short event, a longer programme or a qualification. It will also depend upon the age and experience of your learners, the environment you are in, and your organisation's requirements.

Becoming a good teacher or trainer includes being enthusiastic and passionate about your subject, being approachable and taking pride in your work, which should all be conveyed to your learners when you are with them.

Example

Vic, a new trainer, always arrives early to his sessions. He ensures the training room is tidy and organises the furniture in a way that encourages communication between learners. He delivers his subject with passion and enthusiasm. He uses lots of examples and anecdotes to relate his subject to real life. He includes all his learners by addressing them personally and asking questions, yet he remains fair with the support and advice he gives. He always tidies up afterwards and offers to e-mail handouts and additional learning materials if required. His learners see how conscientious and professional Vic is and they begin to emulate this by being early, being polite and submitting work on time.

A good first impression will help you establish a positive working relationship with your learners. The way you dress, act, respond to questions and offer support, will also influence your learners. They don't need to know anything personal about you, but they will probably make assumptions about you. If asked personal questions, try not to give out any information: by remaining a professional, and not becoming too friendly, you will retain respect. Most teachers are on first name terms with their learners. However, you will need to decide what is appropriate to your situation and the age range of your learners. Establishing routines will help your sessions flow smoothly; for example, always starting on time, setting and keeping to time limits for activities and breaks, and finishing on time.

Activity

How could you create a good first impression with your learners? What would influence this, for example your own previous experiences of attending a session which was either good or bad?

The teaching, learning and assessment cycle

The teaching, learning and assessment cycle is a systematic process which helps ensure your learners have a positive experience and are able to achieve their goals. The process can start at any stage of the cycle and keep on going, however, all stages should be addressed for learning to be effective. Quality assurance should take place continuously to ensure all aspects are being delivered and assessed fairly and accurately, and ensure learning is taking place. The chapters in this book are based on the cycle, which consists of the stages outlined in Figure 1.1. Don't worry if what follows doesn't make sense at the moment, as you progress through the chapters it should become clearer.

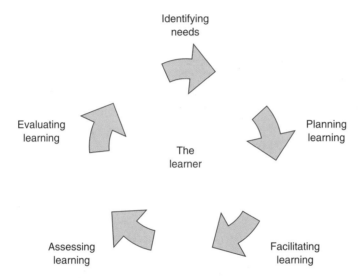

Figure 1.1 The teaching, learning and assessment cycle

Your role might follow the cycle, which includes aspects of quality assurance at each stage, and briefly involve:

- **identifying needs** – finding out what your organisation's, your own, and your potential learners' needs are, finding out why learners are taking the programme and what their expectations are, carrying out initial and diagnostic assessments, agreeing individual learning plans, ensuring learners are capable of progressing to their chosen destination

- **planning learning** – preparing teaching and learning plans, and materials to ensure you cover the requirements of the programme, liaising with others

- **facilitating learning** – teaching, training and facilitating learning using a variety of approaches and resources, obtaining feedback to make improvements

- **assessing learning** – checking your learners have gained the necessary skills, knowledge and understanding at all stages throughout their time with you, using formal and informal types and methods of assessment, obtaining feedback to make improvements

- **evaluating learning** – obtaining feedback from others, evaluating your role, and all aspects involved with the learning process in order to make improvements for the future. Evaluation could also take place after each stage of the cycle

Running throughout the cycle is quality assurance. This is a system of monitoring all aspects of teaching which occur with learners throughout their time of training, from when they commence to when they achieve. Good practice for all programmes is to include a system of *internal quality assurance*. However, this might be a formal requirement if you are delivering and assessing towards a qualification. This means a colleague at your organisation will monitor and sample aspects of everything you do to ensure you are being fair to all learners, making correct decisions and following the relevant policies and procedures. If you are teaching towards a qualification, there might also be an external quality assurance system. This involves a person visiting from the organisation that awards the qualification, to ensure all staff are following the requirements correctly.

Most teachers and trainers follow the cycle from beginning to end; however, your job role might not require you to be involved with all aspects. For example, you might not carry out the *identifying needs* stage as other staff within your organisation will do this. You will, however, need to liaise with them to obtain the information to help you plan your sessions. You might be training a member of staff in the workplace and only carry out the *planning learning* and *facilitating learning* stages, as someone else might assess their progress. Again, you would need to liaise with who else is involved with your learner.

To teach and train effectively involves not only the approaches you use to teach your subject, i.e. discussions, group work and paired activities, but many other factors that go before and after the taught session. This includes planning logically what you will cover in your sessions, preparing your materials and resources, assessing that learning has taken place, giving feedback, keeping records and evaluating yourself and the experiences your learners have had. Never underestimate the amount of time you will need to dedicate to the role.

When teaching or training, your personality and mannerisms will be noticed by your learners. You might do things you are not aware of; for example, waving your arms around or fidgeting. It is really useful to make a visual recording of one of your sessions to possibly see things you would like to change. You may see things you didn't realise you did or things that you would like to change. If you are due to deliver a micro-teach session to your peer group as part of the Award, this would be a good opportunity to record it.

Personal qualities such as arriving early so that you are organised, and smiling when your learners enter will help you all relax at the beginning of the session. Using your learners' names when you get the opportunity will make them feel you are getting to know them as an individual. Observing your learners' body language will help you to see if they are not understanding something, or not paying attention. You can then ask a question to bring them back on track. Don't be afraid of regularly recapping points and repeating aspects – remember, you know your subject, but for your learners it's probably the first time they have seen or heard anything about it.

If you are new to teaching, you may find you are teaching in the same way you were taught at school or college. This could be lecturing, reading from a book or copying information from a board, which might not have been very effective for you. You won't yet know all the other approaches, methods and activities you could use to make learning interesting and engaging. As you become more experienced at teaching and training, your confidence will grow and you will be able to experiment with different approaches, as not everything you do will suit all your learners.

Sue Crowley of the Institute for Learning (IfL) stated:

> *Often new teachers teach as they were taught, then perhaps as they would like to have been taught, and finally they realise different people learn in different ways and a wider spectrum of teaching and learning approaches are needed and available.*

(LSIS, 2009, page 8)

At all times, you should act in a professional manner and give a good impression; for example, time keeping, dress and behaviour towards your learners and others.

The following is a list of examples of roles and responsibilities, in alphabetical order. However, you might not be required to carry them all out depending upon your job role. If there is anything you are unsure of at the moment, don't worry, as you progress through the chapters it should all become clearer.

- acting professionally and with integrity
- attending meetings
- carrying out relevant administrative requirements
- communicating appropriately and effectively with learners and others
- completing attendance records/registers
- complying with relevant regulatory requirements, legislation, policies and procedures, and codes of practice
- differentiating teaching, learning and assessment approaches and materials
- ensuring assessment decisions are valid, reliable, fair and ethical
- ensuring learners are on the right programme at the right level
- establishing ground rules
- following health and safety, and equality and diversity requirements
- giving appropriate information, advice and guidance where necessary
- helping learners develop their English, maths, and information and communication technology skills
- incorporating new technology where possible
- maintaining a safe, positive and accessible learning environment for learners and others
- maintaining records and confidentiality
- partaking in quality assurance processes

- promoting appropriate behaviour and respect for others

- referring learners to other people or agencies when necessary

- reflecting on own practice and partaking in professional development

- standardising practice with others

- teaching and training in an inclusive, engaging and motivating way

- using a variety of assessment types and methods to assess progress formally and informally, and giving feedback to learners (verbal and written)

- using appropriate equipment and resources

- using icebreakers and energisers effectively

Activity

Think about the subject you would like to deliver, the age group of your learners and the environment in which you will teach. Make a list of the roles and responsibilities you might carry out, which might differ from the previous bulleted list. Place these in order from when a learner applies to when they complete.

Boundaries

There are two aspects to boundaries for teachers and trainers: boundaries between your teaching or training role and other professional roles, and other aspects you are *bound by* which might hinder or challenge your role.

- Professional boundaries are those within which you need to work and it's important not to overstep these, for example, by becoming too personal or friendly with your learners. Boundaries are about knowing where your role as a teacher or trainer stops. You should be able to work within the limits of that role, but know that it's okay to ask for help. Don't try to take on too much, or carry out something which is part of someone else's role.

- Other boundaries include the things you are bound by, for example, policies and procedures, the amount of administrative work you are expected to complete, or a lack of funding or resources. These boundaries can often be interpreted as the negative aspects of your roles and responsibilities.

You might have other professional roles besides teaching; for example, you might interview learners and have to decide whether they can attend a programme or not. You might have difficult decisions to make; however, you should always be able to get the support of other staff at your organisation. Never feel you are on your own, find out who can help and advise you when you need support. If you make a decision not to accept a learner, you will need to justify your reasons. You should find out and follow your organisation's policies and procedures. If you are a new teacher or trainer, you might have been allocated a *mentor*, someone to help and support you as necessary and you will find it helpful to keep in touch with them and ask for advice.

When you are with learners, you need to remain in control, be fair and ethical and not demonstrate any favouritism towards particular learners; for example, by giving one more support than the others. You might feel it sensible to make a telephone call to a learner who has been absent but making regular calls would be inappropriate. Giving your personal telephone number to learners could be seen as encouraging informal contact, and you may get calls or texts which are not suitable or relevant. You might not want to take your break with your learners or join their social networking sites as you could become more of a friend than a teacher. It is unprofessional to use bad language, to touch learners in an inappropriate way or to let your personal problems affect your work.

Extension Activity

What other professional roles do you think you might be required to carry out, besides teaching or training? What boundaries do you think you might have between these roles and your other professional roles. How could you overcome them?

Working with other professionals

There will be other professionals with whom you will need to work or liaise with at some point during your teaching or training career. These could include:

- administration staff
- assessors
- budget holders
- caretakers
- cleaners
- co-tutors
- customers
- finance staff
- health and safety officers
- human resources staff
- internal and external quality assurers

- learning support staff
- managers
- other teachers and trainers
- other training providers
- reprographics staff
- safeguarding officers
- staff development personnel
- supervisors
- support workers
- technicians
- union staff
- work placement co-ordinators

You should always be polite and professional and treat others with respect. You will need to find out who these people are at your organisation and how you can contact them. It would also be useful to understand a little about their job role and how they can support you, and how you can support them. However, don't feel you need to support them too much by carrying out aspects of their role for them, otherwise you might be blurring the boundary between your own professional roles.

Examples of working with other professionals might include:

- attending team meetings and contributing towards issues under discussion

- contacting companies to purchase or hire equipment and materials

- communicating with administrative staff to ensure that your learners have been registered with the relevant awarding organisation

- getting handouts photocopied by the relevant department to ensure they are ready in time

- liaising with an internal quality assurer to enable them to sample your work, and/or an external quality assurer from an awarding organisation

- liaising with learning support staff to address particular learner needs

- liaising with the caretaker to ensure the room and/or building is open when you start and secure when you leave

- obtaining technical support staff when using equipment

- team teaching or co-tutoring with other members of staff, i.e. planning who will do what and when

You should never feel you have to resolve a situation on your own, there should be others who can help if necessary. However, you might be delivering a session in a hired venue or a building away from the main premises, in which case it would be useful to know who you could contact and when they are available.

Example

Sarah was due to teach a First Aid session and arrived early to set up the room. She found the computer worked but the interactive whiteboard didn't and there was no internet access. She needed to show a video clip which was only available online. Instead of calling the computer technician, she moved the equipment to check the cables. In doing so, she accidentally broke the internet cable. Had she not overstepped the boundary of her role, she would not have caused further problems.

You might need to liaise with people who are external to your organisation such as parents and guardians if you are teaching younger learners, employers and supervisors if you are training in the workplace, auditors and inspectors if you are assessing qualifications, and other visitors. You should always remain professional when in contact with others and not overstep the boundary of your role. If your organisation requires, you will need to inform reception of their arrival time, perhaps organise parking and refreshments and be accessible as soon as they arrive. They may need to wear a visitors' badge and sign out upon departure. If you are ever in doubt about the boundaries of your role, or how you should act towards others, always ask someone within your organisation.

You might have other roles to undertake such as attending promotional events, conferences or visiting learners who are on a work placement. If so, always remember you are representing your organisation, and therefore you must uphold their values and act professionally at all times. If you have attended a relevant event, you might be required to pass on information to your colleagues, either in the form of a report, a meeting or by delivering a training session to the team. You will therefore need to remain focused upon the facts and not let any personal opinions get in the way.

Extension Activity

Consider the term professionalism, what do you think it means in relation to your job role? How will your role involve you working with other professionals? What boundaries do you think you will encounter between your teaching or training role and other professional roles? How can you effectively overcome them and who would you go to for support and advice?

Quality assurance

Most programmes and qualifications should follow a quality assurance system. This should ensure they are being delivered and assessed accurately, fairly, consistently and reliably. You might not be involved with all aspects of quality assurance at your organisation; however, they will impact upon your role, therefore you should familiarise yourself with the requirements. For example, finding out when policies and procedures are reviewed, analysing surveys and feedback from learners, following up appeals and complaints, and reading feedback from audit and inspection reports.

Quality assurance can be *internal*, i.e. observing delivered sessions, talking to learners, checking assessment decisions, and sampling learners' work and associated records. It can also be *external*, i.e. inspectors, auditors and quality assurers checking compliance with their systems and requirements. Information gained from aspects of quality assurance must lead to improvements for your learners, yourself and your organisation.

Quality *assurance* is an ongoing system to monitor and evaluate a product or a service. To the contrary, quality *control* seeks to find problems, whereas quality assurance seeks to avoid problems. Quality assurance is therefore ongoing and proactive whereas quality control can only be at the end and therefore reactive. Quality controlling a programme once learners have left will not help them; however, quality assuring a programme while the learners are still at the organisation will enable any issues to be resolved.

Internal quality assurance (IQA) also has a supportive element. When you are new to a role, an organisation, or are working with new standards of a qualification, the role of internal quality assurance is particularly important for both you and your organisation. It is far better to identify any areas that need to be resolved early on so that you can have the necessary support and advice to get things right.

The internal quality assurance process relates to a product; for example, a qualification a learner is taking which is accredited by an awarding organisation. It can also relate to a service to develop people; for example, to help staff perform their job roles better or learn a new skill. Internal quality assurance should be carried out from commencement to the completion of the product or service. If there is no external formal examination taken by learners, there has to be a system of monitoring the performance of all staff and all activities involved. If not, staff might make incorrect judgements, or pass someone who hasn't met the requirements perhaps because they were biased. If you are delivering and assessing a qualification, there should be an internal quality assurer within your organisation who will sample aspects of your work. They will not reassess the learners' work, they will audit your work to ensure you have correctly followed the delivery and assessment procedures and made fair, valid and reliable decisions. The types of audit they will carry out will include monitoring how you deliver and assess, and sampling your decisions and records. The amount of auditing will depend upon many risk factors, such as the experience of the staff involved, the number of learners they have, where they are located and the complexity of the qualification.

Example

Ibrahim is delivering and assessing the Level 2 Certificate in Retail Skills. He has been training and assessing staff in a local department store for a couple of months. Jennifer is his internal quality assurer and she has planned to watch him deliver a training session, observe him assess and give feedback to a learner. She will also talk to his learner to ascertain what they think about the delivery and assessment process. At some point, she will sample Ibrahim's records to ensure they are meeting the requirements of the qualification and that he is being fair. Jennifer will give feedback based on her findings, and agree an action plan with him to support his development.

The IQA process can involve:

- advising, supporting and providing developmental feedback to staff
- documenting the quality assurance strategy, process and decisions
- ensuring staff interpret, understand and consistently apply the correct standards and requirements
- ensuring the accuracy and consistency of assessment decisions
- facilitating standardisation activities
- following an audit trail of learner achievements
- holding team meetings

- identifying issues and trends to highlight problem areas

- interviewing learners, assessors and other relevant staff and witnesses

- liaising with external quality assurers

- managing risk

- monitoring and observing all aspects of delivery and assessment from commencement to completion

- partaking in continuing professional development (CPD)

- planning what will be monitored, from whom and when

- sampling assessment records, learners' work and assessor decisions

- upholding the credibility (of the product or service)

Delivery, assessment and IQA systems should be monitored and evaluated continuously to identify any actions for improvement, which should then be implemented. If you are delivering and assessing towards a qualification, an external quality assurer (often referred to as an external verifier) from the relevant awarding organisation will monitor the practice of all involved. They might visit your organisation to do this, or carry out a remote activity whereby they sample aspects electronically, or look at learners' work and records which have been posted to them. All qualifications must be quality assured to enable certificates to be correctly claimed for learners. The awarding organisation must satisfy themselves that the learners have successfully achieved the qualification by their own merit.

Depending upon the product or service you are involved with, you might be audited or monitored based on the internal quality assurance cycle in Figure 1.2. Although the examples are separated, some of them may overlap, or be carried out at the same time as others.

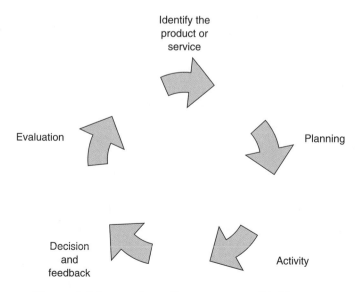

Figure 1.2 Internal quality assurance (IQA) cycle

- **Identify the product or service** – ascertaining what is to be delivered, assessed, quality assured and why. For example, are learners working towards a qualification or are learners being observed performing their job roles? The criteria will need to be clear, i.e. units from a qualification or aspects of a job specification. Assessors should be allocated to learners in a fair way, for example, according to location or work load. Policies and procedures should be in place and up to date.

- **Planning** – devising a sample plan to arrange what will be quality assured, from whom and when. Planning the dates to observe staff in action, talk to learners and sample work. Information will need to be obtained from staff to assist the planning process, and risks taken into account such as their skills, knowledge, understanding, qualifications and experience.

- **Activity** – carrying out the quality assurance activities such as sampling learners' work, following an audit trail of learner achievements, observing training and assessment practice and sampling records and decisions. Activities also include holding meetings and standardisation activities, supporting and developing staff and communicating with others involved in the process.

- **Decision and feedback** – making a judgement as to whether the staff have performed satisfactorily and made fair, valid and reliable decisions. Giving developmental feedback as to what was good or what could be improved. Agreeing action and development points if necessary and following them up.

- **Evaluation** – reviewing the whole process to determine what could be revised, modified and improved. Obtaining feedback from others, i.e. using questionnaires and surveys, analysing these and devising action plans for improvement. Following any action points from external quality assurers and others involved in the process.

The cycle will then begin again with an identification of what needs to be monitored and when. Throughout the cycle, standardisation of practice between staff should take place and records should be maintained.

Standardisation of practice

Standardisation is a process to enable consistency and fairness of all activities carried out with learners. If more than one person is teaching and/or assessing the same qualification, it is important that they all agree how to interpret the requirements, deliver the content and make valid and reliable assessment decisions. Attending a standardisation meeting is also an opportunity to develop and share good practice and be part of a team. It is best to meet prior to the programme commencing to discuss the qualification requirements, design the planning documents, delivery and assessment activities, and any materials and resources. Once assessments have taken place, another meeting can be held to compare and discuss the decisions. Depending on the methods used, double marking can take place, whereby another assessor reviews the work (with or without seeing the original feedback and grade) to ensure consistency and fairness.

Have a look at the quality assurance cycle in Figure 1.2 and describe how each aspect could impact upon your role as a teacher or trainer.

Record keeping

Records must be maintained, not only to support the teaching, learning and assessment process, but to provide an audit trail and supply information to others. Records are needed to satisfy auditors, inspectors, regulators, internal and external quality assurers and to meet your own organisation's requirements. For example, information and data gathering can inform quality assurance, equality and diversity, and health and safety policies. The information contained in records helps to measure learning and the effectiveness and appropriateness of the programme overall. Information such as attendance, progress and achievement could be shared with your colleagues if they are also teaching your learners; for example, to look for patterns of attendance or behaviour issues.

Records should be kept confidential and secure at your organisation; for example, in a locked filing cabinet or password protected electronic file. The Data Protection Act (1998) is mandatory for all organisations that hold or process personal data. It contains eight principles, to ensure that data are:

- processed fairly and lawfully

- obtained and used only for specified and lawful purposes

- adequate, relevant and not excessive

- accurate and, where necessary, kept up to date

- kept for no longer than necessary

- processed in accordance with the individual's rights

- kept secure

- transferred only to countries that offer adequate protection

Records must be kept for a certain amount of time, depending upon your organisation's requirements, which could be several years. They must be up to date, accurate, factual and legible whether they are stored manually or electronically. All records should show an audit trail, i.e. track learner progress from when they commence through to their completion. If you happen to be absent for any reason, a colleague will be able to effectively take over if they have access to your records. Data is also useful to your organisation for purposes such as accidents, appeals, equal opportunities and funding purposes. If accurate records are not maintained, your learners' progress may become unstructured and their achievement might not be recognised or documented.

Example

Nick has set up two lever arch files. One contains all the documentation relevant to deliver and assess the Certificate in Sport and Recreation. This includes a hard copy of the qualification handbook, a scheme of work, session plans, and teaching and learning materials. The other contains alphabetical records relating to each of his learners. In these are: application forms, interview notes, initial assessment results, action plans, tutorial review records and assessment results. These files ensure he has everything to hand, not only to carry out his role effectively, but also for auditors, inspectors and verifiers. His organisation has recently installed computer software to enable all staff to store these records electronically, therefore Nick will be able to use the new system when it's introduced.

Try and keep on top of your administrative work. If you leave it for a while, you may forget to sign or date something. An important record might be the register or record of attendance. You need to know who is in your session not only for fire regulations or other evacuation procedures, but also to keep track of attendance patterns. If a learner is absent regularly you should find out why in case they need any particular support due to certain circumstances.

The following are some of the records and documents you might need to keep, in alphabetical order.

- agreed ground rules
- application and enrolment forms
- assessment and action plans
- continuing professional development (CPD) records
- details of learner progress
- disciplinary and behaviour records
- feedback records and decisions/ grades
- group profile (details of individual learners)
- individual learning plans/action plans
- induction records
- initial and diagnostic assessment results
- learning support records
- minutes of meetings and standardisation activities
- personal details of learners, e.g. address, contacts, disabilities
- questionnaire and survey feedback analysis and action points
- records of what was taught and when
- register/record of attendance
- risk assessments
- teaching and learning plans
- tutorial review records
- resources and equipment (plus electrical test results)

Make a list of the records you should maintain and the reasons why you need to keep them. If you are currently teaching, find out what the exact requirements of your organisation are, where and how long you should keep them, and which records need to be passed on to others.

Legislation, regulatory requirements and codes of practice

Legislation relates to laws passed by Parliament, regulatory requirements are usually specific to certain industries, and codes of practice vary depending upon the organisation within which you will work. It is important for you to keep up to date with all this to ensure you are remaining current with your skills, knowledge and understanding, and with any changes or updates that have taken place.

Legislation

These will differ depending upon the context and environment within which you teach. You need to be aware of the requirements of external bodies and regulators such as Ofsted (in England) who inspect provision, along with awarding organisations who will quality assure their qualifications, and funding agencies who will need data and statistics.

The following information was current at the time of writing; however, you are advised to check for any changes or updates, and whether they are applicable outside England.

- **Children Act (2004)** provided the legal underpinning for the *Every Child Matters: Change for Children* programme. *Well-being* is the term used in the Act to define the five Every Child Matters outcomes:

  ○ be healthy

  ○ stay safe

  ○ enjoy and achieve

  ○ make a positive contribution

  ○ achieve economic well-being

- **Copyright Designs and Patents Act (1988)** relates to the copying, adapting and distributing of materials, which includes computer programs and materials found via the internet. Organisations may have a licence to enable the photocopying of small amounts from books or journals. All copies should have the source acknowledged.

- **Data Protection Act (1998)** made provision for the regulation of the processing of information relating to individuals, including the obtaining, holding, use or disclosure of such information. It was amended in 2003 to include electronic data.

- **Equality Act (2010)** replaced all previous anti-discrimination legislation and consolidated it into one act (England, Scotland and Wales). It provides rights for people not to be directly discriminated against or harassed because they have an association with a disabled person or because they are wrongly perceived as disabled.

There are seven different *types of discrimination*:

1. Associative discrimination: direct discrimination against someone because they are associated with another person with a protected characteristic.

2. Direct discrimination: discrimination because of a protected characteristic.

3. Indirect discrimination: when a rule or policy which applies to everyone can disadvantage a person with a protected characteristic.

4. Discrimination by perception: direct discrimination against someone because others think they have a protected characteristic.

5. Harassment: behaviour deemed offensive by the recipient.

6. Harassment by a third party: the harassment of staff or others by people not directly employed by an organisation, such as an external consultant or visitor.

7. Victimisation: discrimination against someone because they made or supported a complaint under equality legislation.

There are nine protected characteristics: age, disability, gender, gender identity, race, religion and belief, sexual orientation, marriage and civil partnership, maternity and pregnancy.

- **Freedom of Information Act (2000)** gives learners the opportunity to request to see the information public bodies hold about them.

- **Health and Safety at Work etc Act (1974)** imposes obligations on all staff within an organisation commensurate with their role and responsibility. Risk assessments should be carried out where necessary. In the event of an accident, particularly one resulting in death or serious injury, an investigation by the Health and Safety Executive may result in the prosecution of individuals found to be negligent as well as the organisation.

- **Protection of Children Act (POCA) (1999)** was designed to protect children. It gives responsibility to Local Authorities to make enquiries when anyone contacts them with concerns about child abuse.

- **Safeguarding Vulnerable Groups Act (2006)** introduced a vetting and barring scheme to make decisions about who should be barred from working with children and vulnerable adults. Teachers may need to have a Criminal Records Bureau (CRB) check.

Regulatory requirements

Public bodies, corporations, agencies and organisations create regulatory requirements, which must be followed if they are applicable to your job role. For example, in education,

Ofqual is the regulator of qualifications, examinations and assessments in England, and vocational qualifications in Northern Ireland. They are not directly controlled by the government, but report to Parliament. They are responsible for maintaining standards, improving confidence in the system and distributing information about qualifications. Ofqual gives formal recognition to awarding organisations and bodies that deliver and award qualifications. They also monitor their qualifications and activities, including the fees charged, and inspect teaching organisations.

Regulations are often called *rules* and they specify mandatory requirements that must be met.

The following information was current at the time of writing; however, you are advised to check for any changes or updates, and whether they are applicable outside England.

- **Control of Substances Hazardous to Health (COSHH) Regulations (2002)** applies if you work with hazardous materials.

- **Food Hygiene Regulations (2006)** applies to aspects of farming, manufacturing, distributing and retailing food.

- **Health and Safety (Display screen equipment) Regulations (1992)** applies to using display screen equipment e.g. computers.

- **Manual Handling Operation Regulations (1992)** relates to hazards of manual handling and risks of injury.

- **Privacy and Electronic Communications (EC Directive) Regulations 2003** applies to all electronic communications such as e-mail and mobile phone messages.

- **Reporting of Injuries, Diseases and Dangerous Occurrences (RIDDOR) Regulations (1995)** requires specified workplace incidents to be reported.

- **Regulatory Reform (Fire Safety) Order (2005)** places the responsibility on individuals within an organisation to carry out risk assessments to identify, manage and reduce the risk of fire.

Codes of Practice

Codes of practice are usually produced by organisations, associations and professional bodies. They can be mandatory or voluntary and you will need to find out which are applicable to your job role.

Your organisation should have documented codes of practice such as:

- acceptable use of information technology
- behaviour
- code of conduct
- disciplinary

- dress
- environmental awareness
- sustainability
- timekeeping

Policies and procedures
There will be organisational policies and procedures to follow such as appeals, complaints, misconduct, plagiarism and risk assessments. If you are employed, you should have

received a contract of employment and employee handbook which should include your organisation's codes of practice. Alternatively, they might be available electronically.

If you are a work-based trainer, you may have to design your training and assessment activities around the company's policies and procedures (sometimes called *Method Statements* or *Work Instructions*). These will usually have the relevant legislation such as aspects of health and safety built in to them.

There are codes of practice which will apply if you belong a professional association; for example, the Institute for Learning (IfL), which is the independent professional body for teachers, tutors, trainers and trainee teachers in the Further Education and Skills Sector.

IfL Code of Professional Practice (2008)

This was introduced by the Institute for Learning (IfL) to cover the activities of their members. The Code is based on seven behaviours:

1. professional integrity

2. respect

3. reasonable care

4. professional practice

5. criminal offence disclosure

6. responsibility during Institute investigations

7. responsibility

There is a weblink at the end of the chapter if you wish to read the Code in full.

Extension Activity

Identify and research the legislation, regulatory requirements and codes of practice relevant to your role and subject area. Summarise the key aspects of these and state how they could impact upon your role as a teacher or trainer.

Summary

In this chapter you have learnt about:

- *roles, responsibilities and boundaries*

- *working with other professionals*

- *quality assurance*

- *record keeping*

- *legislation, regulatory requirements and codes of practice*

Cross-referencing grid

This chapter contributes towards the following assessment criteria of the units which form the Award in Education and Training, along with aspects of the Professional Teaching Standards. Full details of the learning outcomes and assessment criteria of each unit can be found in the appendices.

Award units	Assessment criteria
Roles, responsibilities and relationships in education and training	1.1, 1.2 3.1, 3.2
Understanding and using inclusive approaches in education and training	
Understanding assessment in education and training	4.1, 4.2
Learning and Development units	**Assessment criteria**
Facilitate learning and development for individuals	1.4, 2.3
Facilitate learning and development in groups	1.4, 2.3
Understanding the principles and practices of assessment	1.4, 3.4 6.1, 6.2, 6.3 7.1 8.1, 8.3
Domain	**Professional Teaching Standards**
A	AS1, AS4, AS5, AS6, AS7, AK2.1, AK2.2, AK4.2, AK6.1, AK6.2, AK7.1, AK7.2, AP6.1, AP6.2, AP7.1, AP7.2
B	BS2, BK1.3, BK27, BP27
C	CS1, CS3, CS4, CK1.1, CK1.2, CK4.1, CP1.1
D	AS3, AS5 DS1
E	
F	FS2, FK2.1, FP2.1

Theory focus

References and further information

Berry, J (2010) *Teachers' Legal Rights and Responsibilities: A guide for trainee teachers and those new to the profession* (2nd Edn). Hertfordshire: University of Hertfordshire Press.

Gravells, A (2012) *Achieving your TAQA Assessor and Internal Quality Assurer Award*. London: Learning Matters.

Gravells, A (2013) *Passing Assessments for the Award in Education and Training*. London: Learning Matters.

HMI (2004) *Every Child Matters: Change for children*. London: DfES.

IfL (2008) *Code of Professional Practice: Raising concerns about IfL members*. London: Institute for Learning.

LLUK (2006) *New Overarching Professional Standards for Teachers, Tutors and Trainers in the Further Education and Skills Sector*. London: Skills for Business.

LSIS (2009) *Centres for Excellence in Teacher Training: CETT Standard*. Learning and Skills Improvement Service Newsletter issue I.

Peart, S and Atkins, L (2011) *Teaching 14–19 Learners in the Lifelong Learning Sector*. Exeter: Learning Matters.

Powell, S and Tummons, J (2011) *Inclusive Practice in the Lifelong Learning Sector*. Exeter: Learning Matters.

Read, H (2011) *The Best Internal Quality Assurer's Guide*. Bideford: Read On Publications Ltd.

Reece, I and Walker, S (2008) *Teaching, Training and Learning: A practical guide* (6th Edn). Tyne & Wear: Business Education Publishers Ltd.

Rogers, A and Horrocks, N (2010) *Teaching Adults* (4th Edn). Maidenhead: Open University Press.

Tummons, J (2010) *Becoming a Professional Tutor in Lifelong Learning Sector* (2nd Edn). Exeter: Learning Matters.

Wilson, L (2012) *Practical Teaching: A guide to assessment and quality assurance*. Hampshire: Cengage Learning.

Wood, J and Dickinson, J (2011) *Quality Assurance and Evaluation in the Lifelong Learning Sector*. Exeter: Learning Matters.

Websites

Criminal Records Bureau – www.crb.gov.uk

Government legislation – www.legislation.gov.uk

IfL Code of Professional Practice – www.ifl.ac.uk/membership/professional-standards

Institute for Learning – www.ifl.ac.uk

National Institute of Adult Continuing Education– www.niace.org.uk

Ofqual – www.ofqual.gov.uk

Ofsted – www.ofsted.gov.uk

Plagiarism – http://plagiarism.org

Regulatory requirements – http://standards.gov/regulations.cfm

2 FACTORS CONTRIBUTING TO LEARNING

In this chapter you will learn about:

- the teaching, learning and assessment environment
- motivation
- learner age ranges and locations
- learning preferences
- theories of learning

There are activities and examples to help you reflect on the above which will assist your understanding of the factors which contribute to learning taking place. At the end of each section within the chapter are extension activities to stretch and challenge your learning should you wish to carry them out. A list of useful references, further information and website links can be found at the end in case you would like to research the topics further.

At the end of the chapter is a cross-referencing grid showing how the chapter's contents relate towards the units of the Award in Education and Training and the Professional Teaching Standards.

The teaching, learning and assessment environment

A suitable teaching, learning and assessment environment is crucial for effective learning to take place. This includes not only the venue, equipment and resources used, but also your attitude and the support you give to your learners. Learning can take place in a variety of contexts; for example, classrooms, the workplace, training rooms, workshops, prisons, outdoors and online. While learning can take place almost anywhere, not all environments will be totally suitable; however, it's *how* you teach your subject and assess it that will lead to effective learning. If you can convey passion and enthusiasm for your subject you will help motivate your learners to want to learn more.

You might be restricted by the availability of particular rooms or resources; therefore you need to be imaginative with what's available to you. Your learners don't need to know of any problems, as your professionalism should enable you to deliver and assess your subject effectively. However, you do need to take into account any health and safety issues and let your organisation know of any concerns. You need to establish a purposeful learning environment where your learners feel safe, secure, confident and valued. The venue, toilets and refreshment areas should be accessible and suitable for everyone, advance knowledge of your learners will help you check that everything is suitable. If your session includes a break, make sure you tell your learners what time this will be and for how long. If you don't, learners might not be concentrating on their learning but thinking about when they can go to the toilet or get a drink.

If you are teaching a practical subject, you will need a suitable environment so that you can demonstrate and your learners can practise, for example, a workshop or a laboratory. If you are teaching a theoretical subject, you may be fine in a room with tables and chairs, but you might need a computer, data projector and/or an interactive whiteboard. You might be delivering a seminar in a venue you have never visited before. If this is the case, it would be useful to telephone or visit in advance to check what facilities are available. Creating a good first impression, being organised and professional should help your learners feel they are receiving a professional service.

The education environment has three aspects: physical, social and learning. Each has an impact on the others and all three aspects should be appropriate, relevant and safe. Some aspects will interact and overlap to ensure teaching, learning and assessment can be effective for everyone.

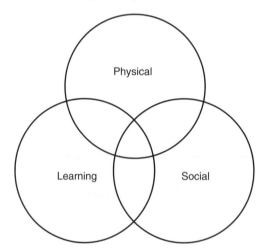

**Figure 2.1 Physical, social and learning aspects and
how they interact and overlap**

Physical

The physical environment is concerned with the surroundings and atmosphere within which learning takes place; this need not be a traditional classroom but could be a training room, workshop, outdoors or another setting such as a community centre. The temperature, lighting and ventilation can all affect the learning that takes place. You may need to close blinds to block out the sun, open a window to let in fresh air or even tidy rubbish away that has been left by the previous occupiers. Different subjects might need different requirements, for example, natural light for drawing and painting, dimmed light to view recorded materials. You will need to find out where light switches are, whether you can adjust heating and ventilation systems, and where fire extinguishers and emergency exits are.

Learners need to know they are safe when they are with you and not in any danger. For example, equipment and resources should not cause harm, tables and chairs should be in an appropriate layout for the subject, and all areas should be accessible. Safe also relates to learners feeling safe to express their opinions without being ridiculed by others. This should inspire confidence, motivate learners and enhance your professional credibility.

While it is your responsibility to ensure the environment is safe and supportive, you might not be able to control some aspects such as external noise. However, what you can do is ensure your session is interesting, meaningful and engaging to your learners. You would need to take into account your organisation's health and safety policy and not do anything outside of your own responsibility, such as moving heavy equipment. Some resources, particularly electrical ones, require regular maintenance checks and testing. If you see a *portable appliance tested* (PAT) label on a resource which shows it hasn't been checked for a long time, you will need to liaise with the relevant personnel to ensure it is safe.

Social

The social environment is concerned with how you help put your learners at ease, establish a rapport with them and help them work and get along together. Using a suitable icebreaker will help learners get to know each other at the beginning of the first meeting. Creating a social and supportive learning environment will include agreeing ground rules, i.e. switching off mobile devices to ensure the session flows smoothly. However, the ground rules will depend upon the age and maturity of your learners. Helping learners relax should lead to effective two-way communication. You should aim to use eye contact with everyone and use their names whenever possible so that they feel valued as an individual.

Learners should know that you, their peers and others if necessary, will make their time meaningful, productive and supportive. Supportive also relates to giving appropriate advice and/or referring your learners to others if you can't help them with a concern they may have. You should demonstrate inclusion (i.e. not exclude anyone) and challenge any inappropriate or anti-social behaviour.

Learning

The learning environment is concerned with giving your session a purpose by having a clear aim of what you want your learners to achieve, using suitable and varied teaching and learning approaches, resources and assessment activities. You should use formal and informal activities during your session. For example, a formal presentation by you followed by an informal group activity. How you plan to deliver and assess your subject will be based upon the requirements of the programme or qualification. It might be left to you to decide in what order you do this and what approaches you take with your learners to achieve it.

Try and plan your session content to flow logically and the subject material should be interesting and stimulating. Encourage your learners to become actively involved, to think for themselves and to use their existing skills and knowledge to build upon. You should give regular feedback regarding individual progress and achievement. You could encourage peer support by using the *buddy* approach. This enables learners to pair up with someone in the group they feel comfortable with. They can then keep in touch between sessions to discuss the topics and this approach is particularly useful if one learner misses a session for any reason and need to catch up.

Knowing your subject, and delivering and assessing it in a meaningful way which includes all your learners, will help them achieve their goals.

Table 2.1 Examples of physical, social and learning aspects

Physical	Social	Learning
Ensure adequate heating, lighting and ventilation	Use a suitable icebreaker to put learners at ease and create a rapport	Have clear aims and objectives/learning outcomes of what will be covered and plan what will take place during each session
Ensure ease of access to all learning areas	Agree ground rules to help promote appropriate behaviour and respect	Engage and motivate learners, give support and encouragement
Ensure the layout of the room is suitable or adjust if possible (e.g. to ensure all learners can see and hear)	Communicate effectively (speaking, listening, body language, eye contact)	Make the session interesting and relevant, summarise and recap regularly
Ensure toilets and refreshment facilities are accessible	Use paired and group activities, draw on learners' skills, knowledge and experiences	Use a variety of suitable teaching, learning and assessment approaches
Ensure safe use of equipment, materials and resources	Encourage learners to listen to you and each other	Differentiate for individual needs, refer learners elsewhere if necessary
Carry out risk assessments and minimise hazards, know who the first aider is	Use learner names and eye contact, include all learners in activities and when communicating	Assess progress and achievement on an ongoing basis (formally and informally)
Know where fire extinguishers and emergency exits are	Give adequate breaks at appropriate times	Provide ongoing constructive feedback
Make sure the room is tidy before and after use	Challenge inappropriate behaviour	Keep records of what has been taught, and the progress of all learners

Activity

Look at the physical, social and learning aspects in Table 2.1 and choose at least three from each column which you feel are important. Draw a diagram like that in Figure 2.1 of three overlapping circles and complete them with your aspects. Which do you think will interact and overlap and why?

Room layouts

If you are teaching indoors, an important influence upon the way your session progresses and how you and your learners can communicate will be the room layout. You may not be able to control this if the furniture is in fixed positions. However, if you can, it is best to create an environment where learners can communicate with each other and see and hear everything you are doing and saying. You should move around the room regularly and interact with your learners rather than stay at the front or sit behind a desk.

Tables or desks in rows

This classroom style does not lead to effective communication between learners. However, all learners can see what is going on. This layout is useful when presenting information if group work is not required. This layout without the tables would enable more chairs to be positioned in rows, allowing many learners to attend a session at the same time. This is known as lecture style. The teacher would need good voice projection to reach all learners at the back of the room, or use a microphone in a large hall. The chairs might have a moveable arm on which to rest notes. If a learner is sitting in the middle of a row and needed to leave for any reason, they would disrupt the rest of the row of learners.

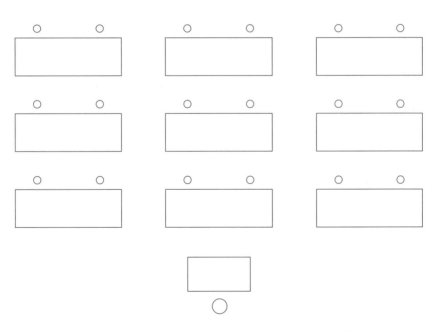

Figure 2.2 Tables or desks in rows – classroom-style layout

Tables or desks in groups
This *cabaret* or *cafe* style is more effective to allow learners to work together and interact during group activities. All learners can still see the teacher and any presentation materials being used. If room permits, tables could be moved so that they are not so close together, or placed at different angles. The teacher could sit beside the desk rather than behind so as not to create a barrier, and move around the room as necessary.

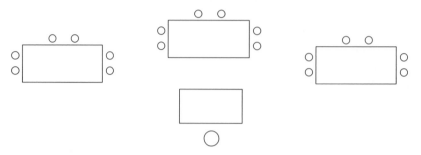

Figure 2.3 Tables or desks in groups (cabaret or cafe style)

Horseshoe or U-shape
This style allows for large group discussions between the learners and the teacher, but is not good for small group work. Learners can still see the teacher and any presentation materials being used. Learners sitting at the very ends of tables may feel excluded from the group if activities are taking place. More tables could be added if necessary to close the gap and create an oblong shape; the teacher then becomes part of the group.

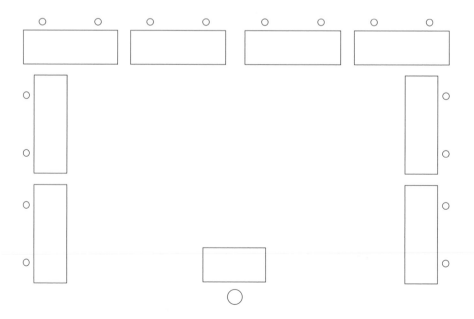

Figure 2.4 Horseshoe or U-shape layout

Boardroom style

This style allows for discussions and group work where a large table area is needed. If the teacher sits at the table with the learners, everyone can communicate and see each other. If the teacher sits separately, some learners will have their back to them and not be able to see a presentation screen if used.

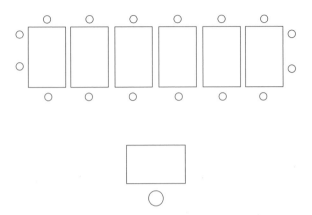

Figure 2.5 Boardroom-style layout

Other layouts

By experimenting with other layouts you can try out how effective they are; for example, having tables in different layouts for individual, small group work and seminars. This can include the teacher as part of the group, with or without tables. Sometimes tables can create barriers between the teacher and the learners. If you are delivering a session at an external venue, such as a hotel or conference centre, you should be able to request certain layouts which will be set up for you. If you need to move the furniture, you should get another member of staff to help you beforehand and again afterwards. You will need to allow space for movement around the room and for bags and coats, to ensure there are no obstructions. Always return the room to its original layout at the end of your session.

Figure 2.6 Other layouts

Activity

Think back to a really good, or a really bad experience you have had as a learner. Explain how the physical, social and learning aspects had an impact upon how you learnt. Were there any other aspects that influenced your learning? What can you do to ensure your learners have a good experience with you and that learning takes place?

You need to manage the learning environment to promote and encourage individual and group learning. The seating arrangements can have a big impact on learning. People like their comfort zones and you may find that learners will sit in the same place each time they are with you. This is often the place they sat during the first session. This is useful to help you remember their names as you can sketch a seating plan and make a note. Remembering and using learners' names will show respect, and encourage them to talk to you in confidence if they have any concerns. Moving learners around or getting them to work with others can either help or hinder their learning depending upon the group dynamics and learner maturity.

If possible, arrive early to set up the environment as you may find it hasn't been left in a suitable condition by the previous user.

Example

Harry arrived at 9.25 a.m. ready for his session which commenced at 9.30 a.m. He was delivering the topic of Sales and Marketing in the conference room. He found the room was untidy with rubbish on the floor, three chairs were missing, writing was on the board and the data projector wasn't working. He became very anxious as his learners arrived while he was trying to prepare the room. He therefore didn't give a professional impression and was flustered when he started the session, missing out some vital information as a result.

You need to ensure the physical environment is suitable not only for learning, but for social interaction too. If possible, aim for 70 per cent of the time for learner involvement and activities, and 30 per cent of the time for teaching activities. This will of course depend upon the subject you are teaching and the environment you are in. However, using activities, projects, discussions, paired and group work for your learners to carry out should aid the learning process by keeping them active, interested and motivated.

Health and safety considerations

Learners are entitled to learn in a healthy and safe environment. If you see a potential hazard, be proactive and do something about it or report it: don't wait for an accident to happen. Under the Health and Safety at Work etc Act 1974 (HASAWA), health and safety is your responsibility as well as your organisation's. Your learners may need to wear protective clothing or use hazardous substances for some activities; you will therefore need to find out what your organisation's procedures are for these. You might be using electrical equipment which will need checking regularly by an appointed person in your organisation. You also need to make sure that any floor surfaces are not slippery, that any trailing wires are out of the way and any equipment your learners will be working with is safe and reliable. If you are teaching a subject that could be dangerous or hazardous, you may need to carry out risk assessments, which should be documented. If safe to do so, you could include your learners in this process to help them identify any issues or concerns, prior to their use.

You will need to know your organisation's accident and fire procedures, such as the location of fire exits and meeting points, extinguishers and first aid facilities. You should inform your learners of these during their first meeting with you. If you have any learners who started after the programme commenced, you should always give them this information when they start. You could include it in a handout or it may already be in a learner handbook or accessible electronically.

You may have learners who have individual needs such as epilepsy or diabetes, therefore it's important to find this out. You will need to know who they are, what you need to do, and who you need to contact in case of an emergency.

Extension Activity

Think about the subject you would like to teach and the environment you will use. What health and safety considerations might there be? Are there any restrictions regarding the resources your learners need to use; for example, cutting equipment? Are there any records or checks you need to complete beforehand, or anyone you need to liaise with?

Motivation

Motivation is the incentive or reason why someone chooses to do something. You need to be aware of what motivates your learners, as their keenness will affect their learning and behaviour during your sessions. A learner attending a session because they have been told to, may not be as motivated as a learner who is there for personal or professional fulfilment. You also need to know what your learners are expecting from you, as what you expect to deliver might differ from what they expect to receive. Finding out the expectations of your learners, and what motivates them, should help you deliver the programme in a way that will lead to successful achievement.

Motivation is either intrinsic (from within), meaning the learner wants to learn for their own fulfilment, or extrinsic (from without), meaning there may be an external factor motivating the learner; for example, a promotion at work. Table 2.2 lists some examples of internal and external reasons why people are motivated to learn.

Table 2.2 Intrinsic and extrinsic motivation factors

Intrinsic	Extrinsic
• desire to achieve something new	• acceptance and approval of others
• enjoyment and fulfilment	• achievement of a qualification
• overcoming personal challenges	• career progression
• passion for subject	• pay rise
• personal reasons	• professional reasons
• social interaction	• promotion
• to complete something previously not achieved	• requirement of job role
	• resolving professional situations
• to gain confidence	• to please others or make them proud
• to improve self-esteem and self-worth	• to prove to others something can be achieved
• to prove to self something can be achieved	• to receive a bonus or commission

If learners are keen and active towards learning, they should be self-motivated and keen to learn. For example, obtaining the relevant resources and text books, asking for help when necessary, getting actively involved and taking control of their studies. Conversely, if learners are passive, their motivation to learn will be less. For example, expecting the teacher or trainer to supply their resources, not asking for help when necessary, not participating and not wanting to take control of their studies. Passive learners might blame the teacher or trainer when they don't achieve, whereas active learners might just blame themselves.

Try and make things interactive by involving your learners as much as you can. Some popular live television programmes are becoming interactive by encouraging their audiences to get involved. For example, using social networking to communicate, carrying out an online poll, and encouraging people to phone or text. This way, people feel engaged, are involved and active, rather than passive.

Whatever level of motivation your learners have, will be transformed, for better or worse, by what happens during their experience with you. You therefore need to promote a professional relationship that leads to individual trust and learning. Some learners may seem naturally enthusiastic about learning, but many need or expect you to inspire and engage them.

Many factors affect a learner's motivation to work and to learn; for example, interest in the subject matter, perception of its usefulness, a general desire to achieve, self-confidence and self-esteem, as well as patience and persistence. Not all learners are motivated by the same values, needs, desires, or wants. Some of your learners will be motivated by the approval of others and some by overcoming personal challenges.

To help motivate your learners you can:

• ask open questions (ones that begin with *who, what, when, where, why* and *how* – not closed questions, which just lead to *yes* or *no* responses)

- avoid creating intense competition, although some competition can be engaging and fun
- be aware of attention-span limits
- give ongoing constructive feedback
- give praise and encouragement
- maintain an organised and orderly atmosphere
- make tasks interesting, practical and relevant
- negotiate realistic targets
- stretch and challenge learners' potential
- support those who need it
- treat learners with respect and as individuals
- use icebreakers and energisers to get learners actively working together
- vary your teaching and assessment approaches to reach all learning preferences

Attention spans

An attention span is the amount of time that a learner can concentrate without being distracted. This will vary due to the age of your learners; often younger learners will concentrate less and older ones more. Being able to focus without being distracted is crucial for learning to take place. There are two types of attention, *focused* and *sustained*.

- Focused attention is a short-term response to something that attracts awareness and is very brief. For example, the ring of a telephone or an unexpected occurrence. After a few seconds, it is likely that the person will return to what they were originally doing or think about something else.

- Sustained attention is a longer-term response which will enable the achievement of something over a period of time. For example, if the task is to take a few photos, choose the best three and upload them to a website, then the person showing sustained attention will stay on task and achieve it fully. A person who loses attention might take a few photos but move on to doing something else before choosing and uploading the best three.

Most healthy teenagers and adults are able to sustain attention on one thing for about 20 minutes (Cornish and Dukette, 2009, page 73). They can then choose to refocus on the same thing for another 20 minutes. This ability to renew concentration enables people to stay on task for as long as necessary. However, there are other factors to take into consideration, such as self-motivation, ability, tiredness, thirst and hunger. If a learner is really hungry their concentration may lapse as a result. If you find your learners losing focus, ask them if there's anything distracting them as you might be able to resolve it, for example, opening a window if it's too warm.

When planning to deliver your sessions, try and use several short tasks to enable your learners to stay focused. If you do need to use longer tasks, try and break these down into 20 minutes for each, with a chance for a discussion or something different in between. If you teach longer sessions, for example over an hour, try and include a break to enable your learners to experience a change of scenery, obtain refreshments and visit the toilet if necessary.

You might find that attention spans are decreasing due to the use of modern technology. For example, searching the internet, changing television channels and using electronic devices and mobile phones can reduce concentration time. If you have learners who use a lot of electronic devices, they may have reduced attention spans and need to move on to other tasks more frequently. If applicable, you could incorporate the use of information and communication technology (ICT); for example, researching current topics online and creating a presentation regarding their findings.

Maslow's (1987) Hierarchy of Needs

Maslow (1987) introduced a *Hierarchy of Needs* in 1954 after rejecting the idea that human behaviour was determined by childhood events. He felt that obstacles should be removed that prevent a person from achieving their goals. He argued there are five needs which represent different levels of motivation which must be met. The highest level was labelled *self-actualisation,* meaning people are fully functional, possess a healthy personality, and take responsibility for themselves and their actions. He also believed that people should be able to move through these needs to the highest level provided they are given an education that promotes growth. Figure 2.7 shows the needs expressed as they might relate to learning, starting at the base of the pyramid.

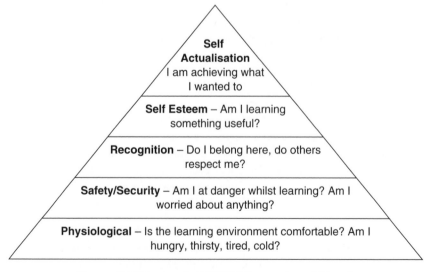

**Figure 2.7 Maslow's (1987) Hierarchy of Needs
expressed in educational terms**

When learners satisfy their needs at one level, they should be able to progress to the next level. Something may set them back a level, but they should need to keep striving upwards. It is these needs that motivate learning to take place. However, some people may not want to progress through the levels, and may be quite content where they are at that moment in their life.

To help your learners' motivation, always ensure that the environment you create meets your learners' first-level needs. This will enable them to feel comfortable and secure enough to learn and progress to the higher levels. You will need to appreciate that some learners may not have these lower needs met in their home lives, making it difficult for them to move on to the higher levels.

Always try to establish a purposeful environment where your learners can feel safe, secure, confident and valued.

Example

Susan was due to teach a session from 5 p.m. to 7 p.m. She arrived early and noticed the room was hot and stuffy so opened the windows. She also realised that most of her learners might not have had a chance to eat something prior to the session. When they arrived she told them they could have an early break to enable them to get refreshments. After break, she kept one window open to let some fresh air in the room and also allowed her learners to have bottled water if they wished. This ensured her learners' first-level needs were met, enabling learning to take place.

While you may be very good at delivering your subject, you might have no control over the environment and will need to create a suitable atmosphere if you can. However, your enthusiasm and passion for your subject should help engage your learners. If you can also make your session interesting, active and varied, your learners will enjoy the experience and remember more about the subject and you, rather than the environment or lack of facilities.

Extension Activity

How can you engage and motivate your learners? Can you create an activity or task for them to carry out which is relevant to the subject, yet includes their interests and also relates to their reasons for learning?

Learner age ranges and locations

Learners in the Further Education and Skills Sector include a breadth of people aged 14 and above, who will be from a variety of backgrounds, with diverse levels of experience and knowledge, and in different locations. All learners will have different reasons for learning something new and you have the opportunity to help them achieve their aspirations.

The age ranges you might be involved with will bring interesting challenges, whether you are teaching in a small or large group, or training individually on a one-to-one basis. This section will explore some of the types of learner you might come across such as:

- 14–16 year olds
- 16–19 year olds
- adult learners

- workplace learners
- distance learners
- offender learners

14–16 year olds

The 14–16 age group are still attending compulsory education and certain regulations, safeguarding and disciplinary procedures will apply. You could be teaching in an academy, public, private or free school, college or other organisation which may have different requirements to a secondary or comprehensive school. You might be teaching learners who are in residential care; for example, physically disabled youngsters who are entitled to education but are not necessarily integrated within mainstream establishments.

Teaching this age group might bring with it issues that you will have to deal with such as challenging behaviour, truancy, peer pressure, negative attitudes, disruption, bullying and discreet use of mobile phones. Learners might want to be treated as adults but they are still classed as children. It would be beneficial to set clear boundaries and establish routines so that a climate of respect and organisation can exist. You will need patience and understanding and must treat everyone in the group as an individual, remaining firm but fair to all. To help maintain respect, you might not want to be on first name terms, nor reveal anything too personal about yourself.

If you are teaching this age group, you may need to modify your delivery style and methods to those you would use with adults. You might be teaching within the school environment and have to follow their rules and regulations. Alternatively the learners might come to your organisation and therefore act more maturely, or act over confidently and become disruptive in front of their peers.

You may need to liaise with colleagues or specialist staff on a regular basis. Some learners may have learning difficulties; others may come with a support assistant to help them. However, all learners will have something positive to contribute to the session and you will need to ensure your delivery enables everyone to participate in the learning experience. You might also need to deliver other topics such as Personal, Social and Health Education (PSHE).

Ensuring your sessions are meaningful, with lots of interesting and practical tasks, will help classroom management. If you can't use practical tasks, break your session down into lots of smaller aspects, recapping each before moving on. Younger learners need lots of praise and encouragement, they appreciate you listening to them and supporting them when necessary. They also like to use technology whenever possible. Try and be approachable, and listen to what they have to say. If you ask a learner a question and they answer wrongly, don't dismiss it, but try and relate their answer to a real situation which is relevant to the subject. Include all learners when asking questions and make them feel their contribution is valued, if you are enthusiastic about the subject, hopefully they will be.

16–19 year olds

The 16–19 age group will include some learners still in compulsory education and those attending part time or full time to achieve qualifications perhaps in a college. Learners might be taking an apprenticeship programme or attend day release from work. Non-attendance might affect their funding allowance and you might be required to sign records of attendance to prove they were present. Some problems that you may encounter with the 14–16 age range might be the same as those encountered with the 16–19 age range. For example, if they have to attend as part of a work experience programme and are not attending voluntarily they might not pay as much attention. However, some learners may have been in (or are still in) employment and will have knowledge and experience that can be drawn on during the sessions. You might, therefore, have learners who have recently left school in the same group as learners who have been in employment for a while; as a result, levels of maturity may differ. However, some school leavers might prefer being in an adult environment to a school environment and as such pay more attention. Never assume, under or over estimate your learners' skills, knowledge and understanding or make any presumptions about them or their past.

You might be teaching a broad spectrum of ages ranging from 16 upwards, in groups or as individuals. Some learners might be apprehensive if they have not attended education for a few years. You will therefore need to reassure them that you are there to help them. Depending upon your subject, there will be ways of integrating your learners' experiences to benefit everyone.

Example

Haani teaches a weekly two-hour Information Technology programme which will last eight weeks. There are ten learners aged 16 to 65. As part of the first session he asked them all to introduce themselves and say a little about their experience of using a computer. He soon realised the older learners have very little experience and three have never even switched on a computer before. The younger learners are more confident and have used computers at school and home. He therefore decides to sit a younger learner next to an older one so they can help and support each other. Each learner will be working individually through a series of tasks, at their own pace and can ask each other questions, learning from each other as well as from Haani.

Depending upon your subject, you will find your own ways to reach each individual, giving them confidence to progress with their learning. Always give positive encouragement to retain motivation and treat all questions from learners as valid, no matter how silly they may seem to you (or them) at the time.

Adult learners

Adult learners are usually motivated to learn, either for their own personal benefit or to learn new skills and knowledge. They might attend for professional reasons, retraining to enhance their job role, or as a result of redundancy or wanting a new opportunity. Their motivation ensures they are keen and enthusiastic learners, usually attending voluntarily in their own time and probably at unsociable hours. However, some adults might have been told to attend a programme either by their employer or as part of programme to help them gain employment. Therefore, their motivation might not be as high as you would like. You might find with some adult learners that they feel they know more than they do. You will therefore need to be tactful at finding out what they can and cannot do to help them realise this.

Adults tend to have a lot of experience, whether it is practical or theoretical and are often used to being active and having self-discipline when it comes to learning. Adults are often confident to ask questions and challenge theories and like to relate new learning to their own situations. If you are asked a question you cannot answer, say you will find out, and make sure you do. While you are expected to have an in-depth knowledge of your subject, you won't know everything and it's best to be honest and admit when you don't know something.

Often, adults are not afraid of making a mistake as they have learnt this through experience, whereas younger learners would not want to embarrass themselves in front of their peers. Adults are often keen to tell you and the group their experiences and how they have learnt from them. Conversely, some adults might lack confidence to discuss things in front of their peers until they get to know them well.

When teaching adults, plan tasks in a logical order, relate theory to practice and involve them with discussions of their own experiences. Always clearly state the aim of your session and how the objectives and/or learning outcomes relate to their goals. Objectives and learning outcomes will be covered in detail in Chapter 4. With all learners, you should recap and summarise topics, repeat key points and ask questions on an ongoing basis to check learning is taking place.

Adults will usually make the effort to arrive on time, have the necessary materials, e.g. pens, paper and text books, and not be disruptive. However, you need to consider their personal circumstances and situations, especially if you are delivering an evening class and some of your learners have been at work all day or looking after children.

You could be on first name terms with adults and have a more informal delivery style (depending upon your subject and your learners). Some adults might have had negative experiences at school or of previous programmes they have attended which might have stayed with them, therefore affecting their current learning. Try and get to know each learner as an individual to enable you to support their learning in an appropriate way.

Workplace learners

Workplace learners are those who are learning in their place of work. They might be learning a new task or procedure, being assessed for a qualification, or as part of an apprenticeship programme. The way you teach or train will usually be on an individual or small group basis. If you are also based in the same environment, it will give you the opportunity to spend more time with your learners. Hopefully, your learners will be self-motivated and keen to learn, therefore being quite attentive. However, you will have other priorities such as the commitments and deadlines of your own job role to take into consideration. You might be training a learner who is with your organisation as part of a work experience programme, they might be with you one day a week or for a full week or more. Even though they might not be in paid employment, you should treat them as a member of staff and make them feel welcome. They might have certain tasks they need to learn and carry out as part of their training programme, therefore you might need to assess their progress and liaise with staff from the organisation they are from.

Distance learners

Distance learners are those that are learning away from the formal teaching environment and might therefore be isolated from the teacher and other learners. Learning is increasingly taking place online via the internet, enabling it to occur at a time and place to suit. Programmes can be tailored to meet individual requirements and learners can work at their own pace. If you are teaching online, you might never meet your learners, but communicate via the computer program, e-mail or face-to-face online applications. Learners need to be self-motivated, committed and able to devote a suitable amount of time to this type of study.

Learning can be *synchronous*, i.e. the learner and teacher are online at the same, or *asynchronous,* i.e. at different times. Some programmes require learners to attend a few sessions somewhere, and support the rest of their learning through a virtual learning environment (VLE). This is known as *blended learning*, and handouts, activities and resources can be uploaded by the teacher at any time for access by the learner. Activities, communication and assessment can also be carried out via the VLE. There can still be issues with motivation as learners need to be disciplined with aspects such as time management. There could also be concerns with behaviour in that some inappropriate comments could be made online. Agreeing a code of conduct from the start could help alleviate this.

Offender learners

These learners might be in a young offender institution, on remand or detention, or in a prison. It might be compulsory that they attend various sessions and while some will be keen to learn, others may not. This will bring its own challenges regarding motivation, and there might also be some behavioural issues to contend with. You will need to allow extra time before and after a session to go through the security procedures. If you are teaching or training in this type of environment you will need to be careful not to allow yourself to become conditioned to situations, i.e. forgetting that your learners are there to gain skills and knowledge which will help them upon their release. You will also have strict guidelines to follow. It could be that some of your learners are released or moved part way through the programme. Others might start at different points and will need to catch up on what has been taught so far. Some may drop in and out of your sessions due to the prison regime where offenders are attending other activities such as physical educa-tion. You might even arrive to teach a session and find that the learners have been locked in due to operational issues. Some might be with visitors or have been moved elsewhere and therefore will not be attending. Keeping an accurate and up-to-date track of individual progress and achievement will therefore be important.

Extension Activity

Think back to when you attended school, college or university and compare this to a more recent learning experience as an adult. Were your experiences positive or negative? What age group would you like to teach and will your previous experiences influence the way you treat your learners?

Learning preferences

Most people learn in different ways, known as *learning preferences*, what suits one learner might not suit another. For example, you might like to watch someone perform a task, and then carry it out yourself, or you might just want to try it out for yourself first. What you might tend to do is deliver your sessions in the style in which you learn best – although it will suit you, it might not suit your learners. If you can find out what your learners' prefer-ences are, then you can adapt your teaching and learning approaches to suit. There are many different ways that people learn, often known as *learning styles* and this section will explore some of these.

There is an old Chinese proverb: *I hear – I forget, I see – I remember, I do – I understand.* When you hear lots of information you may find it difficult to remember it all. If you can see something taking place that represents what you hear, you should remember more. However, if you actually carry out the task which relates to what you have heard and seen, you will understand the full process and remember how to do it again.

Pike (1989) stated: *Studies show that over a period of three days, learning retention is as follows.*

- 10% of what you read
- 20% of what you hear
- 30% of what you see
- 50% of what you see and hear
- 70% of what you say
- 90% of what you say and you do

If your learners can incorporate *reading, hearing, seeing, saying* and *doing* during your sessions, their learning retention should increase. Once learners put theory into practice they should begin to understand what they have learnt. Some people learn by imitating others, while they might then be able to perform the task, they might not know *why* they are doing it. There-fore, skills and knowledge should be learnt together to ensure understanding takes place.

Example

Gill was demonstrating how to correctly prune roses to a group of learners taking a Horticulture programme. As she did so, she explained why it's important to prune them in a certain way, and at a set point in the gardening calendar. If Gill hadn't explained this, her learners would not know when to do it or why, and might apply their knowledge wrongly in future as they didn't fully understand.

Fleming (2005)

Fleming stated that people can be grouped into four styles of learning: visual, aural, read/write and kinaesthetic, known by the acronym VARK. However, not all learners fall into just one style as they may be *multi-modal*, i.e. a mixture of two or more styles enabling learning to take place more quickly.

Table 2.3 Examples of VARK styles of learning

Visual Visual (seeing) learners usually:	Aural Aural (listening and talking) learners usually:
• are meticulous and neat in appearance • find verbal instructions difficult • memorise by looking at pictures • notice details • observe rather than act or talk • like watching videos/DVDs	• are easily distracted • enjoy talking and listening to others • have difficulty with written instructions • hum, sing and whisper or talk out loud • ask questions • don't like noisy environments
Read/write Read/write (reading and writing) learners usually:	Kinaesthetic Kinaesthetic (doing) learners usually:
• are good spellers and have good handwriting • enjoy research • like rewriting what others have written • like to read books • use a dictionary and thesaurus • write lists and make notes	• are tactile towards others • do not like reading and are often poor spellers • enjoy worksheets and discussions • fidget with pens while studying • like practical activities • use their hands while talking

Activity

If you have access to the internet, go to www.vark-learn.com and carry out the online questionnaire. See what your results are for each of V, A, R and K. This is something you could ask your learners to do if you have the opportunity.

It is always useful to get your learners to carry out a learning preferences questionnaire. It can be fun and lead to an interesting discussion, as well as helping you plan your teaching, learning and assessment approaches to reach their learning preferences. It also empowers learners to adapt information in a way that they are comfortable with, for example, using a digital voice recorder rather than hand writing notes. Table 2.4 gives some examples of VARK learning preferences.

Table 2.4 Examples of VARK learning preferences

Topic	Visual	Aural	Read/write	Kinaesthetic
Answering the telephone	Watching a demonstration, viewing a presentation and/or video Looking at a handout	Listening to instructions and recordings, asking questions	Making notes, reading instructions and handouts	Carrying out the task or a role play
Decorating a cake	Watching a demonstration, viewing a presentation and video	Listening to instructions, asking questions	Making notes, reading instructions and handouts	Carrying out the task
Remembering historical dates	Viewing a video Looking at a handout or presentation	Listening to instructions, discussing with others	Reading text books and handouts, writing facts and dates	Researching the internet, carrying out a role play or quiz
Practising interview skills	Viewing a video or simulation	Listening to instructions, asking questions	Reading handouts, making notes	Carrying out a role play
Using a word processor	Watching a demonstration, viewing a presentation and video	Listening to instructions, asking questions	Making notes, reading instructions and handouts	Carrying out the task on a computer
Learning a foreign language	Viewing a video	Listening to conversations and recordings of people speaking, talking to others	Reading text books, writing words and phrases	Holding a conversation
Changing a fuse	Watching a demonstration, viewing a presentation and video	Listening to instructions, asking questions	Making notes, reading instructions	Carrying out the task for real

Honey and Mumford (1992)

Honey and Mumford suggest learners are a mixture of four styles: activist, pragmatist, theorist and reflector.

Activist
Activist learners like to deal with new problems and experiences, often learning by trial and error. They like lots of activities to keep them busy and enjoy a hands-on approach. They love challenges and are enthusiastic.

Pragmatist
Pragmatist learners like to apply what they have learnt to practical situations. They like logical reasons for doing something. They prefer someone to demonstrate a skill first before trying it for themselves.

Theorist
Theorist learners need time to take in information, they prefer to read lots of material first. They like things that have been tried and tested and prefer reassurance that something will work.

Reflector
Reflector learners think deeply about what they are learning and the activities they could do to apply this learning. They like to be told about things so that they can think it through. They will also try something, think again about it, and then try it again.

Activity

Consider something you have recently learnt; for example, using a new mobile phone. Did you: jump right in and press all the buttons (activist); ask someone to show you before having a go (pragmatist); read the instructions thoroughly, then carry them out (theorist); or become confident at using the phone for calls and texts before considering its other uses (reflector)?

However, there are critics of learning preferences. In 2004, Professor Frank Coffield of The University of London carried out a systematic and critical review of learning preferences and pedagogy in post-16 learning. The report reviewed the literature on learning preferences and examined in detail 13 of the most influential models. The report concludes that it matters which is chosen. The implications for teaching and learning, he states, are serious and should be of concern. Coffield has since written widely on the subject and states ... *it was not sufficient to pay attention to individual differences in learners, we must take account of the whole teaching-learning environment.* (2008, page 31).

Extension Activity

Think about the subject you will deliver, what activities could your learners do to cover the visual, aural, read/write and kinaesthetic learning preferences? Do you agree with Coffield that the whole teaching and learning environment has an impact rather than the learning preferences? If so, how?

Theories of learning

There are lots of theories regarding how people learn. These theories will have been based on ideas, thoughts and experiences. Some are quite old, but are trusted; others are fairly recent. You may even come up with your own theory or challenge existing ones. All people learn differently, perhaps influenced by experiences in their childhood, school, personal or professional relationships. When you learn something new, you will probably adapt, change or modify your behaviour as a result, and the same will apply with your learners. This section will briefly explain some of these theories, which you may wish to research further.

Learners need to know why it is important for them to learn, what they are going to learn and how they will do this. Setting clear aims and objectives of what you want your learners to achieve is the starting point; summarising and recapping regularly and varying your approaches will all help. Having a sense of humour and making learning interesting and fun should help your learners remember key points. Your learners need to believe that what they are learning has real value and meaning. You also need to treat each learner as an individual and with respect. You should always introduce yourself to your learners; you could keep your name visible somewhere or wear a name badge in the early stages. This should encourage them to feel comfortable to approach you or ask questions.

Sensory theory

Laird (1985) stated that learning occurs when the five senses of sight, hearing, touch, smell and taste are stimulated. Laird's theory suggests that if multi-senses are stimulated, greater learning takes place. You could therefore adapt your approaches and resources to enable your learners to use as many of their senses as possible.

Example

When you were a child, if you saw something that interested you, you would touch it, probably putting it in your mouth if it was small, shaking it to hear if it made a noise and putting it near your nose to smell it. You would soon learn if something tasted nasty not to put it in your mouth again. Therefore, a change in your behaviour took place as a result.

Conditions of learning

Gagne (1985) stated that there are several different types or levels of learning. Each different type requires different types of teaching. Gagne identified five major conditions of learning. These are:

- verbal information

- intellectual skills

- cognitive strategies

- motor skills

- attitudes

Different internal and external conditions are required for each. For example, for motor skills to be learnt, there must be the opportunity for your learner to practise new skills rather than just observe them. For attitudes, your learner must be able to explore these; for example, by discussing them. In addition, this theory outlines nine events that activate the processes needed for effective learning to take place. Gagne believed all teaching and learning sessions should include this sequence of nine events. Each event has a corresponding cognitive process (in brackets below).

1. Gaining attention (reception)

2. Informing learners of the objective (expectancy)

3. Stimulating recall of prior learning (retrieval)

4. Presenting the stimulus (selective perception)

5. Providing learning guidance (semantic encoding)

6. Eliciting performance (responding)

7. Providing feedback (reinforcement)

8. Assessing performance (retrieval)

9. Enhancing retention and transfer (generalisation)

Example

Ellie, a new teacher can ensure all these events take place in her sessions by:

1. *Gaining attention – showing an example of what the learners will achieve during the session, e.g. an iced wedding cake.*

2. *Identifying the objective – stating that the learners will be able to ice a wedding cake by the end of the session.*

(Continued)

(Continued)

3. *Recalling prior learning – asking the learners if they have ever iced a wedding cake before.*

4. *Presenting stimulus – explaining how they will ice the wedding cake and what they will need to use.*

5. *Guiding learning – demonstrating how to ice a wedding cake.*

6. *Eliciting performance – encouraging the learners to begin icing a wedding cake.*

7. *Providing feedback – informing the learners how they are progressing.*

8. *Assessing performance – ensuring the learners are correctly icing the wedding cake by observing and asking questions.*

9. *Enhancing retention/transfer – summarising the learning, relating it to real life events and explaining what will be covered in the next session.*

Experiential

Kolb (1984) proposed a four-stage experiential theory, known as the experiential learning cycle. It is a way by which people can understand their experiences, and as a result, modify their behaviour. It is based on the idea that the more often a learner reflects on a task, the more often they have the opportunity to modify and refine their efforts. The process of learning can begin at any stage and is continuous, i.e. there is no limit to the number of cycles which can be made in a learning situation. This theory suggests that without reflection, people would continue to repeat their mistakes.

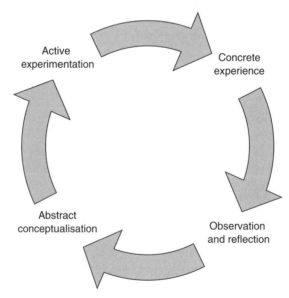

Figure 2.8 Kolb's (1984) experiential learning cycle

- Concrete experience is about experiencing or immersing yourself in the task and is the first stage in which a person simply carries out the task assigned. This is the *doing* stage.

- Observation and reflection involve stepping back from the task and reviewing what has been done and experienced. Your values, attitudes and beliefs can influence your thinking at this stage. This is the stage of *thinking* about what you have done.

- Abstract conceptualisation involves interpreting the events that have been carried out and making sense of them. This is the stage of *planning* how you will do it differently.

- Active experimentation enables you to take the new learning and predict what is likely to happen next or what actions should be taken to refine the way the task is done again. This is the *redoing* stage based upon experience and reflection.

Example

Wang is taking an accounting programme which has an examination at the end. If he fails he will not know why he has failed. He will need to wait another three months before he can retake the examination. During the programme, he could experience the learning process, but not reflect upon what he might be doing wrong that may lead to him failing the examination. He therefore could not modify his behaviour and try again. If he took a programme with ongoing assessment instead of an examination at the end, he would have the opportunity to go through the full cycle. He would have the experience, reflect upon it due to ongoing feedback, think how he could improve and then experiment to try again.

You are probably familiar with the saying *you learn by experience*. You might find that doing a task, then thinking about it, leads you to plan how you would do it differently next time. Repeating and reflecting on tasks will help your learners learn, whether this relates to skills or knowledge.

Humanist theory

Rogers (1983) and others developed the theory of facilitative learning based on a belief that people have a natural human eagerness to learn and that learning involves changing your own concept of yourself. This theory suggests that learning will take place if the person delivering it acts as a facilitator. The facilitator should establish an atmosphere in which their learners feel comfortable, are able to discuss new ideas and learn by their mistakes, as long as they are not threatened by external factors.

Example

Vicky is due to teach a Digital Photography for Beginners evening class. There is no qualification handbook as the programme does not lead to a qualification. Therefore she has planned to deliver what she thinks is relevant, based on the last time she taught it. However, she remembered being told by an observer of her class last term that she should consider the needs of her learners more. Therefore, at the first session, she has decided to encourage her learners to tell her what their expectations are. This will enable her to facilitate her sessions to cover these. It will also ensure her learners feel included, comfortable to discuss topics and as result learning will take place.

Behaviourist theory

Skinner (1974) believed that behaviour is a function of its consequences, i.e. learners will repeat the desired behaviour if positive reinforcement is given. The behaviour should not be repeated if negative feedback is given. Giving immediate feedback, whether positive or negative, should enable your learners to behave in a certain way.

Positive reinforcement or rewards can include verbal feedback such as *That's great, you've produced that document without any errors* or *You're certainly getting on well with that task* through to more tangible rewards such as a certificate at the end of the programme or a promotion or pay rise.

Example

Jamie was sawing a piece of wood as part of a carpentry programme and hadn't paid attention to the health and safety regulations. The saw kept slipping and he cut his hand. His teacher gave him negative feedback and this, along with his cut, ensured he was more careful in future.

The Peter Principle

Peter and Hull (1969) devised the principle that people are promoted to their highest level of competence, after which further promotion raises them to a level just beyond this and they become incompetent. These levels are as follows.

- Unconscious incompetence – you don't know how to do something, but don't know that you don't know this. To reach the next level, you need to know what it is that you don't know.

- Conscious incompetence – you know what you want to do, and start to appreciate the gap in your competence. To reach the next level, you need to know how to become competent.

- Conscious competence – you can do what you set out to do, but have to give it a lot of attention. Through repeated practise, you can reach the next level.

- Unconscious competence – you can perform a skill easily without giving it a great deal of thought. Once you achieve unconscious competence, you are at a level which suits your ability at the time.

If you are promoted or try something different, you might return to the first level and become unconsciously incompetent again. This is useful to know, as your learners may reach and stay at one of these levels, or reach the highest level and then return to a lower level due to further progression.

Example

Renuka has just started a Using Spreadsheets programme, having previously only used a computer for e-mails and accessing the internet. She doesn't yet know how to use a spreadsheet or the functions it can perform – she is at the unconscious incompetence level. After learning how to set up a spreadsheet, she now wishes to perform some calculations; she knows she wants to do this but doesn't know how. This is the conscious incompetence level. Renuka soon learns how to perform calculations and does this at the conscious competence level. She isn't quite at the unconscious competence level yet, where she could do it without thinking.

Domains of learning

Bloom (1956) stated that learning often goes through five stages, which should lead to a change in behaviour These stages are:

- attention

- perception

- understanding

- short-/long-term memory

- change in behaviour

Starting with gaining your learners' attention and progressing through the stages should ensure learning takes place, therefore leading to a change in behaviour. The stages relate to your learners' *thinking, emotions* and *actions* which Bloom called *domains* of learning. These domains are known as *cognitive, affective* and *psycho-motor*. Think of cognitive as the head (thinking), affective as the heart (emotions) and psycho-motor as the hands (actions). When delivering your subject, you need to consider which domain you want to reach and how you can progress your learners through the five stages. It's useful to know which domain you want to reach when planning your session's aim and objectives. More information regarding Bloom, and the setting of aims and objectives can be found in Chapter 4.

Example

- *cognitive domain (subject – geography) learners will state the reasons for coastal erosion*

- *affective domain (subject – the environment) learners will discuss their ideas for recycling*

- *psycho-motor domain (subject – bricklaying) learners will build a two-foot high wall*

Knowing a little about the different theories will help you realise which teaching, learning and assessment approaches to use, and why things happen in a certain way. You might like to research other theories; therefore relevant texts and websites are listed at the end of this chapter.

Extension Activity

How will these theories affect the way you deliver and assess your subject? Do you agree with them, or do you have your own theory of how learning takes place?

Summary

In this chapter you have learnt about:

- *the teaching, learning and assessment environment*

- *motivation*

- *learner age ranges and locations*

- *learning preferences*

- *theories of learning*

Cross-referencing grid

This chapter contributes towards the following assessment criteria of the units which form the Award in Education and Training, along with aspects of the Professional Teaching Standards. Full details of the learning outcomes and assessment criteria of each unit can be found in the appendices.

Award units	Assessment criteria
Roles, responsibilities and relationships in education and training	1.1, 1.4 2.1
Understanding and using inclusive approaches in education and training	1.1 2.1, 2.2, 2.3
Understanding assessment in education and training	
Learning and Development units	**Assessment criteria**
Facilitate learning and development for individuals	1.1
Facilitate learning and development in groups	1.2
Understanding the principles and practices of assessment	
Domain	**Professional Teaching Standards**
A	ASI, AS2, AK1.1, AK2.1, AK2.2, AK4.1, AP1.1, AP2.2, AP3.1, AP4.1, AP6.2
B	BSI, BK1.1, BK1.2, BK1.3, BK2.1, BK2.2, BK2.3, BPH, BPI.3
C	CK3.1.CP3.1
D	
E	
F	

Theory focus

References and further information

Bloom, BS (1956) *Taxonomy of Educational Objectives: The classification of educational goals*. New York: McKay.

Carr, N (2010) The Web Shatters Focus, Rewires Brains. *Wired* magazine, 24 May. Available at: wwwwired.com/magazine/2010/05/ff_nicholas_carr/all/l (accessed October 2011).

Coffield, F (2004) *Learning Preferences and Pedagogy in Post-16 Learning*. London: Learning and Skills Research Centre.

Coffield, F (2008) *Just Suppose Teaching and Learning Became the First Priority*. London: Learning and Skills Network.

Cornish, D and Dukette, D (2009) *The Essential 20: Twenty components of an excellent health care team*. Pittsburgh: RoseDog Books.

Fleming, N (2005) *Teaching and Learning Preferences: VARK strategies*. Honolulu: Honolulu Community College.

Gagne, R (1985) *The Conditions of Learning* (4th Edn). New York: Holt, Rinehart & Winston.

Gould, J (2012) *Learning Theory and Classroom Practice in the Lifelong Learning Sector* (2nd Edn). London: Learning Matters.

Gravells, A (2013) *Passing Assessments for the Award in Education and Training*. London: Learning Matters.

Honey, P and Mumford, A (1992) *The Manual of Learning Preferences* (3rd Edn). Maidenhead: Peter Honey Associates.

Illeris, K (2010) *The Fundamentals of Workplace Learning: Understanding how people learn in working life*. Abingdon: Routledge.

Kidd, W and Czerniawski, G (2010) *Successful Teaching 14–19*. London: SAGE Publications Ltd.

Knowles, M, Elwood, FH and Swanson, A (2011) *The Adult Learner* (7th Edn). Oxford: Butterworth-Heinemann.

Kolb, DA (1984) *Experiential Learning: Experience as the source of learning and development*. New Jersey: Prentice-Hall.

Laird, D (1985) *Approaches to Training and Development*. Harlow: Addison Wesley.

Learning and Skills Council (LSC) (2007) *Learner Health, Safety and Welfare: The safe learner blueprint*. Coventry: LSC.

Maslow, AH (1987) (edited by Frager, R) *Motivation and Personality* (3rd revised Edn). New York: Pearson Education Ltd.

Peart, S and Atkins, L (2011) *Teaching 14–19 Learners Practice in the Lifelong Learning Sector*. Exeter: Learning Matters.

Peter, LJ and Hull, R (1969) *The Peter Principle: Why things always go wrong*. New York: William Morrow and Company.

Pike, RW (1989) *Creative Training Techniques Handbook*. Minneapolis MN: Lakewood Books.

Rogers, CR (1983) *Freedom to Learn for the 80s*. Columbus, OH: Charles Merrill.

Rogers, A and Horrocks, N (2010) *Teaching Adults* (4th Edn). Maidenhead: Open University Press.

Skinner, BF (1974) *About Behaviorism*. San Francisco, CA: Knopf.

Wallace, S (2007) *Getting the Buggers Motivated in FE* (2nd Edn). London: Continuum.

Websites

Bill Gates – Creating great teachers video – www.youtube.com/watch?v=1IcZbRY_bYs&feature=related

Health and Safety Executive – www.hse.gov.uk

Learning preferences questionnaire – www.vark-learn.com

Learning theories – www.learning-theories.com

Peter Honey – www.peterhoney.com

Teaching and learning theories -http://classweb.gmu.edu/ndabbagh/Resources/IDKB/models_theories.htm

Tips for teaching adults – www.helium.com/knowledge/61278-tips-for-teaching-adult-learners-instead-of-younger-learners

In this chapter you will learn about:

- identifying needs of the organisation, teachers and learners
- initial and diagnostic assessment
- potential needs of learners and points of referral
- inclusive learning
- equality and diversity

There are activities and examples to help you reflect on the above which will assist your understanding of how to identify the relevant needs of learners on which to base the teaching, learning and assessment process. At the end of each section within the chapter are extension activities to stretch and challenge your learning should you wish to carry them out. A list of useful references, further information and website links can be found at the end in case you would like to research the topics further.

At the end of the chapter is a cross-referencing grid showing how the chapter's contents relate towards the units of the Award in Education and Training and the Professional Teaching Standards.

Identifying needs of the organisation, teachers and learners

Identifying and understanding the needs of all those involved in the teaching, learning and assessment process will help ensure your practice is effective and that learning can take place.

Organisation needs

The starting point for planning teaching, learning and assessment is usually based upon the needs of your organisation: for example, the curriculum which is to be offered. The qualifications and programmes which make up the curriculum might be decided by local needs; for example, business and employment. Other considerations may include priorities attached to funding from external agencies, as some programmes are offered only if financial support or loans can be obtained by learners. External agencies such as awarding organisations will give approval for accredited qualifications to be delivered at your organisation. They will produce a syllabus, more often known as a *qualification handbook* for each subject. This will give details of what must be delivered and assessed. If learners successfully achieve the requirements, they will receive a certificate endorsed by the awarding organisation. Organisations are responsible for recruiting relevant experienced and qualified staff to meet their curriculum needs.

If there is a demand, *bespoke* programmes could be created to meet a particular need and be offered at a place of employment or in a local venue or hotel. These are often known as *non-accredited* programmes as an awarding organisation does not usually issue a qualification. However, your organisation might issue certificates of attendance. These will prove a person was there, but not that they necessarily learnt anything. Assessment would need to take place to determine what that person actually learnt, enabling a certificate of achievement to be issued. These types of programme are often paid for by the employer or the learner. Some bespoke programmes could lead to an accredited qualification if the learners were able to achieve units from qualifications which matched the programme content, or if a qualification was created to meet a particular need.

Programmes and qualifications can be short, medium or long term and may be offered at various times of the day or evening and at various locations, depending upon needs. Different models of delivery can be used such as formal attendance, open to anyone, online, distance learning, flexible, or blended learning, which combines technology with traditional learning.

If the programme you teach is advertised on your organisation's website, in a prospectus, leaflets or in the local press, make sure you read it to check it is correct. If what you plan to offer is different from that advertised, there will be confusion when your learners commence. Your future learners should be able to have access to information, advice and guidance. This will help them make a choice about the programme they wish to take, which will help them progress to reach their goals.

Different models of delivery will influence what you *must* and what you *could* do with your learners. The *product* model of delivery focuses upon the requirements of a programme; for example, what learners *must* know to pass an examination, test or assignment. The teacher often just teaches what *must* be taught to get the learner through. What *could* be taught isn't taken into consideration, often due to time constraints, and therefore doesn't benefit the learner in the long term.

Example

Samantha is taking a Spanish qualification at evening classes. Her teacher covers only what is in the programme requirements (what must be taught) and does not cover anything else which could help Samantha if she visits Spain in the future (what could be taught).

The *process* model of delivery focuses on the content of the programme *and* other relevant skills and knowledge that *could* be learnt and applied.

> ## Example
>
> *Kelly is taking a word-processing qualification. She is paying for the programme herself and is prepared to continue until she feels capable. As she has never used a computer before, she has asked her trainer to help her learn keyboard skills and file-management skills. These are in addition to word-processing skills. She is therefore getting the benefit of what could be taught as well as what must be taught.*

Additional aspects that could be taught to add value to the programme will be based upon how much time you have and the needs of your organisation and learners.

Teacher and trainer needs

Your needs as a teacher or trainer might include updating your subject knowledge, working towards teaching qualifications and/or learning new skills. All teachers and trainers should not only be knowledgeable and current in their specialist subject but they should also know how to use innovative ways to deliver and assess their subject to enable learning to take place.

Ideally, you need a suitable environment in which to teach your subject. You may not be able to change this; however, you could make it more stimulating by displaying posters or changing the layout of the furniture (if possible). You will also need various resources to deliver your subject effectively; for example, computers, equipment, books and handouts. Whether you can have these might depend upon the finances available. If your organisation can't afford to buy up-to-date textbooks you could place the onus upon your learners to purchase them, access them from a local library or download an electronic version.

There are certain things you must know before you begin to plan your sessions; for example, what and who you will be teaching, for how long, where and when. Knowing this will help you plan your sessions effectively. You will also need to know the people at your organisation who can support you; for example, administration staff, caretakers and managers. When you start teaching, you should have a mentor, someone in the same subject area as yourself. They should show you around the premises, introduce you to relevant staff members and give you advice and support as necessary. If you encounter situations with learners that you can't deal with, you must feel you can approach someone such as your mentor.

You might find it useful to create a *toolkit* of items you will regularly use when teaching. This could contain pens, board markers, a wireless remote control for electronic presentations, paper, a small clock, stapler, hole punch and other relevant items for your subject. It's useful to have a few extra pre-prepared activities or quizzes that you could use if you have spare time during your sessions, or if some learners finish an activity earlier than others.

Learner needs

Identifying any individual learner needs prior to commencement will help you plan your teaching to meet these. Learner needs will vary, they could simply be a need to know where to park their car, the need to have privacy to take insulin for diabetes at certain times, or the need to know the qualification will meet their career aspirations. Depending upon the type of programme you are teaching, you might not always be able to find out this information in advance. As a result, some learners may take a programme which is unsuitable for them or their needs won't be met.

It might be that you don't have the opportunity to identify your learners' needs as they are just attending a short session, for example, a one-day programme. In this case, you could find out at the beginning of the session if anyone has any particular needs, for example, sitting closer to the front as they are hard of hearing.

Identifying your learners' needs can take place as part of the application process, during an interview or when they commence the programme. Information, advice and guidance (IAG) should be given to learners regarding their programme choice, and this should be clear, unambiguous and impartial to ensure it meets their needs and capability. The application process should ensure learners are on the right programme to help them reach their destination, i.e. the correct qualification for their career path. You should also inform learners of how they will be assessed during the programme, e.g. assignments, observations or tests. This will ensure there are no surprises once they have started.

Some learners may be embarrassed or not wish to divulge personal information on application forms or at an interview. You could have an informal chat with them to find out if they have any needs or specific requirements; for example, if they have dyslexia. Some of the indicators of dyslexia in adults include:

- a low opinion of their capability
- difficulty filling in forms and writing reports
- difficulty structuring work schedules
- losing and forgetting things
- the tendency to miss and confuse appointment times

An indicator checklist is available at www.dyslexia.uk.net, or your organisation might be able to arrange for a dyslexia test.

If you are unsure about how to help your learners, just ask, as they are best placed to know how you could support them.

If you have a learner requiring support for any reason, there is a difference between *learning support* and *learner support*. *Learning* support relates to the subject, or help with English, maths, study skills or information and communication technology (ICT). *Learner* support relates to help they might need with any personal issues, and/or general advice and guidance such as financial support.

You should discuss the requirements of the programme or qualification with your learners, along with the range of services and agencies that are available to assist with any specific needs. Impartial advice should be available from the National Careers Service regarding job search, preparation for interviews and more.

Extension Activity

What do you consider the needs of your organisation, yourself, and your learners might be? How could you find out and use this information?

Initial and diagnostic assessment

Initial and diagnostic assessments are the formal ways of ascertaining your learners' prior skills, knowledge and understanding of the subject to be taken, and whether they have any specific *learning* or *learner* needs. The process should be carried out prior to, or at the beginning of the programme. There could be particular entry requirements for your subject and an initial assessment or interview would ascertain if these have been met prior to your learners commencing.

Initial assessment

Using initial assessments will help you to find out about your learners and identify any particular aspects which might otherwise go unnoticed. It's best to do this prior to the programme commencing. This will allow time to deal with any issues that might arise, or to guide learners to a different, more appropriate programme if necessary.

Initial assessment can:

- allow for differentiation and individual requirements to be met
- ascertain why the learner wants to take the programme along with their capability to achieve
- find out the expectations and motivations of your learner
- give your learner the confidence to negotiate suitable targets
- identify any information which needs to be shared with colleagues
- identify any specific additional support needs

Example

Jennifer had applied to take a Conflict Management programme and was attending an interview with the trainer. After discussing her current skills and knowledge, and her aspirations for using the qualification to improve her career, she decided it wasn't for her at the moment. She felt she lacked the confidence at this point in time, therefore the trainer referred her to the National Careers Service where she could get further advice.

Diagnostic assessment

Diagnostic assessments can be used to evaluate a learner's skills, knowledge, strengths and areas for development in a particular subject area. It could be that your learner feels they are capable of achieving at a higher level than the diagnostic assessments determine. The results will give a thorough indication of not only the level at which your learner needs to be placed for their subject but also which specific aspects they need to improve on. Skills tests can be used for learners to demonstrate what they can do, knowledge tests can be used for learners to demonstrate their understanding.

Diagnostic tests can also be used to ascertain information regarding English, maths and ICT skills. Information gained from these tests will help you plan your sessions to meet any individual needs and/or to arrange further training and support if necessary.

You should not accept learners onto a programme just because you need the numbers to make a group viable. The programme may not be suitable for them and they may leave, therefore wasting their time and yours.

Diagnostic assessment can:

- ascertain learning preferences
- enable learners to demonstrate their current level of skills, knowledge and understanding
- ensure learners can access support such as study skills
- identify an appropriate starting point and level for each learner
- identify gaps in skills, knowledge and understanding to highlight areas to work on
- identify previous experience, knowledge, achievements and transferable skills
- identify specific requirements: for example, English, maths and ICT skills

The results of initial and diagnostic assessments should help you negotiate individual learning plans (ILPs) or action plans with your learners, ensuring they are on the right programme at the right level with the support they need to succeed.

Extension Activity

Find out what initial and diagnostic assessments are available at your organisation. Will it be your responsibility to administer these, or is there a specialist person to do this? How will you use the results? If you are not yet teaching, research suitable assessments that you could use with your learners in future, perhaps via the internet.

Potential needs of learners and points of referral

Some learners will have needs, barriers or challenges to learning that may affect their attendance, progress and/or achievement. If you can ascertain these prior to your learners commencing, you will hopefully be able to refer them to someone that can help. However, other issues may occur during their time with you, which you would need to deal with. You would therefore need to plan a suitable course of action to help your learners, or refer them to an appropriate specialist or agency to alleviate any impact upon their learning.

Potential needs of learners

It's difficult to help your learners if they don't tell you about any specific issues, needs or concerns they might have. You could ask if there is anything you could do to help make their learning experience a more positive one. However, anything you do would have to be reasonable, and not seen as favouritism by other learners. Encouraging them to tell you when you are on your own at an appropriate time, would save your learner any embarrassment they might feel when in front of their peers. Learner needs, barriers or challenges might include a lack of finance, transport issues, childcare concerns or English as a second or other language.

Example

Dave informed his teacher that he has dyslexia and asked if any handouts could be printed on cream paper as this helps him read them better. He also asked if anyone minded if he used a digital recorder during the sessions, as he preferred to listen to this afterwards rather than make notes. His teacher asked the group if they were all happy to have handouts on cream paper and whether they minded Dave recording the session. All the group agreed to his requests. The teacher also uploaded all the programme materials to the virtual learning environment (VLE). This enabled everyone to access them in their own time, save or print them in a suitable font and colour.

If you can be proactive and notice potential needs before they become issues, you might be able to alleviate your learners' concerns. Otherwise, you will need to be reactive to the issue and deal with it professionally and sensitively.

You could create a *risk register* to document any concerns and/or issues with individual learners. You can update it with any occurances to keep track of progress before anything serious occurs. Your learners may trust you and tell you something confidential; however, you may need to pass this information on to more experienced people, particularly if your learner is vulnerable and/or in need of expert help. See Table 3.1 for examples of potential needs and possible points of referral.

Points of referral

You should always refer your learners to an appropriate specialist or agency if you can't deal with their needs. Never feel you have to solve any learner problems yourself and don't get personally involved, always remain professional. You will need to find out what is available internally within your organisation or where you could refer them externally. You may encounter learners with varying degrees of needs; therefore you should remain impartial, but sensitive. You may feel you can deal with some of these yourself; however, it's best to seek advice or refer your learner to someone who can help.

Table 3.1 Examples of potential needs and possible points of referral

Potential need of learner	Possible point of referral
• access to, or fear of technology	• local library or internet cafe • specialist colleagues and/or training programmes
• alcohol or substance misuse	• telephone helplines • relevant support agencies
• childcare concerns	• childcare agencies
• death in the family	• bereavement support agencies
• emotional or psychological problems	• health centres, general practitioners • Samaritans or other professionals
• English as a second or other language	• interpreters, bilingual staff or other specialist colleagues
• financial issues	• banks, building societies • Citizens Advice Bureau • specialist staff with knowledge of funding, grants and loans
• health concerns	• health centres, general practitioners, hospitals
• limited basic skills such as English and maths	• specialist colleagues • online programmes and training centres
• transport problems	• public transport websites and timetables
• unsure which career path to take	• National Careers Service • specialist staff within the organisation

Extension Activity

What needs or challenges do you think your learners might have and how can you identify them? Make a list of the people or agencies you could refer them to if you are not able to help the learners yourself.

Inclusive learning

Inclusive learning is about ensuring all your learners have the opportunity to be involved, to contribute and to be included in the learning process. It's also about treating all learners equally and fairly, without directly or indirectly excluding anyone. Inclusion is about attitudes as well as behaviour, as learners can be affected by the words or actions of others. You are not teaching your subject to a group of learners who are all the same, but to a group of individuals with different experiences, abilities and needs which should be recognised and respected.

Example

A group of four learners decide to go out for dinner to celebrate their achievements. One is a vegetarian, the second is dairy intolerant, the third doesn't eat fish and the fourth has no preference. They all want to eat at the same restaurant and choose from the same menu. They checked in advance that the restaurant they had chosen will cater for all nutritional needs. This ensured they will all be included as part of the group, and can order from the same menu and therefore be treated equally. The diverse requirements of the group are being taken into account to differentiate for their needs and ensure all learners are included in the activity.

Ways to promote inclusion include:

- ascertaining individual needs, learning preferences and goals
- being approachable and accessible, enabling learners to feel comfortable to disclose concerns
- challenging stereotyping, discrimination and prejudice as it happens
- differentiating activities to address individual differences; for example, different abilities and levels
- encouraging group work where learners can mix and participate with all members of the group over a period of time
- ensuring the environment is accessible to all learners
- identifying where modifications or changes are needed to equipment or activities
- involving all learners, e.g. using their names, using eye contact and asking individual questions
- recognising and valuing individual contributions and achievements
- using a wide range of teaching, learning and assessment approaches based upon learner needs
- using resources and materials which positively promote all aspects of community and society, equality and diversity

When you are with your learners, try to promote a positive culture of equality of opportunity whereby all your learners can attend, participate and feel safe and valued. Ways of including your learners can simply be by using their names when they arrive and when talking to them, using eye contact and speaking personally to them during each session. If possible, try and ask an open question to every learner during each session (ones that begin with *who, what, when, where, why* and *how*). Using the pose, pause, pick (PPP) technique of questioning can be a way of including all your learners. This is where you ask a question, then pause for a few seconds so that all learners are thinking about a response, while you use eye contact with everyone. You can then pick a learner to answer the question, stating their name as you look at them. This is better than stating a learner's name before the question, as the other learners will not be thinking about the answer as they know someone else has been asked. You might need to prepare some questions in advance, or use opportunities which occur during the session. If possible, ask a question to each learner so that they have all been included.

Activity

Think about the subject you will deliver and assess. Compose several open questions that you can use during a session, enough for one for each learner. If you have the opportunity, use the PPP technique and see how effective it was.

If you can develop the conditions for learning that are based on respect and trust, and address the needs of individual learners, you will have created an effective teaching, learning and assessment environment.

Extension Activity

Imagine you have a group of 14 learners for your subject: six females and eight males aged between 16 and 65 from a variety of backgrounds. Three have never used a computer before, one has dyslexia and one is a wheelchair user. Their learning preferences are: nine kinaesthetic, two visual, two read/write and one aural. Regarding the subject you will teach, how could you ensure you differentiate for individual needs yet include everyone in the session?

Equality and diversity

Equality is about the rights of learners to have access to, attend, and participate in their chosen learning experience. This should be regardless of age, ability and/or circumstances. Any inequality and discrimination should be challenged to ensure fairness, decency and respect among your learners. Equal opportunity is a concept underpinned by legislation to provide relevant and appropriate access for the participation, development and advancement of all individuals and groups. In the past, equality has often been described as *everyone being the same* or *having the same opportunities*. Nowadays, it can be described as *everyone being different, but having equal rights*.

Diversity is about valuing and respecting the differences in learners, regardless of age, ability and/or circumstances, or any other individual characteristics they may have. If you have two or more learners, you will experience diversity. You may have a mixed group of learners with different past experiences who are aiming to achieve the same qualification but at a different level. You could therefore set different activities and targets for the different levels of assessment criteria.

When teaching and training, you should always ensure you:

- are non-judgemental

- challenge any direct or indirect discrimination, stereotyping, prejudice, harassment, bullying and biased attitudes by yourself or others

- do not have favourite learners or give some more attention than others

- do not indulge the minority at the expense of the majority

- ensure particular groups are not offended; for example, faith or religion

- ensure particular learners are not disadvantaged or overly advantaged

- reflect on your own attitudes, values and beliefs so that you are not imposing these upon your learners

- treat all learners with respect and dignity

- use activities and assessments which are pitched at the right level

- use questions which are worded so as not to cause embarrassment to learners

Whenever possible, you should try and embrace, embed and advance all aspects of equality and diversity. You could use pictures in handouts and presentations which reflect different abilities, ages, cultures, genders and races. You can also help your learners by organising the environment to enable ease of access around any obstacles (including other learners' bags and coats), and around internal and external doors. If you are ever in doubt as to how to help a learner, just ask them.

Incorporating activities based around equality and diversity and the local community and society within which your learners live and work could help your learners be more understanding and tolerant of each other. You also need to prepare them for the world outside their own living and working environment in case they move elsewhere in the future.

Try and have discussions regarding your subject which are based around areas of learners' interest, cultural topics, popular television programmes and relevant news stories. Place the focus on them to choose rather than you. This should get them thinking about the concept of equality and diversity in society and how to be accepting and tolerant of others.

Activity

If you are currently teaching or training with groups, ask your learners to think of something involving equality and diversity, or to watch the news or a particular television programme. They can then note the key issues for discussion at the next session. During the following session, place your learners in pairs or groups and ask them to discuss their topics. You can then place the pairs into fours if you have time for further discussion. From this activity, you will be able to see how your learners view equality and diversity, enabling you to link their discussions to the subject area.

If you have access to the internet during your session, you could search for a short equality and diversity video which you could show to help generate discussions. Other activities could involve discussions around perceptions and stereotypes, for example, most: fire-fighters are male, nurses are female, male footballers are heterosexual and male hairdressers are gay.

The Equality Act 2010

The Equality Act (2010) replaced all previous anti-discrimination legislation and consolidated it into one Act (for England, Scotland and Wales). It provides rights for people not to be directly discriminated against or harassed because they have an association with a disabled person or because they are wrongly perceived as disabled.

To ensure you comply with the Equality Act (2010), you need to be proactive in all aspects of equality and diversity. You should make sure your delivery style, teaching, learning and assessment resources promote and include all learners in respect of the Act's nine *protected characteristics* (known as personal attributes):

- age
- disability
- gender
- gender reassignment
- marriage and civil partnership
- race
- religion and belief
- sexual orientation
- pregnancy and maternity

Finding ways of integrating these characteristics might occur naturally during your sessions.

Example

Marta was teaching a catering programme to a mixed group of learners from various backgrounds and faiths. As Chinese New Year was approaching she decided to use it as a theme and create different menus around it. This opened up a discussion about the Chinese culture, which the group found interesting and meaningful. She decided she would research other cultures, faiths, religions and beliefs to incorporate them during her sessions throughout the year.

Other opportunities could include:

- celebrating local and national events
- creating and using crosswords, word searches, puzzles or quizzes based around aspects of equality and diversity

- discussing issues when they arise during your sessions, such as their perceptions of disability, older people, different races

- discussing events in the news such as racist attacks, or an issue in a particular television programme such as disability or ageism

- drawing upon the experiences of learners within your group

- embracing differences

- encouraging research activities which relate to the subject

- mixing different learners during group and paired activities

- using pictures to represent the Equality Act's characteristics in your resources and on publicity and marketing materials

- visiting museums and cultural buildings

Example

Leah was teaching a group of Hair and Beauty learners who were three weeks into a two-year day release programme. There were 12 females and two males. During a group activity, Leah overheard one of the females make a remark that the males must be gay if they were taking this programme. After the activity, Leah took the opportunity to open up a group discussion as to why the perception was that males must be gay if they are in this profession. Leah ensured each learner was able to voice their opinion and by the end of the session their perceptions had changed.

Try to encourage learners not to make assumptions: for example, *foreigners always take the jobs of British people,* or *mothers always take time off work to look after their children.* If conversations like these occur, take the opportunity to challenge them.

The Act has seven different *types of discrimination:*

- associative discrimination: direct discrimination against someone because they are associated with another person with a protected characteristic

- direct discrimination: discrimination because of a protected characteristic

- indirect discrimination: when a rule or policy which applies to everyone can disadvantage a person with a protected characteristic

- discrimination by perception: direct discrimination against someone because others think they have a protected characteristic

- harassment: behaviour deemed offensive by the recipient

- harassment by a third party: the harassment of staff or others by people not directly employed by an organisation, such as an external consultant or visitor

- victimisation: discrimination against someone because they made or supported a complaint under equality legislation

You should watch for any type of discrimination occurring between your learners, and indeed whether you or a colleague are perhaps discriminating without realising.

Extension Activity

How can you promote equality and value diversity within your sessions? Design an activity you could use with your learners which will enable them to discuss relevant topics relating to equality and diversity. If you have chance, carry it out and evaluate how effective it was.

Summary

In this chapter you have learnt about:

- *identifying needs of the organisation, teachers and learners*

- *initial and diagnostic assessment*

- *potential needs of learners and points of referral*

- *inclusive learning*

- *equality and diversity*

Cross-referencing grid

This chapter contributes towards the following assessment criteria of the units which form the Award in Education and Training, along with aspects of the Professional Teaching Standards. Full details of the learning outcomes and assessment criteria of each unit can be found in the appendices.

Award units	Assessment criteria
Roles, responsibilities and relationships in education and training	1.1, 1.2, 1.3, 1.4 2.1, 2.2 3.1
Understanding and using inclusive approaches in education and training	1.1 2.1 4.2
Understanding assessment in education and training	

Learning and Development units	Assessment criteria
Facilitate learning and development for individuals	1.5 4.3
Facilitate learning and development in groups	2.3 4.3
Understanding the principles and practices of assessment	4.1 8.3
Domain	Professional Teaching Standards
A	ASI, AS2, AS3, AS5, AS6, AS7, AK1.1, AK2.1, AK3.1, AK5.2, AP1.1, AP2.1, AP2.2, AP3.1, AP5.1, AP5.2, AP6.2
B	BSI, BS3, BS4, BK2.5, BK3.4, BK3.5, BK4.1, BP2.5, BP3.5, BP4.1
C	CK3.2, CK3.5, CP3.2, CP3.3, CP4.2
D	DSI, DS2 ,DK2.2, DP1.1
E	ESI, ES3, EK1.1, EK2.1
F	FSI, FS2, FS4, FK1.1, FK1.2, FK2.1, FK4.1, FK4.2, FPU, FP1.2, FP2.1, FP3.1, FP4.1, FP4.2

Theory focus

References and further information

Ayers, H and Gray, F (2006) *An A to Z Practical Guide to Learning Difficulties*. London: David Fulton Publishers.

Clark, T (2010) *Mental Health Matters for FE: Teachers toolkit*. Leicester: NIACE.

Farrell, M (2006) *Dyslexia and Other Learning Difficulties*. London: Routledge.

Gravells, A (2013) *Passing Assessments for the Award in Education and Training*. London: Learning Matters.

Gravells, A and Simpson, S (2012) *Equality and Diversity in the Lifelong Learning Sector* (2nd Edn). London: Learning Matters.

Powell, S and Tummons, J (2011) *Inclusive Practice in the Lifelong Learning Sector*. Exeter: Learning Matters.

Websites

Citizens Advice Bureau – www.citizensadvice.org.uk

Database of self help groups – www.self-help.org.uk

Dyslexia Association – www.dyslexia.uk.net

Equality and Diversity Forum – www.edf.org.uk

Equality and Human Rights Commission – www.equalityhumanrights.com

Inclusion, Equality, Diversity and Differentiation resources – http://reflect.ifl.ac.uk/viewasset.aspx?oid=3201642&type=webfolio&pageoid=3201743

Inclusive teaching resources, weblinks and videos – www.open.ac.uk/inclusiveteaching/pages/general/a-z.php

Initial and diagnostic assessment – http://archive.excellencegateway.org.uk/page.aspx?o=BSFAlearning difficulty%2Finitialassess

National Careers Service – https://nationalcareersservice.direct.gov.uk/Pages/Home.aspx

Open University inclusive teaching – www.open.ac.uk/inclusiveteaching/pages/inclusive-teaching/index.php

In this chapter you will learn about:

- teaching and learning plans
- differentiation
- resources
- opportunities for English, maths and wider skills
- using information and communication technology

There are activities and examples to help you reflect on the above which will assist your understanding of how to plan your teaching and learning sessions. At the end of each section within the chapter are extension activities to stretch and challenge your learning should you wish to carry them out. A list of useful references, further information and website links can be found at the end in case you would like to research the topics further.

At the end of the chapter is a cross-referencing grid showing how the chapter's contents relate towards the units of the Award in Education and Training and the Professional Teaching Standards.

Teaching and learning plans

To effectively deliver and assess your subject, you need to plan and prepare what you are going to do and when. Using a document known as a *teaching and learning plan* (also known as a *session plan*) will help you formalise this. It might be for a short one day event, a series of daytime or evening classes to groups, on the job one-to-one training, distance learning, online learning or another style of learning. It's useful to plan various aspects in advance so that you are organised and can give a professional service to your learners. It might be that you are delivering a programme that already has the documentation prepared for you, in which case you might just need to adapt it slightly to meet the needs of your learners. However, you might have to prepare the planning documents yourself and your organisation should supply you with the correct forms to use.

A scheme of work (sometimes referred to as a *learning programme* or *scheme of learning*) is a document you can use to structure the teaching, learning and assessment of your subject in a logical and progressive way over several sessions. The content should be flexible to allow for any changes, for example, a cancelled session due to adverse weather; and detailed enough in case a colleague needs to cover for you. If you meet your learners for one session rather than a series of sessions, you will not need a scheme of work, just a session plan. Individual learning plans (ILP) might be better than a scheme of work if you have learners who are all working to different requirements during your sessions, or if you train on a one-to-one basis. A session plan is a detailed breakdown of each date on your scheme of work. It will outline all the teaching and learning activities, with allocated timings, assessment activities and resources required. It will also take into account the individual requirements of your learners, for example their learning preferences.

A scheme of work can be for a whole programme or just a unit of a qualification. You will need to prepare one whether you teach groups or individuals. If you teach the same subject as your colleagues, you could all work together to produce a standardised scheme of work. This will enable all learners to have the same learning experience no matter who they are with. Templates or pro-formas for schemes of work and session plans, and the amount of detail you are expected to include, will vary depending upon the context within which you teach. The requirements of your organisation and external inspectors might also need to be taken into account.

Creating a scheme of work

A scheme of work is a document you can use to plan a sequence of sessions. If you are delivering an accredited qualification, you will need the qualification handbook to ensure you deliver and assess all the required content. If you are delivering a non-accredited programme, you will need to devise your own programme content, along with suitable delivery and assessment materials to meet the needs of your learners.

When creating your scheme of work, it is useful to know something about your learners; for example, their previous knowledge and/or experience, their learning preferences or any particular requirements or needs they may have. This will enable you to plan your teaching and learning activities in a progressive way to achieve maximum potential. You might like to put yourself in the place of your learners when planning the order of what you will teach. This way you can see things from a beginner's perspective to ensure you keep things simple during the earlier sessions. Start with the known and move onto the unknown or unfamiliar, checking the progress of your learners as you go. Because you are a knowledgeable teacher, you might tend to want to achieve too much in the early stages, which could confuse your learners, even though it's very clear to you. Always ask yourself *what am I going to do with my learners and why?*

Your scheme of work should show a variety of teaching, learning and assessment activities to suit all learning preferences. Your sessions should follow in a logical order, which might not be the order printed in the qualification handbook. You might have to state how you will include skills such as English, maths and information and communication technology (ICT). These are covered later in this chapter.

Make sure you check all dates carefully in case there are any bank or public holidays on the dates you would normally be with your learners. The first session should include an induction to the programme and organisation, an icebreaker to help your learners get to know each other, and the setting of ground rules; for example, timekeeping and switching off electronic devices. You might also need to assess prior skills, knowledge and under-standing in this session, or before your learners commence. You will need to check if you will have the same venue for all the sessions, and what facilities, equipment and resources will be available. The more time you take to plan your scheme of work, the easier it will be to create your session plans.

All subsequent sessions should begin with a recap of the previous session and allow time for questions, and end with an explanation of the next session. Depending on how long the programme will last, it would be useful to include an evaluation activity to obtain feedback part way through as well as during the final session. At the end of the programme you should give details of how your learners can progress, i.e. what steps they can take to further their development. See Table 4.1 for a basic example of a scheme of work.

A rationale such as using 'five Ws and one H', *who, what, when, where, why* and *how*, will help you plan your scheme of work, for example:

- who the sessions are for, and what you want your learners to achieve (who and what)

- the objectives or learning outcomes of the qualification or programme (why)

- the dates and times, number of sessions, and venue (when and where)

- teaching and learning approaches, resources and assessment methods (how)

Activity

Consider the five Ws and one H for the subject you will be delivering and assessing. Can you obtain all this information easily? What else will you need to know prior to producing your scheme of work?

Most qualifications have *contact* and *non-contact* time allocated to them. Contact time is when you are in contact with your learners, for example during sessions, tutorial meet-ings and assessing progress and achievement. Non-contact time is for the learner and can be used for reading, research, completing assignments and gathering evidence of work towards meeting the requirements of the qualification. It's useful to inform your learners of their non-contact time and suggested activities prior to them commencing, so that they are aware of what is required.

What you want to achieve with your learners is known as an *aim*, and what your learners will do to achieve it are known as *objectives*. These will be covered in more detail later in this chapter.

There are various aspects you will need to consider prior to creating your scheme of work. For example, do you need to:

- obtain the qualification handbook (if it's an accredited programme)?

- create your own programme content?

Table 4.1 Example – basic scheme of work showing first, second and last sessions

Teacher/trainer A G Smith		Venue Room 3		
Programme/qualification Introduction to Information Communication Technology Level 1		**Group composition** 10 adults with little or no previous experience		**Dates** from: 8 Sept to: 13 Oct
Number of sessions Six		**Contact hours** 18 (3 per week) Non-contact hours 2		

Aim of programme To enable learners to use a computer (for basic word processing, spreadsheets, database, internet and e-mail)

Dates	Objectives *Learners will:*	Teaching and learning activities	Resources	Assessment activities
Week 1 8 Sept	• obtain and discuss information regarding the organisation, programme content and assessment • switch on a computer and use a keyboard and mouse • complete an online initial assessment and learning preferences questionnaire • discuss previous knowledge/experience of using ICT • use the ICT applications	Induction, icebreaker, ground rules Explanation of programme and organisation Video Practical and theoretical demonstration and discussion Initial assessment Discussion and differentiated activities based upon results of learning preferences and to meet individual needs Practical activities Recap of session and explanation of next session	computers interactive whiteboard workpacks internet access flipchart handout exercises quiz	Oral questions and discussion Observation and questions Online initial assessment Discussion Observation Questions
Week 2 15 Sept	• create, save and print documents using a word-processing program	Recap previous session Demonstration of word processing Discussion of uses Differentiated activities and informal assessments Explanation of next session	computers interactive whiteboard workpacks handouts	Observation Oral and written questions Gapped handout Practical activities Quiz
Week 6 13 Oct	• use all ICT programs • carry out a formal assessment activity • complete an evaluation form • discuss opportunities for progression	Recap all sessions Explain and discuss formal assessment process, those not taking it will continue with individual exercises Explain case study activity Facilitate programme evaluation Explain progression opportunities	computers interactive whiteboard workpacks exercises case study activity assignments evaluation form	Formal assignment Observation Questions

- break the content down into a logical order and manageable chunks of learning (remember what *must* and *could* be learnt depending upon how much time you have)?
- know aspects about your learners, e.g. age range, ability, prior knowledge, learning preferences?
- obtain any information about the subject or partake in any training yourself?
- allow time to check if learners have had effective information, advice and guidance?
- allow time for an induction, initial assessment, icebreaker and ground rules in the first session?
- find out what rooms, facilities, equipment and resources are available or need to be obtained?
- embed English, maths and ICT?
- plan activities and materials which can be differentiated and are inclusive to all?
- know the dates and times when learners will be attending, and bank, public and religious holiday dates?
- liaise with others?
- plan non-contact activities?
- upload materials to an online or virtual learning environment (VLE)?
- devise teaching, learning and assessment materials?
- allow time for an evaluation to take place?
- evaluate the programme and your own performance?

The more time you take to plan your scheme of work, the easier it will be to create your session plans and enable learning to be effective.

Aims and objectives

These are terms used to express what you want your learners to achieve and how they will go about it. The aim is a broad statement of intent of *what* you want your learners to achieve; for example, *to enable learners to use a computer*. The objectives are *how* your learners will achieve the aim; for example, *switch on a computer, use a keyboard and mouse*. Once you have your aim for a particular session, you can plan what you want your learners to achieve, i.e. the objectives.

When writing objectives, try not to use words such as *know, learn* and *understand,* i.e. don't say... *Learners will know how to use a computer* because *how do you know they know?* The only way you will know, is if your learners can do something to prove it, i.e. they can *use* a computer. The key to good writing of aims and objectives is to use words that are *verbs,* i.e. things that the learner has to *do* to prove their understanding.

Example

Learners will know the Kings and Queens of England from 1066 to the present day, *is vague and will not show you that learning has taken place.*

Learners will state the names of the Kings and Queens of England from 1066 to the present day *is better as your learners have to do something that enables you to assess learning has taken place.*

Objectives should always be SMART to enable you to deliver and assess learning effectively. This is an acronym for:

- **S**pecific – are the objectives clearly defined and stated to meet the required outcomes?

- **M**easurable – can they be achieved at the right level?

- **A**chievable – can they be met by all learners?

- **R**elevant – do they relate to the aim, the subject, and the learners?

- **T**ime bound – can agreed target dates and times be met?

Being SMART is all about being clear and precise with what you expect your learners to achieve. SMART objectives should always be the right level for your learners; for example, to *list* is easier than to *evaluate*. Knowing your learners and the level of the qualification or programme they are taking will help you plan which verbs to use. Objectives should be challenging enough to ensure learning is progressive, yet be inclusive to all learners to ensure they can achieve.

There are two types of objectives: *behavioural* which demonstrate skills and *non-behavioural* which demonstrate attitudes, knowledge and understanding.

- Behavioural – this is when your learners can demonstrate a skill; for example, *learners will change a fuse in a plug*. If you are teaching *skills*, your objectives might include: demonstrate, perform and use.

- Non-behavioural – this is when your learners can demonstrate they have the right attitude and/or have gained the required knowledge and understanding. Non-behavioural objectives are more difficult to assess and often contain the words *know, learn* or *understand*; for example, *learners will know the law of gravity*. If you use non-behavioural objectives, try to make them SMART; for example, *learners will know the law of gravity by explaining how it occurs*. The addition of the word *explaining* enables you to assess that learning has taken place. Being able to perform a skill and knowing how to do it should not be in isolation from having the understanding to know *why* the skill is being performed. If you are teaching *knowledge*, your objectives might include: describe, explain and list. If you are teaching *attitudes*, your objectives might include: define, differentiate and evaluate.

If you are going to deliver a micro-teach session as part of the Award, you will need to use SMART objectives when producing your planning documents.

Learning outcomes and assessment criteria

Another term widely used in the Qualifications and Credit Framework (QCF) is *learning outcomes*. These might be longer in terms of time taken for your learners to achieve, i.e. they might not achieve them within one session. The word *understand* often appears in the QCF learning outcomes. However, it's the assessment criteria that underpin them that make them SMART. For an example, look at the learning outcomes and assessment criteria of the units of the Award in Education and Training which are in the Appendices at the back of this book.

Although the learning outcomes and assessment criteria for QCF qualifications will have been defined for you, you will still need to write aims and objectives to help you break down your subject into more manageable topics. Having clear aims and objectives will help you plan the content for your scheme of work and individual sessions. Learning outcomes are what *the learner will* do and assessment criteria are what *the learner can* do. Therefore the learning outcomes will help you plan what you will deliver, and the assessment criteria will help you assess that learning has taken place.

Levels of learning

Bloom (1956) identified six progressive levels of learning which have associated objectives (verbs) to denote what learners will be able to know and/or do. These are:

- knowledge for remembering and recalling facts, e.g. list, recall
- understanding for demonstrating comprehension, e.g. describe, explain
- application to apply knowledge to real situations, e.g. demonstrate, operate
- analysis for considering and working things out, e.g. appraise, calculate
- synthesis for compiling ideas and generating new ones, e.g. compose, design
- evaluation for making and defending judgements, e.g. argue, critically appraise

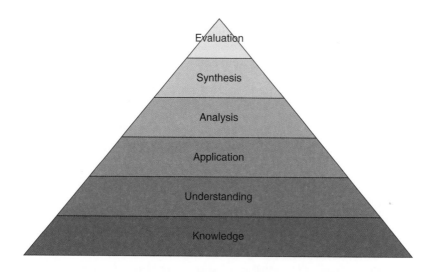

Figure 4.1 Bloom's (1956) six levels of learning

Using Bloom's theory will help you differentiate the objectives you want your learners to achieve to enable them to meet the correct level they are aiming for. Your learners might achieve at different levels throughout their time with you, starting with an expression of their knowledge and leading up to an evaluation of their learning. Table 4.2 lists some objectives which can be used for the different levels ranging from knowledge to evaluation.

You might have groups of learners at different levels within the same session, therefore all might be able to *list* (to demonstrate knowledge), most might be able to *explain* (to demonstrate understanding), and some might be able to *operate* (to demonstrate application), depending upon their progress at the time.

Table 4.2 Objectives to meet Bloom's levels

Objectives					
Knowledge	Understanding	Application	Analysis	Synthesis	Evaluation
define	describe	apply	analyse	arrange	argue
list	discuss	demonstrate	appraise	assemble	assess
name	estimate	devise	calculate	compose	choose
match	explain	illustrate	categorise	construct	critically appraise
recall	identify	interpret	compare	create	differentiate
recognise	locate	modify	criticise	design	estimate
repeat	recognise	operate	debate	invent	evaluate
state	select	use	test	summarise	judge

Example

Barbara teaches health and safety to a group of 20 learners. To test the knowledge of the full group she asks them to list three important Acts of Parliament. To test understanding of this legislation, she asks everyone to explain three points of each Act. Only eight learners were able to. Of those eight, she asks how they could apply the content of the Acts to a real working situation. Only two learners were able to. This shows Barbara what level her learners are at, enabling her to differentiate the teaching and learning approaches accordingly.

Once you know the subject you are going to deliver and assess, you should be aware whether it relates to skills, knowledge and understanding, and/or attitudes. This will help you use appropriate objectives for your learners to achieve. Table 4.3 gives some examples of objectives for skills, knowledge and understanding, and attitudes at different levels of learning. If you are delivering a qualification which is on the QCF it will be at one of the levels in Table 4.3, which range from foundation to level 8. However, your qualification might have assessment criteria which are repeated at different levels, for example, *explain* could occur at level 3 and level 4. It is the underpinning knowledge and understanding that differentiates the level. Although your learners will be working towards assessment criteria at a set level to achieve the qualification, you can still use different levels of objectives during your sessions. For example, your learners could start with lower level objectives such as *state* and progressively work through the others such as *explain* and *demonstrate,* until they reach the assessment criteria at the level of the qualification.

Activity

Obtain a scheme of work template, or create one with similar headings to the one in Table 4.1. Plan a scheme of work for six sessions based on your specialist subject. Make sure you have an appropriate aim for your subject and suitable objectives for the level of your learners.

Table 4.3 Objectives at different levels (note – some might occur or be repeated at different levels on the QCF)

Level	Skills		Knowledge and understanding	Attitudes	
Foundation	Attempt Carry out Learn Listen Read		Answer Match Recall Repeat Show	Adopt Assume Contribute Listen	
1	Arrange Help Imitate Obtain	Switch Use View Watch	Access Know List Locate	Name Recap Recognise State	Adapt Co-operate Familiarise
2	Assist Change Choose Connect Demonstrate Draw	Perform Practise Prepare Present Rearrange	Compare Describe Identify Reorder Select Write	Accept Consider Develop Express Question Understand	
3	Apply Assemble Assess Build Create Construct Design	Devise Estimate Facilitate Illustrate Make Measure Produce	Compose Explain Paraphrase Test	Apply Appreciate Challenge Defend Determine Discriminate Enable	Participate Predict Relate Review Study Visualise
4	Calculate Complete Convert Diagnose Explore Generate Maintain	Modify Plan Quality assure Research Search Solve	Analyse Invent Contextualise Outline Revise Summarise Verify	Appraise Command Criticise Debate Define Discuss Influence	Judge Justify Persuade Rationalise Reflect
5	Accept responsibility Encapsulate Establish	Interview Manage Organise Teach	Categorise Classify Contrast Evaluate Interpret	Argue Critically appraise Define	Differentiate Dispute Formulate Suggest
6	Operate Utilise		Extrapolate Synthesise Translate	Conclude Hypothesise Justifiably argue	
7	Modify		Strategise	Critically differentiate	
8	Lead		Redefine	Critically discriminate	

Creating a session plan

A session plan, also known as a *teaching and learning plan* is a document which should be produced prior to each session and relate to your scheme of work if it's a series of sessions. Although it's very similar to the scheme of work, it is much more detailed and helps you manage the time that you are with your learners. It should also state the activities you use to assess your learners, which can be formal and/or informal. Formal activities will count towards learner achievement, whereas informal activities demonstrate learner progress.

You need to consider what you want your learners to be able to *know* and/or *do* by the end of the session, i.e. your *aim*. SMART objectives will help you focus on this and enable you to assess that learning has taken place.

Example

Aim: learners will:

- *switch on a desktop computer and access the internet*

Objectives: learners will:

- *locate a suitable desktop computer*
- *switch the power on*
- *use a keyboard and mouse to locate appropriate applications on the screen*
- *access the internet*
- *search for a particular website*
- *view the website*

Try not to prepare too many session plans in advance, as circumstances or dates may change and you want the information to be fresh in your mind. You also might change a subsequent plan based upon how a current session went. Once you have a set of session plans, providing the programme doesn't change, you can adapt them in the future for different groups of learners, rather than starting again. However, don't think that because everything worked well last time, it will again this time, as you will have different learners with different needs and abilities.

Each plan should have an introduction, development and conclusion/summary stage; in other words, a beginning, middle and end, with times allocated to the activities within each. Your introduction should include the aim of the session and a recap of the previous session (if applicable). This should hopefully arouse interest and link to previous learning. You could carry out a *starter activity* to gain attention and focus learning, for example, a short quiz. If this is your first meeting with your learners, make sure you introduce yourself, explain the facilities of the organisation, the requirements of the programme, carry out an icebreaker and agree the ground rules. You can also carry out any practical matters such as taking a record of attendance, or reminding learners of any important issues.

The development stage is where teaching and learning should take place and should be in a logical sequence for learning to progress. Imagine you are teaching someone to make a cup of tea. You can probably do it without thinking; however, for a learner who hasn't done it before you need to appreciate just how many steps are involved. It's the same with your subject: you know it well, but for a new learner you need to break it down into smaller logical steps. You should include a variety of theory and practical approaches, activities and assessments to help maintain motivation and interest. You need to engage and include your learners by asking questions, holding discussions and carrying out various activities. If you don't vary your activities your learners may become bored, lose concentration or be disruptive. Don't be afraid to try something different, for example, a paired activity instead of a group discussion if something's not going too well. Try to use 70 per cent of the session for learner involvement and activities, and 30 per cent of the session for teaching activities.

Don't expect too much from your learners at first; they don't know what you know and will need time to assimilate new skills and knowledge before they fully understand. Don't forget to allow time for a break if necessary. Before concluding your session, you might like to ask questions to check knowledge (one aimed at each learner if you have time). If you have a large group, you could split them into teams and ask questions in the form of a quiz. This is a fun way of ending the session and shows you how much learning has taken place.

Your conclusion should include a summary of your original aim and relate to the objectives which have been achieved during the session. You should allow time for any questions and to discuss any homework or other issues. You can then state what the aim of your next session will be (if applicable).

Activity

Watch one of the main news programmes on television. Notice how the presenters introduce the stories, then explain them in more detail and recap them at the end. Often there are two presenters, one male and one female, the camera shots change and there are videos and pictures to back up the stories. They will have planned and prepared well, having a contingency plan in case anything goes wrong. Did you take into account what the presenters look like and what they were wearing? Did this distract you in any way from the news?

Newsreaders have an autocue to read from; they also have the news written in hard copy as a contingency plan in case anything goes wrong. They will have a script which shows the timings for the news stories and who will read them. As the news is always a live programme, timings are crucial. This is just like your session plan, it has to follow the introduction, development and summary stages, and be interesting and engaging to keep you watching. On your plan, your timings can be expressed as actual times e.g. 6 p.m., 6.10 p.m., or how long each activity will take place, e.g. 10 minutes, 5 minutes. Don't feel you have to strictly adhere to these, if something isn't working well, you can cut it down, and increase the timing for something else that is.

Be prepared – better to have too much than not enough. Unused material can be carried forward to another session or given as work to be carried out during non-contact time. Also, consider learners who may finish tasks early: can you give them something else to do? You should always evaluate your session; this could be afterwards when you have time to reflect, and/or by making notes as you progress, i.e. if something didn't work well you could put a cross next to it on your session plan. You could note your strengths, areas for development and any action and improvements required for the future. Your plan may even change as you progress through your session to take into account the needs of your learners. See Table 4.4 for a basic example of a session plan.

Activity

Look at the objectives in Table 4.3. List the ones which would be appropriate to use when planning your sessions. Now identify which are SMART and which are not SMART. Can you make your non-smart objectives SMART by adding another objective? For example, learners will watch a video and explain three key points.

There are a number of aspects to consider when creating your session plan.

- The overall topic aim – what you expect your learners to achieve during the session.

- Objectives – how your learners will achieve your aim, are they SMART, how do they link to the programme or qualification, in what order will you deliver them, what timings will you allocate to each activity? Remember to include breaks if applicable.

- Group composition – details of individual learners, their needs and learning preferences to enable differentiation to take place.

- Teacher activities – what you will be doing. Use a variety of theory and practical approaches to meet all learning preferences and retain motivation.

- Learner activities – what your learners will be doing and for how long – how will you keep them active and interested? How will you ensure inclusion and differentiation? Do you have spare activities in case some learners finish before others? What could you remove or cut down on if you run out of time?

- Resources – what do you need to effectively deliver your session – do you need to check something is working, or reserve anything in advance? Do you have a contingency plan in case something goes wrong?

- Assessment activities – how will you assess that learning has taken place?

- The next session – how will you link to the next session (if applicable)?

Table 4.4 Example – basic session plan for the first session from the scheme of work

Teacher/ trainer	A G Smith	Date	8 September	Venue	Room 3
Subject/level Qualification reference	Introduction to Information Communication Technology Level 1 Ref 1.1	Time Duration	6–9 p.m. 3 hours	Number of learners	10
Aim of session	\multicolumn{5}{To induct learners to the programme, organisation and assessment requirements. To enable learners to use a computer}
Group composition	10 adults with little or no previous experience of computers (4 female, 6 male, age range 19–55) Initial assessment during this session will identify any prior skills, knowledge and understanding, along with learning preferences. One learner has dyslexia and requires handouts on pastel coloured paper, therefore all handouts issued will be the same colour. All learners will complete all the planned activities, most will complete a gapped handout and some will complete an additional activity if they finish early.				

Timing	Objectives Learners will:	Teacher activities	Learner activities	Resources	Assessment activities
6.00	Obtain and discuss information regarding the organisation, programme and assessment requirements	Explanation and discussion	Gain knowledge Listen and ask questions	Handouts Flipchart and paper Interactive board	Oral questions
6.20	Complete an icebreaker	Facilitate icebreaker	Partake in icebreaker	Handout	Observation
6.40	Agree ground rules	Facilitate ground rules	Discuss ground rules	Flipchart	Discussion
6.50	Switch on a computer and use a keyboard and mouse	Practical demonstration	Observe teacher Use keyboard and mouse	Computers Workpacks Exercises Interactive board	Oral questions
(7.30 Break)					
7.45	Complete an online initial assessment to ascertain learning preferences	Facilitate initial assessment	Complete online initial assessment and learning preferences test	Computers connected to the internet	Observation Online test
8.15	Identify previous knowledge/experience and test results	Discussion	Discussion	Printed test results	Oral questions
8.25	Describe and use ICT applications	Show video Facilitate practical activities	View video Use computer Complete gapped handout	Interactive whiteboard	Oral questions Observation Gapped handout
8.55	Switch off computers	Summarise session Explain next session	Log off Hear a summary of the session Ask questions	Flipchart	Oral questions
9.00 End	Tidy work area and leave	Ensure computers are off			

Your session plan should be visible at all times for you to refer to and to check how your timings are progressing. You may need to remove an activity if you are overrunning, or add something if you have spare time. You could highlight key words on your session plan to quickly glance at as an aid to help you keep focused. Or you could prepare *cue cards* – small pieces of card with key words or statements that you hold in your hand or have visible close by. These will act as prompts, particularly if you have a lot of complex information to remember.

If you are training individuals, you should still use a plan, but it will be known as an individual learning plan (ILP) rather than a session plan. The ILP will cater purely to your individual's learning and needs rather than to a group's.

Extension Activity

Obtain a session plan template, or use a similar format to the one in Table 4.4, and plan a session for one date from your scheme of work. Make sure you have an appropriate aim and suitable objectives for the level of your learners. You could add a column to show how the teaching and learning activities will meet different learning preferences, i.e. whether they are visual, aural, read/ write or kinaesthetic. Think about the assessment activities you will use, and whether they will check progress or count towards achievement a qualification. If you are training individuals rather than a group, you could create an individual learning plan instead of a session plan which is geared towards one person.

Differentiation

Differentiation is about using a range of different approaches and resources to meet the needs of individuals and groups. It is very rare that a teacher or trainer has a group of learners who are all at the same level of ability, with the same prior knowledge and experience, and have the same needs. You don't have to individualise everything you do, you just need to take individual needs into account. Small group work and paired activities are a good way to use differentiation. You could group your learners for different activities by their learning preference, level of ability, level of qualification, past experiences or current knowledge.

> *Differentiation can be defined as an approach to teaching and learning that both recognises the individuality of learners and also informs ways of planning for learning and teaching that take these individualities into consideration.*

(Tummons, 2010, page 93)

You could plan different activities which *all* your learners are capable of achieving, as well as what *most* or *some* can achieve according to their level and ability.

Paul has a mixed group of level 2 and 3 learners taking a Certificate in Customer Service. He knows the full group will be able to answer questions based on the level 2 programme, most will be able to answer from both levels and some will be able to answer questions based on the level 3 syllabus. He has therefore devised and used a differentiated questioning technique for his group of learners.

Differentiated questioning can help support learners; for example, learners for whom English is a second language may need longer to process information or need questions rephrasing. A learner who has dyslexia may prefer to work with more images, have handouts printed on pastel coloured paper, wish to make an audio recording of the session to listen to afterwards, or key in notes directly to a laptop or tablet. An older learner might shy away from using new technology whereas younger learners may expect to access and use it.

Acknowledging and embracing the diverse nature of your learners' ages, experiences, culture and backgrounds should help you include all learners and bring your subject to life. Some learners may work quicker than others; giving them another activity known as an *extension* activity could help develop, stretch and challenge their learning further, without compromising the learning of others.

Initial assessment is crucial to gain the information you need to plan effectively; however, not all your learners may reveal things during this process. If you can encourage your learners to let you know of anything that you can do to help them, you will improve their learning experience. Simply asking, *Is there anything I can do to help your learning?* should ascertain this. Alternatively, ask yourself *What can I do to give everyone a valuable learning experience?*

You could keep a record known as a *group profile*. This will include details of each learner, i.e. learning preferences and any particular requirements to enable differentiation to take place.

Differentiating your teaching, learning and assessment approaches should lead to more confident learners who feel included, are motivated to learn and are able to achieve. While it may take longer to plan and prepare your sessions to differentiate effectively, you will find your learners are more engaged and motivated rather than being bored and uninterested.

Extension Activity

What will you need to know about your learners to plan for effective differentiation of teaching, learning and assessment? How can you differentiate your objectives to take into account the needs of your learners?

Resources

Resources are all the aids, books, handouts, items of equipment, objects and people that you can use to deliver and assess your subject. They should stimulate learning, add impact and promote interest in the subject. Resources should be accessible and inclusive to all learners, while enabling them to acquire new skills, knowledge and understanding. When using or creating resources, ensure they promote equality of opportunity, reflect diversity and challenge stereotypes. For example, text and pictures in a handout should portray all aspects of society. Resources should be appropriate in terms of level, quality, quantity and content and be relevant to the subject and the learning expected. Handouts and presentations should be checked for spelling, grammar, punctuation and sentence construction errors. You could put your name, date and organisation details as a footer on any documents to show where they originated. You may also find it useful to add a file name and version number to keep track of any changes. If you create any resources as part of your job role (even in your own time), you might find your contract doesn't allow them to remain your property, but entitles your organisation to have them.

If you give a handout at the beginning of the session, you may find your learners fiddle with it and become distracted. If you can, issue handouts at an appropriate time and talk through the content, asking questions to ensure your learners have understood the topic. Otherwise, issue them at the end of the session and ask learners to read them later to help reinforce what has been covered. Alternatively, to aid sustainability, you could upload handouts to a VLE or e-mail them to your learners. Handouts can also be used as activities; for example, a gapped handout can contain sentences with missing words that learners need to fill in. These are useful to assess lower-level or new learners, as a fun team activity or to fill in time at the end of a session. If a resource you are using is not effective with some learners, try changing the experience rather than the resource. You might need to explain the resource differently or change a group activity to become an individual one. Table 4.5 gives examples of resources you might be able to access and use.

Activity

Look at the list of resources in Table 4.5 and make a list of the ones you could use for your subject. Choose three resources and consider how they will stimulate learning, add impact and promote interest in the subject.

Depending upon your subject and what is available, you may need to create your own or adapt someone else's resources. This could be a handout of useful information, an exercise, practical activity or worksheet or it could be a complex working model used to demonstrate a topic. If you can search the internet, you might find resources for your subject area are freely available. Publishers are often happy to give away free inspection copies of text books for your subject, providing you give feedback or recommend them to your learners. Whatever resources you use, it's important to ensure they meet the differing needs of your learners. Putting posters on the wall of the room will help to reinforce points. Learners may not always look at them consciously, but subconsciously will glance at them, taking in the information. You might have to acknowledge your organisation's resource constraints and make best use of what is available. You should always evaluate the effectiveness of any resources you use, to modify or change them for future use.

Table 4.5 Examples of resources

Information and communication technology	Objects
• Audio, visual and digital recorders • Calculators • Camcorder • CDROMs • Computers/laptops/netbooks/tablets • Digital cameras • DVDs • Epidiascope • Interactive whiteboards • Internet • Intranet • Microscope • Mobile phones and smart phones • Personal digital assistants • Photocopier • Presentations • Projectors and data projectors • Radio • Recording devices • Scanners • Social networking • Television • Video conferencing • Video recorder • Virtual learning environment (VLE) • Voting technology • Webcam • Whiteboards	• Animals • Apparatus • Games • Models • Plants • Puppets • Puzzles • Samples of products • Specimens • Sports equipment • The *real thing* • Tools • Toys
	People
	• Colleagues, teachers, trainers, managers, mentors, technicians, administrative staff, support staff, employers, supervisors • Friends and relatives • Information, guidance and careers staff • Learners • Manufacturers/suppliers • Other professionals: internal/external agency staff, quality assurers, Awarding Organisation personnel, subject experts • Specialist speakers • Volunteers • Yourself

Outside events	Visual aids
• Cinema/theatre/concert • Conferences • Exhibitions • Field trips • Lectures • Libraries • Museums • Specialist shops • Sports/leisure centres	• Charts/posters • Display board • Flannel/sticky/magnetic boards • Flip chart, paper and pens • Maps • Overhead or slide projector • Presentations • Photographs • Whiteboard/chalk board

Other resource materials	
• Advertisements • Books • Catalogues • Comics • Handouts • Information leaflets • Journals • Magazines • Maps • Manuals	• Newspapers • Original documents • Periodicals/journals • Photocopies of documents • Promotional literature • Publicity materials • Puzzles and quizzes • Reports • Text books • Wordsearches/crosswords • Worksheets

When designing resources, any individual needs should be taken into account; for example, dyslexia, a hearing impairment, visual impairment, physical or mental disability. You may need to produce handouts in a larger-sized font, on different coloured paper, or ensure there is plenty of white space surrounding the text (the blank area around the text/pictures). You also need to consider the location, cost, challenges and benefits of using certain resources. If you are using, adapting or copying work, you will need to check you are not in breach of copyright legislation. Using pictures as well as text and not putting too much information on a handout will help learning. If you were given one handout with a lot of written information in small text, and another with text in a larger more pleasing font with a few pictures, which one would you prefer to read? It would probably be the latter.

You may have to deal with unexpected situations which relate to resources. It is useful to have a contingency plan just in case.

Example

Jack was due to deliver a Food Hygiene session to a group of 12 learners at 2 p.m. He had created a computerised presentation and saved it to a memory stick. He arrived at the venue half an hour early, only to find a notice on the door stating he had been moved to another room. In the other room were two circular tables that would seat six learners comfortably, but only four chairs at each. He switched on the computer and realised the version of his presentation was newer and it wouldn't open. If he didn't have a contingency plan he would have been unable to deliver the session effectively. However, because he was early he was able to locate and ask the caretaker to bring four extra chairs. He had printouts of the presentation which he could hand out to each learner, but he also had time to go to the office and resave the document in a previous version. While there, he saved it to the organisation's hard drive which was accessible from any room, just in case a problem occurred with his memory stick.

Preparing for unforeseen circumstances comes with experience. Whenever you are due to meet your learners, ask yourself, *What would I do if something wasn't available or doesn't work?* You might prepare a computerised presentation and make copies as handouts that you can give your learners. However, if you can't get copies made in time, you can still deliver your presentation and offer to e-mail a copy to your learners, upload it to a VLE, or get photocopies made later. Try not to rely totally on presentation software when teaching: use different approaches and activities to add variety.

Evaluating resources

You should always evaluate the resources you use to improve or amend them for future use. It could be that a handout you used with your learners was not read thoroughly, for example there was too much text on it or they found it too complex. Or it could be you have used a working model to demonstrate something but it didn't function on the day.

Always practise with your resources in advance of using them with your learners, just in case anything could go wrong.

What works with one learner or group might not work well with others, perhaps due to their learning preferences or other influences. Don't change something for the sake of it; if it works, hopefully it will continue to work.

When evaluating the resources you have used, ask yourself the following.

- Did the resource do what I expected? If not why not?
- Did it support and reinforce learning effectively?
- Did it reach all learning preferences, i.e. was there something to look at (visual), did I talk about it and could learners discuss it (aural), was there something written and/or could learners make notes (read/write), was there something practical for learners to do (kinaesthetic)?
- Were all learners able to use it with ease and was there enough for everyone?
- Did it motivate the learners to learn more?
- Was it up to date and relevant to the subject?
- Was it active or passive? Do my learners prefer to be actively engaged when using resources, such as a working model rather than passively reading a handout?
- Was it easy for me to create? Can I update it easily?
- Did I encounter any problems setting it up and using it? Was it too time consuming?
- Did I carry out any necessary risk assessments?
- Was it of a high quality and professional looking?

After evaluating your resource, you can make any necessary changes before using it again. Don't forget to ask for feedback from your learners as they are best able to inform you how effective it was.

Extension Activity

Create a suitable resource that you could use for your subject. If possible, use it during one of your sessions and evaluate its effectiveness. If you don't know how to use the equipment at your organisation, for example, presentation software or an interactive whiteboard, ask a colleague how you can arrange for a training session.

Opportunities for English, maths and wider skills

English and maths

Whenever possible, you should try and improve the English and maths skills of your learners. This will help them improve their personal skills, knowledge and understanding and hopefully increase their career aspirations. English includes other terms such as literacy and language, and maths includes numeracy. These skills have had many labels in the past such as Basic Skills, Skills for Life, Key Skills, Core Skills, Essential Skills and Functional Skills. The latter consist of English, maths and information and communication technology (ICT). They provide the essential skills, knowledge and understanding that will enable people to function confidently, effectively and independently in life and at work. Functional skills can be taken by apprenticeship learners and adults on other programmes where it would help improve their skills.

You shouldn't have to be highly qualified with English and maths, but know enough to make it relevant to the subject you are delivering. For example, maths doesn't have to be complex equations, it can be about using numerical skills such as planning a household budget, working out the cost of a shopping list, calculating the amount of paint needed to decorate a room, or comparing gas and electricity prices.

However, you might feel your own skills do need improving, therefore you could partake in further training yourself. If you are not competent you will not set a good example to your learners. For example, if you spell words wrongly in a handout, have difficulty making calculations or can't use a computer, your learners may lose confidence in you.

Example

Sanjay is due to teach Cookery for Beginners and plans to improve his learners' skills as follows:

English (literacy) – reading recipes, researching and reading healthy eating magazines and books, writing a list of ingredients.

English (language) – discussing recipes, talking, listening and asking questions.

Maths (numeracy) – calculating weights and costs of ingredients, measuring amounts, estimating calorific values, cooking times and temperatures, dealing with money to buy ingredients and sell completed products.

ICT – using a word processor to type the menu, researching relevant websites, e-mailing other learners. Giving a presentation to their peers using the electronic whiteboard, creating a podcast, taking photos of finished products and uploading them to a website or electronic portfolio.

Wider skills

Wider skills is the term used for other skills which will help your learners improve their knowledge and skills in areas which relate to their personal learning and thinking skills (PLTS).

The overall aim of the PLTS framework (QCA, 2007) is to: help young people ... become successful learners, confident individuals and responsible citizens ... The framework comprises six groups of skills that, together with the functional skills of English, mathematics and ICT, are essential to success in learning, life and work.

(Learning and Skills Network, 2008, page 2)

Learners are likely to encounter skills from several groups in any one learning experience. The groups comprise of:

- independent enquirers
- creative thinkers
- reflective learners

- team workers
- self-managers
- effective participators

Ways to improve these skills with your learners include:

- Independent enquirers: planning and carrying out investigations and taking informed decisions
- Creative thinkers: generating ideas, tackling problems and finding imaginative solutions
- Reflective learners: setting goals for learning and work, monitoring performance and reviewing progress
- Team workers: working collaboratively with other people, taking responsibility and resolving issues
- Self-managers: being organised, showing enterprise and responding to new challenges
- Effective participators: playing a full part in studies and the workplace or the wider community

Your organisation might want you to integrate the above groups of skills with your learners during your sessions; if so, consider how you could use activities which could improve and develop them for your particular subject.

Wider skills also include skills which are valued by employers such as:

- *Working with Others* which focuses on teamwork, planning, organising and carrying out work with other people
- *Improving Own Learning and Performance* which focuses on recognising the skills of being an effective learner and the importance of reflection
- *Problem Solving* which focuses on the skills of recognising problems and identifying, evaluating and seeing through possible solutions

There are other areas in which you could promote skills, knowledge and understanding, which also fall under the term of wider skills. Your organisation or the programme you are teaching might require you to incorporate some or all of these skills within your sessions. For example:

- Citizenship – discussions based on nationality, politics and the state
- Employability – creating a curriculum vitae (CV) and applying for jobs
- Enterprise – setting up a small business, creating a website and online ordering system
- ICT – using smart phones, computers, tablets, laptops, etc. for e-mail, web-based research, social networking, viewing videos, word-processing assignments, and using presentation packages for projects

- Social responsibility – time keeping, personal development, behaviour and professionalism, confidence, health and well-being

- Sustainability – how to recycle, reuse and reduce usage

To help improve the skills of your own learners, you could use activities which integrate them in the context of the programme such as naturally occurring opportunities. Learners who possess skills in these areas should be able to progress in education, training and employment and make a positive contribution to the communities in which they live and work.

Example

Ravi teaches plumbing in a realistic working environment (RWE), and has realised that many aspects of the job naturally include the use of English and maths. Talking to customers and suppliers, reading manuals and writing orders all involve English. Measuring pipes, calculating the amount of materials to use and working out invoices all involve maths. Ravi also encourages his learners to use ICT by researching materials on the internet, e-mailing suppliers, word-processing invoices, taking digital photos before, during and after jobs, and maintaining an electronic diary. He also encourages discussions based around sustainability and the environment, i.e. recycling.

You could create the opportunity to use board games or other educational and online games, which can help learning while being fun. These can be carried out individually, in pairs or groups and help to improve the wider skills as well as English and maths. There are many free educational games available via the internet, just carry out a search for *educational games* and see what appears. There are also some useful websites listed at the end of the chapter.

When integrating and embedding the skills during sessions, you need to ensure they are realistic and relevant to enable your learners to engage with real situations in their subject area. You can also encourage your learners to carry out activities in their own time to help them improve their skills. There might be free courses in your area or via the internet that learners could take. If there are library facilities locally you could give your learners an activity to carry out as research. They could produce a short presentation, individually or in groups, and report back on their findings. If you upload materials to a VLE, your learners could access these at a later date, amend them to an appropriate font or size, and save or print them.

Extension Activity

Find out which of the wider skills you need to incorporate into your subject. If you are not required to use any, consider the ones you feel would help your learners the most. How could you provide opportunities for your learners to practise these skills? Design an activity to incorporate English, maths and ICT. If possible, try out the activity with learners and evaluate how effective it was.

Using information and communication technology

Information and communication technology (ICT) includes all the uses of digital media, equipment, tools and equipment that are currently available, and which will enhance the teaching, learning and assessment process.

ICT covers all products which will store, retrieve, display, manipulate, send or receive information electronically in a digital format. For example, personal computers, tablets, smart phones and interactive whiteboards. Technology is advancing very quickly and there are new products becoming available all the time. ICT products should be used whenever possible to engage and stimulate your learners. They will also help raise learner confidence if they haven't used ICT much in the past. You might deliver and assess your subject via an online program or use a blended approach of traditional teaching supported with access to technology. Learners today live in a world of easy access to the internet, and often use tablets and/or smart phones as part of their everyday activities. Therefore you need to consider how you can incorporate this technology into your sessions to make learning interactive. However, don't be too keen to overload your learners by using too much technology, make sure you get the balance right with other resources.

ICT can encompass a wide variety of activities, for example, using:

- audio, video and online clips (creating or viewing, recorded or live)
- blogs
- calculators
- chat rooms
- computer programs
- digital cameras, camcorders and video recorders
- discussion boards
- e-assessments
- electronic brain games
- e-mail (text and video, with or without attachments)
- e-portfolios and e-assessment
- e-readers
- interactive and online programs and educational games
- interactive whiteboards linked to the internet
- internet and intranet access
- laptops and netbooks
- mobile and smart phones
- online discussions
- online voting
- podcasts
- presentation packages
- scanners
- social networking (if appropriate)
- smart phones
- tablets
- using applications (apps) which are relevant
- video conferencing
- virtual learning environments (VLE)
- webcast, weblog, short message, podcast, etc.

You would need to feel confident using ICT equipment yourself and may therefore need further training. You would also need to ensure everything is accessible, in working order and appropriate for your learners.

Some 42 per cent of adult learners most like to learn by doing practical things, a figure that is unchanged since 1998. However, now almost a quarter (23 per cent) mentioned using computers, mobile phones and the internet, not feasible options for most in 1998.

(Campaign for Learning, 2009)

When using ICT, remember to vary your methods to address individual needs. Technology can help overcome barriers to learning; for example, pairing an experienced learner with an inexperienced learner so that someone who hasn't used it before doesn't feel alone. You also need to be careful that learners are using it appropriately, i.e. not accessing unsuitable websites or checking e-mails while you think they are working. Some learners may be concerned about using ICT; for example, a learner with epilepsy may need regular breaks from a computer screen. You could let your learners bring laptops, tablets and e-readers to use for reading downloaded texts and/or writing notes rather than using hard copy text books, pen and paper. Learners could use these and/or their smart phones during sessions to carry out research. When using ICT during sessions, it's useful to have agreed some ground rules in advance, such as not accessing social networking sites.

You might use equipment such as an interactive or electronic whiteboard. With a normal whiteboard, once you have written on it, you need to clean it before using it again. With the interactive whiteboard, you use a special pen-like device directly onto the board, information is displayed and can be transferred to a computer for saving, printing, uploading to a VLE and/or e-mailing. You can open documents, move between pages and add text and pictures, link to the internet and show video clips. You can involve your learners by getting them to use the system to create and use documents, quizzes, pictures and presentations.

Example

Angela is teaching a new group of learners how to use a computer. She is able to demonstrate how to use various functions by displaying each program on the interactive whiteboard, enabling everyone to see what she does. Previously, she would have had to gather the group around one small computer screen. She can also link to the internet to demonstrate how to use e-mail, access websites and show short video clips. Her learners all have e-readers to view the relevant text book, and have access to a VLE to download work, partake in online forum discussions, share information and upload assignments.

Other equipment you could use includes specialist software for creating and delivering presentations. This would enable you to use graphics as well as text to make your presentation more visual. You can prepare your presentation in advance and save it to a disk, memory stick and/or upload it to a VLE or accessible website. Therefore, as long as a computer and data projector are available, you can use any room with access. A wireless remote control is useful as it enables you to move around the room rather than stand next to the keyboard to move between the slides. Always have a contingency plan in case anything doesn't work, i.e. an activity learners can carry out while you resolve the situation.

Hints for using handouts and presentations

Handouts and presentations are useful resources to add variety to your session and focus attention. You should always check the spelling, grammar and punctuation of any materials you use, otherwise you could come across as unprofessional. If a learner does see an error, don't make excuses but thank them and say you will amend it for future use. Hard copies of your materials will enable your learners to refer to them during and after the session to go over important points. However, you might not always be able to get them copied in time. You could consider uploading handouts and presentations to an intranet or VLE to aid sustainability. Learning doesn't have to stop just because the session has.

The following are some hints which you could refer to when creating handouts and presentations.

Handouts

- Make the text easily readable, in an appropriate font and size. Don't put too much text or too many pictures on one page and don't mix fancy fonts. It might look good to you, but might not be easily readable by your learners. Keep plenty of *white space* (the blank area around the text/pictures). This makes the information stand out clearly and will allow your learners to make notes if necessary. If there is too much on a handout your learners may find it difficult to read and not absorb all the information.

- A single sheet, one sided or double sided, is best; too many pages will take too long for your learners to read and assimilate the information. If you do use more pages, always staple in the top left corner and number each page.

- If you have created the handout yourself, type your name, filename, version number and date as a footer. This will enable you to find it easily to make future changes and ensures you are using the most recent version.

- Make sure the information is up to date. You may need to revise something if there have been changes to your subject.

- Consider numbering paragraphs or using numbers instead of bullet points. That way you can direct your learners to important points.

- If you have a learner who has dyslexia they might prefer handouts on pastel coloured paper, use the same colour for everyone so that no one is singled out. If you can't get coloured copies, give the learner a coloured plastic wallet within which they can place the handout. This will change its colour and hopefully make it easier to read.

- If you are issuing several handouts during a session, you could print them on different coloured paper for ease of reference when you are talking about their content.

- If you use pictures of people, make sure they represent all aspects of society.

- If you use any quotes, make sure you reference them correctly. A list of relevant references or websites is useful to encourage your learners to research further after the session.

- Handouts can be useful if incorporated into an activity, for example a gapped handout containing sentences with missing words for learners to complete.

- If possible, give handouts towards the end of the activity they refer to. If you give them too early, your learners may fiddle with them and read through them rather than concentrating on you.

Activity

Create a handout for your subject, taking into account the previous bulleted points. If possible, use the handout with your learners and then evaluate its effectiveness.

Presentations

- Always check the equipment and data projector are connected and working. As a backup, store your work to an external drive as well as the internal one or a memory stick. Check that the program and version in which you have saved your presentation is compatible with the one to be used.

- Don't include too much text or use fancy fonts, colours and animations as this could distract from the points you want to make.

- Check if you need to insert a logo on each slide as a footer, or use a particular font and size for consistency throughout the organisation.

- Large, bold plain fonts are easier to read than smaller type, for example **Arial, Comic Sans** or **Verdana.** Serif and script fonts are thought to be more difficult to read, for example Times New Roman and *Brush Script.* The font size should be readable from the back of the room. Using combined upper and lower case is preferable to using all upper case as the latter can appear as though you are shouting.

- Blue-eyed people often struggle to see red, orange, green or yellow text, particularly if on a coloured background. Red and green can cause confusion for learners who are colour blind. Be consistent with the colours and backgrounds you use, for example use black text on a white background. Check which colours your learners prefer. How you see the colours on the slides may be very different to how your learners see them.

- Use bullet points, three or four per slide, and don't read them verbatim. Schedule them to come in line by line otherwise your learners will be reading ahead. Expand on each point and discuss it with your learners. Involve them where possible by asking open questions to make the presentation a two-way process and use anecdotes to bring your subject to life.

- Graphs and diagrams are often easier for learners to understand than tables; however, don't make them too complex. It's better to use several slides with a few pieces of information on rather than one slide with too much on.

- If you have time, incorporate a short video to bring your topic to life and add variety, however, do check any copyright restrictions and/or fair use policies. If you are connected to the internet you can insert the website link into your slide for easy access. Always check in advance that the site is still accessible.

- If you need to refer to the same slide more than once, copy it rather than moving back through your presentation, otherwise you could lose your place.

- Use a remote control for moving through your slides. This enables you to move around the room pressing a pointer rather than standing next to the keyboard. The remote control communicates via a device which plugs into a slot in the computer. Don't forget to remove it at the end or you may lose it.

- Press the letter B on the keyboard to black out the screen, or W to white out, for example if you don't want a slide on display for a few minutes while you focus on something else. Pressing B or W again will restore it.

- If your presentation is given via an electronic whiteboard, you could use features such as writing on the slides with the pen-like device. You can then save and e-mail it to your learners, or upload it to a VLE.

- Involve your learners; ask them to use the presentation equipment and/or electronic whiteboard whenever possible.

- Don't rely on using presentations; vary your delivery by using other types of equipment, and teaching and learning approaches.

- Have a hard copy of the presentation for yourself in case something goes wrong. You can then refer to it rather than having nothing. You can also hold it during the presentation and remain facing your learners, rather than looking at and talking to the screen.

- If you want your learners to make notes throughout the presentation, you can print a copy using the *handout* function. That way, they can have several slides on one A4 page with room for making notes. Printing one slide per A4 sheet is just a waste of paper. If you are not sure how to do this, ask someone to show you.

- Supporting handouts can be given at the end, which include further information, rather than squashing it onto the slides.

Online qualifications and programmes

Increasingly, qualifications and programmes are delivered online, i.e. where learners access learning via a specialist website. This is ideal for learners who might have difficulty attending a venue, or wish to learn at times convenient to them. Learners will need a computer or device with a reliable internet connection; however, this could be in a library or another suitable location rather than at home.

Teaching and learning can be *synchronous* (where both teacher and learner are online at the same time) and/or *asynchronous* (where the teacher and learner are not online at the same time).

Some programmes are taught purely online, in which case the teacher may never meet their learners. Other programmes use a blended approach with some aspects carried out online and others in a suitable environment. Online programmes can be individual or group based, and usually allow the learners to progress at their own pace. Aspects such as icebreakers and ground rules should still be carried out with learners to agree boundaries within which to work.

Learners can easily upload their work for you to access, assess and give feedback online. Be careful how you write your feedback and messages, as they could be interpreted differently when read. You also need to remember that whatever you write might be permanent and accessible for a long time, therefore don't use any inappropriate language or anything you might regret later.

Technology is advancing rapidly where online teaching and learning is concerned. Unfortunately, there isn't room in this book to explain it in detail, therefore please refer to other appropriate texts such as those listed at the end of this chapter.

Extension Activity

What ICT resources could you use within your subject? Research new and emerging technologies and create an activity to use with your learners. If possible, use the activity and then evaluate its effectiveness. If you are not yet confident with ICT, find out where you could receive training or support. There are a few free online websites listed at the end of this chapter.

Summary

In this chapter you have learnt about:

- *teaching and learning plans*
- *differentiation*
- *resources*
- *opportunities for English, maths and wider skills*
- *using information and communication technology*

Cross-referencing grid

This chapter contributes towards the following assessment criteria of the units which form the Award in Education and Training, along with aspects of the Professional Teaching Standards. Full details of the learning outcomes and assessment criteria of each unit can be found in the appendices.

Award units	Assessment criteria
Roles, responsibilities and relationships in education and training	1.3, 1.4
Understanding and using inclusive approaches in education and training	1.1, 1.3 2.1, 2.2 3.1, 3.2
Understanding assessment in education and training	
Learning and Development units	**Assessment criteria**
Facilitate learning and development for individuals	1.1, 1.2, 1.7 2.1
Facilitate learning and development in groups	1.7 2.2
Understanding the principles and practices of assessment	8.2
Domain	**Professional Teaching Standards**
A	ASI, AS2, AS3, AS4, AK3.1, AP3.1
B	BS5, BK2.1, BK2.2, BK2.4, BK5.1, BK5.2, BP2.1, BP5.1, BP5.2
C	CSI, CK3.3, CK3.4, CK3.5, CK4.1, CK4.2, CP3.4, CP3.5
D	DSI, DK1.1, DK1.2, DK1.3, DK2.1, DK2.2, DP1.1, DP1.2, DP1.3, DP2.1, DP2.2, DP3.1
E	
F	

Theory focus

References and further information

Becta (2009) *Harnessing Technology Review 2008: The role of technology and its impact on education.* Coventry: Becta.

Bloom, BS (1956) *Taxonomy of Educational Objectives: Handbook I.* New York: Longman.

Campaign for Learning (2009) *State of the Nation Survey 2008.* London: Campaign for Learning.

Gravells, A (2013) *Passing Assessments for the Award in Education and Training.* London: Learning Matters.

Haythornthwaite, C and Andrews, R (2011) *e-learning Theory and Practice*. London: Learning Matters.

Hill, C (2008) *Teaching with e-learning in the Lifelong Learning Sector* (2nd Edn). Exeter: Learning Matters.

Holmes, B and Gardner, J (2006) *e-learning Concepts and Practice*. London: SAGE Publications Ltd.

Tummons, J (2010) *Becoming a Professional Tutor in the Lifelong Learning Sector* (2nd Edn). Exeter: Learnin Matters.

Websites

Copyright – www.copyrightservice.co.uk

Dyslexia Association – www.dyslexia.uk.net

English and Maths free support – www.move-on.org.uk

Further Education Guide to using learning technology – http://feweek.co.uk/2013/02/22/guide-to-fe-learning-tech/?goback=.gde_4139923_member_217969739

ICT free support – www.onlinebasics.co.uk and http://learn.go-on.co.uk

Learning and Skills Network (2008) *Personal Learning and Thinking Skills: Lessons from the wider key skills* http://archive.excellencegateway.org.uk/media/post16/files/keyskillspltspublication.pdf

Online free courses in various subjects – www.vision2learn.net

Online games – www.npted.org/schools/sandfieldsComp/games/Pages/Game-Downloads.aspx

Online presentations – www.prezi.com

Qualifications and Credit Framework – http://tinyurl.com/447bgy2

Resources Centre – www.heacademy.ac.uk/resources

Teacher training videos for using ICT – www.teachertrainingvideos.com/latest.html

Using computers and technology: free guides – http://digitalunite.com/

Using IT – www.reading.ac.uk/internal/its/training/its-training-index.aspx

Using VLEs – www.ofsted.gov.uk/resources/virtual-learning-environments-e-portfolio

Video e-mail – http://mailvu.com/

In this chapter you will learn about:

- induction, icebreakers and ground rules
- teaching and learning approaches
- communication, behaviour and respect
- working with groups and individuals
- maintaining a safe and supportive learning environment

There are activities and examples to help you reflect on the above which will assist your understanding of how to facilitate the learning process. At the end of each section within the chapter are extension activities to stretch and challenge your learning should you wish to carry them out. A list of useful references, further information and website links can be found at the end in case you would like to research the topics further.

At the end of the chapter is a cross-referencing grid showing how the chapter's contents relate towards the units of the Award in Education and Training and the Professional Teaching Standards.

Induction, icebreakers and ground rules

When you begin teaching a new group or an individual, there will be lots of information you must explain regarding your organisation, the facilities available and the programme. This is known as an *induction* and will usually take place during the first meeting with your learners. An *icebreaker* is an activity you can carry out with your learners to help them feel comfortable and get to know each other and you. Establishing *ground rules* once your learners have relaxed a little will help underpin appropriate behaviour and respect throughout their time with you, for example, by switching off mobile devices during sessions.

Induction

Your organisation might have a checklist of general points for you to follow and you may need to add specific points regarding your subject and the learning environment. This is known as an *induction*.

An induction should include aspects such as:

- introducing yourself and giving a little information about your experience and knowledge regarding the subject

- an icebreaker to introduce learners to each other

- dates and times of attendance/meetings

- break times and refreshment facilities

- checking your learners have received relevant information, advice and guidance

- programme/qualification content and assessment requirements

- a tour of the site (if applicable) including location of study areas, toilets, catering venues, parking and smoking areas

- organisational policies such as health and safety, equality and diversity, appeals and complaints

- organisational procedures such as fire and accidents

- the setting of ground rules

If you are delivering a short event, you might carry out certain *housekeeping* aspects rather than a detailed induction. This might include stating the times of breaks, where certain facilities are such as toilets and refreshments, along with information regarding fire procedures.

There may be some administrative aspects to be completed during the first meeting with your learners, such as filling in relevant forms. Don't let this take over – your learners will want to leave their first session having learnt something interesting about the subject. If you have any learners who commence late, make sure you spend time with them to cover what they have missed, and introduce them to the others.

Activity

Imagine you are to begin delivering your subject to a new group of learners. Devise a checklist of the information you would need to cover. You could think back to when you started a new programme, i.e. the information you received and the questions you asked. If you are currently teaching, obtain a copy of your organisation's checklist, if there is one, and compare it with yours.

Giving your learners a copy of the induction checklist, or making it available electronically, will act as a reminder of what was covered. Often, so much information is given out during the first session that learners can easily forget some important points. You could keep a signed copy as a record that the induction process took place.

Icebreakers

Some learners can be quiet, shy, nervous or apprehensive when they commence a new programme. Carrying out an icebreaker is a good way of everyone getting to know each other's name, and encouraging communication to take place. Some learners may already know each other, or have carried out an icebreaker with another teacher or trainer they currently have. Knowing this beforehand will help you decide upon an appropriate and suitable icebreaker to carry out, and saves repetition. You could carry out the icebreaker before covering the induction requirements as this will encourage your learners to relax, and give them confidence to speak or ask questions in front of others. Always introduce yourself first otherwise learners may be wondering what your name is, or whether you are just someone facilitating the first session. First impressions count, therefore you need to portray that you are a professional, knowledgeable person who is competent and approachable.

Icebreakers can be quite simple; for example, asking your learners to introduce themselves in front of the group. However, this can be a bit intimidating if none of the learners have met before. A way round this is to form the group into pairs and ask them to talk to each other for five minutes about their interests, reason for attending and their expectations. They may find they have something in common and create a bond. You can then ask each person to introduce the person they have been talking to. People may not feel comfortable talking about themselves to a group of strangers, so another person introducing them might take any anxiety away. A good idea is to note down your learners' names when they introduce each other, on a rough sketch of a seating plan. This will help you remember their names as it's likely they will return to the same position at the next session. You could also note something about them which you could use in a future conversation. This shows that you are taking an interest in each learner as an individual. Making a note of their expectations will help you match what they expect with what the programme involves. If there are any expectations that will not be covered as part of the programme, make sure you explain why this is.

If you don't have time for introductions, you could issue name badges for learners to wear or name cards to place in front of them. This acts as a visual reminder to others, and helps you remember and use their name when speaking to them.

More complex icebreakers can involve games or activities, but the outcome should be for your learners to relax, enjoy the activity, communicate and ascertain each other's names. Icebreakers help retain attention, keep motivation high and help the group to bond and work together. All learners should be included and you should manage the activity carefully to ensure everyone can actively take part. You may wish to include yourself in the icebreaker, or just observe what is happening. If you include yourself, don't get too personal, resist the temptation to be everyone's friend and remain professional throughout.

Icebreakers can also be used during an established session, perhaps after a break to help learners refocus. These are called *energisers* and can be subject-specific such as a quiz or a fun activity or game which gets learners moving about. Always have a contingency plan in case anything you planned to use isn't available, or if some learners finish before others or don't wish to take part.

Whichever way you use an icebreaker or an energiser, it should be designed to be a fun and light-hearted activity to:

- build confidence

- create a suitable learning environment

- enable learners to talk confidently in front of their peers

- encourage communication, motivation, interaction, teamwork and inclusion

- establish trust and respect

- get the programme off to a good start

- help learners relax

- introduce learners to each other

- minimise barriers

- reduce apprehension and nervousness

- reduce intimidation

Activity

Imagine you have a new group of 16 learners starting next week who have never met before. What sort of icebreaker would you carry out with them and why? There are lots available via the internet if you have access.

Your organisation may have icebreakers for you to use, you could design your own or search the internet for ideas. Keep your icebreaker short and simple and always evaluate how it went to enable you to modify or improve it for the future.

Ground rules

Ground rules are boundaries and rules to help create suitable conditions within which learners (and yourself) can safely work and learn. They should underpin appropriate behaviour and respect for everyone in the group, including yourself, and ensure the session runs smoothly. If they are not set, problems may occur which could disrupt the session and lead to misunderstandings or behaviour problems. It is best to agree the ground rules during the first meeting, perhaps after the icebreaker once everyone is feeling more relaxed.

Ground rules should always be discussed and negotiated with your learners rather than forced upon them. Using an activity to do this will help learners feel included, take ownership of, and hopefully follow them. Some ground rules might be renegotiated or added to throughout the programme; for example, changing the break time. Others might be non-negotiable: for example, health and safety requirements. These might already be listed in a learner handbook, agreement or learner contract and you would need to ensure all learners have a copy, and know that they are in addition to any rules agreed as a group. The types of ground rules you agree with your learners will depend upon their age and maturity.

When establishing ground rules, you need to have an idea of what will be non-negotiable, i.e. because of organisational requirements, and what can be negotiable.

Example

Non-negotiable ground rules:

- *no anti-social behaviour*
- *everyone is to respect the views and beliefs of others*
- *the area is to be left tidy*

Negotiable ground rules:

- *no eating or drinking during sessions*
- *mobile phones and electronic devices to be switched off*
- *breaks will last a maximum of 20 minutes*

Whatever method you use to collate the ground rules, make sure they are not open to any misinterpretation. Having clear ground rules will help your learners feel comfortable and able to participate. You might like to change any negative ground rules into positive ones; for example, *no eating or drinking during sessions* could become *eat and drink outside of the session*. You should be a role model and set a good example for your learners by not breaking any of the ground rules yourself. If you have too many ground rules, learners might become over cautious of what they can and can't do and this could affect the learning process.

If your learners attend sessions taken by others, it is a good idea to discuss with them what your group has agreed, to ensure consistency. You might also take your learners for other subjects and therefore have a core list of ground rules for all sessions, with some specific ones for each particular subject.

Ways to establish ground rules

One way is where both you and your learners work together by a process of discussion and negotiation. This enables your learners to recognise what is and is not acceptable, giving them a sense of ownership and responsibility. It also enables learners to begin working together as a group and encourages aspects such as listening, compromise and respect for others. Alternatively, your learners could write down the rules individually, then discuss in pairs and join into fours to create a poster or a list on flipchart paper. One or two learners could present this to the full group and agreement can then take place. Another way would be to ask your learners what others have done during previous events they have attended which made learning difficult. They will usually come up with answers like mobile phones ringing and people interrupting others. You can then start creating a list to build upon with the group. Even if you only have one or two learners, you should still agree some ground rules.

Depending upon the age of your learners, you could use the term *group contract* instead of ground rules. Ideally, the ground rules should be on display each time your group meets, and/or a typed version could be given to each learner, or uploaded to a virtual learning environment (VLE) or intranet if applicable.

Ways to maintain ground rules

Keeping the ground rules visible throughout the sessions will act as a reminder of what is not acceptable, and enable them to be amended or added to as necessary. Any learners who have commenced the programme late will be able to see them. It's useful to refer to the rules at the beginning of the session and when a rule is broken. For example, if a learner is late, they must be reminded that it is a requirement that all sessions start promptly, otherwise they might not make the effort to arrive on time for subsequent sessions. If other learners see that you don't say or do anything, they will feel the ground rules have no value. You could also refer to the ground rules when they are not broken as positive reinforcement of good behaviour. However, there will be occasions when a learner cannot help being late due to no fault of their own.

If a learner breaks a ground rule, you may find their peers reprimand them before you need to. You might like to ask your group to decide upon penalties or consequences for when a ground rule is broken. This could be a token penalty: for example, donating 50 pence to a group fund. Your learners can then decide what to do with the fund at the end of the programme such as giving it to a local charity. It could be more serious; for example, with younger learners, writing their name on a wall chart and allocating a point every time a rule is broken. Three points could lead to disciplinary action or removal from the session. Ultimately, you will need to find your own strategy for dealing with learners who break the ground rules, depending upon the age and maturity of the group. At the end of your session you could thank your learners for following the ground rules; this will act as a reminder of their existence.

If you can lead by example, you will help create a culture of mutual compliance which should enable effective teaching, learning and assessment to take place.

Extension Activity

What methods would you use to establish ground rules with your learners? Give examples of ground rules which would be non-negotiable and ones that you could negotiate depending upon your subject. What would you do if a learner broke a ground rule?

Teaching and learning approaches

Teaching and learning approaches are the methods you will use to facilitate the learning process. Think of these as techniques which can focus on learners being *actively engaged* during the session and not just *passively listening* to you. The approaches you use will depend upon the subject you are teaching, the context and environment you are teaching in, the length of each session and any particular learner needs. It's not about *what you will teach*, but *how they will learn*. Approaches should always be fit for purpose, i.e. to enable learning to take place, and not just used for the sake of it, or because you like to do things in a certain way. To give you some ideas, see Table 5.2 later in the chapter. It lists teaching and learning approaches and activities along with their strengths and limitations.

Formal teaching approaches include lectures, demonstrations, instruction and presentations which are usually teacher-centred, known as *pedagogy*. Informal approaches include discussions, group work, practical activities and role plays and are usually learner-centred, known as *andragogy*. Wherever possible it's best to use a mixture of the two and vary the approaches you use. This will ensure all learning preferences are met, that all learners are included and can participate, and will enable you to assess that learning is taking place.

Example

Zak teaches History by lecturing to groups of learners. He feels that although he uses a computerised presentation and handouts, his learners are not actively participating in any way. He decides to make his session more practical by introducing group discussions, and role plays of historical events. Several learners approach him after the session to say how much they enjoyed it and how it enabled them to understand the subject more. He has set up the VLE to encourage interaction outside of the sessions, and he uploads videos and audio clips for learners to access. He now finishes each session with a quiz to assess knowledge in a fun way. Zak's sessions are more inclusive and enable him to assess how much learning has taken place.

Teaching and learning should not be in isolation from the assessment process. You can assess that learning is taking place each time you are with your learners. This can simply be by observing practice or asking questions. If your learners are taking a qualification, there will be formal methods of assessment such as an assignment, or an observation in the workplace. However, you can devise informal methods to use with your learners to check progress. For more information regarding assessment please see Chapter 6.

Knowles et al. (2011) are the theorists who brought the concept of pedagogy and andragogy to the fore. The *pedagogical approach* places the responsibility for making decisions about the learning process upon the teacher, who may decide to teach the same material in the same order, at the same time to all learners. This doesn't allow any flexibility for a learner who may miss a session, or is learning more slowly or quickly than others, i.e. to allow for differentiation to take place. Pedagogy often relates to formal teaching methods. However, it is possible to teach in a formal manner, yet involve the learners throughout a session to help make the learning process more engaging.

The *andragogical approach* places the emphasis on the learner to take responsibility for the learning process; they can then ensure they are learning in a way that suits them. This approach allows you to adapt your teaching approaches and materials to suit each learner's progress and development. If your sessions are mainly pedagogical, try to include your learners by asking individual questions to check their understanding, or asking pairs to talk about a topic and then discussing it as a whole group. Your subject should never bore your learners; you need to inspire them to maintain their motivation and interest. Learners will only be bored if the session is delivered in a boring way. To help your confidence, imagine you are an actor playing a role, that role is of the teacher or trainer, not you as a person. If you are nervous, breathe deeply and pause for a second or two; it might seem a long time to you; however, it isn't. Focus your thoughts, relax and enjoy what you are doing. A tip if nerves do take over is to place your tongue on the roof of your mouth for a few seconds, no one will notice and you should feel better.

The following table shows a few examples of how learning might take place depending upon the teaching approach you choose, and how that learning could be assessed. The more teaching and learning approaches you can use, the more opportunities there are for assessment to take place.

Table 5.1 Examples of teaching, learning and assessment approaches

Teaching approach	Learning approach	Assessment approach
facilitating activities with learners	practical involvement, i.e. paired and group work, discussion, looking, listening, asking questions, problem solving, reflecting, writing notes	asking questions observing practice peer and self-assessment written questions
demonstrating a skill	watching, listening, asking questions and writing notes	asking questions
discussing a topic	listening, asking questions and voicing opinions, problem solving	written or oral questions
instruction regarding a practical task	watching, listening, asking questions and attempting the task	asking questions observing practice peer and self-assessment
lecturing	listening and writing notes	asking questions
presentation with video	watching, listening and writing notes	asking questions quiz
facilitating role plays	watching, listening and practical involvement	asking questions observing practice peer and self-assessment

Sometimes, if learners are quite passive, i.e. listening or reading, then not much learning will take place, as they are doing little else, unless that is their particular learning

Activity

Look at the list of teaching and learning approaches and activities in Table 5.1, which would you use and why? How can you use a mixture of different approaches to engage and motivate your learners to ensure learning takes place?

preference. If you can get learners to demonstrate that they have learnt from their listening and reading then you will know that they have understood. For example, asking open questions, asking them to summarise what they have heard, or to demonstrate a task.

Dale's (1969) cone of learning and experience

Dale (1969) devised the *cone of learning and experience* to express how people remember what they read, hear, see and do. Using activities from the top of the cone (passive) through to

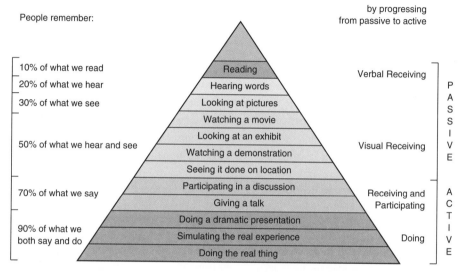

Figure 5.1 Dale's cone of learning and experience

the bottom of the cone (active) will enable your learners to realistically experience your subject. They should then remember more because they have *said and done* what they have *read and heard,* i.e. they have put theory into practice. The bands within the cone are not rigid but flexible, and the cone has been adapted and revised over the years.

Using a variety of teaching and learning approaches will help meet all learning preferences and enable learning to take place. If you expect your learners to listen to you and then to remember everything you have said, as well as understand it, then very little learning will

Activity

Read the following list of words once, cover it up, and then write down the words you remember.

cat	deck	table	snow	storm
sky	plant	book	smile	sky
lulu	lala	sky	plant	music
tree	bottle	money	cat	plant

have taken place, unless it is their particular learning preference. If you can involve your learners with discussions, questions and activities which they can engage with, it will bring the subject to life and help learning to take place. However, not all approaches will work with all learners and you will need to find out what does and doesn't work for the type of learners you have, for example, different age groups.

Among your words are probably cat, plant, sky, lulu and lala. This is because they occur at the beginning, the end, are unusual or are repeated words. Use this approach with important points when teaching, i.e. by doing something different or unusual, and repeating points.

Engaging and motivating learners

Engaging your learners is all about obtaining and maintaining their attention, involving them during the session and keeping them motivated. When commencing a session, if you are unsure what to say to gather your learners' attention, start with *Welcome to the session, today we will...* in a louder than normal but assertive voice. To settle your learners and focus their attention towards learning, you could use a *starter activity*. This could be a quiz to test knowledge gained so far, a discussion to open up thinking about the current topic, or an energiser activity focusing upon the session topic. You can then state your aim and the objectives from your session plan. Always check if your learners have any prior knowledge and/or experience by asking them; you can then draw upon this during the session. Never assume your learners know or don't know something.

As you progress, allow time for questioning, repeating and summarising important points. Incorporate the knowledge and experience of your learners and, if you can, give relevant anecdotes to bring the subject to life. Ensure your session flows progressively, i.e. is delivered in a logical order and assesses progress before moving on to the next topic. When changing topics, try to link them together somehow or summarise one before moving on to the other. Break aspects down into small manageable chunks; for example, if you are teaching a learner how to spell the dog breed of Chihuahua, break it down into three small chunks, i.e. Chi, hua, hua.

Try not to use the word *obvious*, as things are only obvious to you. Show interest, passion and enthusiasm for your subject and encourage your learners to take pride in their work. Use tone and inflection to emphasise key points and don't be afraid of silent pauses; they will give you time to refocus, and your learners time to consider what you have said.

If you make a mistake, don't draw attention to it, but continue professionally; your learners probably won't know any different. However, if they do notice, acknowledge your mistake and don't bluff your way through it. Your learners will respect your honesty.

If you feel you are overrunning on your timings, don't be afraid to carry something over to the next session, cut it out altogether or give it as homework. Alternatively, you can adjust the timings of the activities to reduce or increase them as necessary. Don't feel you must keep to the number of minutes you have written on your session plan. It's more important to ensure learning is taking place, than keeping to your timings. If you finish earlier than planned, make sure you have some extra activities you could use; for example, worksheets or a quiz. If particular learners finish earlier than others, you could give them an *extension activity* to stretch and challenge their learning further. It's always useful to carry a few spare activities around with you, or to have access to them electronically. When you summarise at the end of the session, don't introduce anything new as this might confuse your learners.

If you are delivering a sequence of sessions, always recap the previous session before commencing the current session. While teaching, notice the reactions of your learners; you might need to change your pace of delivery or introduce something practical to energise them. If you are demonstrating something in front of your learners, always check if they are left- or right-handed as this could change the way they see things. When they look at you, your right hand will be on their left. It's helpful to show a completed item if you are demonstrating how to make something: for example, a finished pipe weld. This will help them visualise what they are aiming for. Make sure your session includes activities which cover all learning preferences, i.e. visual, aural, read/write and kinaesthetic.

When you are planning break times, make sure you inform your learners when these will be and for how long, otherwise they may be thinking about when they can get refreshments, which will distract them from learning. If there is a break, state what time you expect them back, rather than saying how many minutes they can have. This way, they know exactly what time they are due back. When your learners return, ask if they have any questions. Sometimes they will have been thinking about the topic during the break, and would like an opportunity to clarify aspects or ask questions.

During the session, if possible, move around the room regularly to ensure your learners are not using electronic devices inappropriately. If your learners are using information, communication technology (ICT) equipment as part of the session, make sure you agree the boundaries of which websites can or cannot be accessed, and whether they can use social networking sites or access their e-mail. If you have younger learners who have worked particularly well, it could be a reward that they have 10 minutes at the end to check their messages.

If you find you have spare time towards the end of your session, there are a few things you can do. For example, ask each learner in turn to state the *one significant thing* they have learnt which they could apply to their practice. This is good if you have a small group; however, if you have a large group you could approach it differently, for example, ask the

Example

Ellie had five minutes to spare at the end of her session. She decided to ask each of her 12 learners to give her one word that summarised the session. If the word was negative she would ask the learner to expand. Words included 'great', 'brilliant', 'fun' and 'boring'. She asked the learner who had said 'boring' to explain why. He said it was because he had been thinking about other things rather than paying attention.

learners to write it on a sticky note and hand it to you on the way out. Depending upon how much time you have, you could use the *one word* approach to gain feedback from your learners.

If Ellie had more time, she could have asked each learner to expand on the positive as well as the negative points as this would give her more feedback on which to improve certain aspects. Alternatively, she could ask for two, three or four word feedback. This makes learners think a bit more about what they will say, and by limiting the words it keeps them focused.

Keeping some spare activities handy in case you have time can be a useful way to finish your session. You could create a worksheet, a crossword or a few multi-choice questions to use when necessary. For example, you could hold a quiz by placing your learners in groups and letting them confer on the answers. If so, quickly think of a few questions regarding the topic your learners have just learnt. A point could be allocated to the winning team and this method could be used more regularly as a fun way of finishing the session. It is also a good way to informally assess learning has taken place. Points could be built up over the sessions and lead to some sort of reward at the end of the programme.

When you finish your session, summarise the content, relate it to your aim and the objectives and allow time for learner questions. Explain what will be covered in the next session (if applicable). If you are setting any homework, be clear about your requirements and hand in dates. Qualifications on the Qualifications and Credit Framework (QCF) require learners to study in their own time, known as *non-contact time*. You will need to plan various activities for learners to carry out as homework, i.e. reading, research and assignments. Always follow up or check on their progress.

If you are unsure what to say to formally end your session, simply say *Thank you, I've enjoyed my session with you today*. If you are due to see your learners again for another session, you could say *Thank you, I look forward to seeing you all again on...* Plan time at the end for clearing up; you don't want to be rushed.

If you are facilitating a session with a colleague, you will need to plan in advance which aspects will be covered by whom, and who will deal with any questions or behaviour issues. You will also need to plan who will introduce and close the session. Team teaching takes practice as personalities and delivery styles may differ. However, it is useful where a complex subject is being taught as different techniques of delivery can be utilised, and the experience and knowledge of the teachers drawn upon.

A mixture of different approaches within your sessions will ensure you meet all learning preferences, engage your learners, retain motivation and ensure learning is successful. Never be afraid to try something new and always evaluate how it went afterwards.

Table 5.2 contains examples of teaching and learning approaches and activities which you might like to use with your learners. The strengths and limitations of each are also stated.

Extension Activity

Make a list of at least six different teaching and learning approaches you could use for your subject to engage and motivate your learners. Consider the advantages and limitations of each and which are best suited to group or individual learning. You might like to refer to Table 5.2 for some ideas.

Table 5.2 Teaching and learning approaches and activities: strengths and limitations

Approach/ activity	Description	Strengths	Limitations
Activities	Tasks carried out by pairs, a group or individual, relevant to the topic being taught	Learners are active Develops group interaction	Not all learners may want to participate Clear objectives should be set, activity must be clearly explained Time limit required Time needed for feedback or de-brief
Assignments	A longer-term activity based around the qualification or topic, which provides evidence of learning Can be practical or theoretical	Can be produced by the teacher to challenge a learner's potential or consolidate learning Can be formative or summative	If set by an Awarding Organisation, ensure all aspects of the syllabus have been taught beforehand Must be individually assessed and written feedback given which can develop learning further
Blended learning	Using more than one method of teaching, usually including technology. For example, a teaching session can be supported with learning materials and resources available via the organisation's website, with e-support/assessment from teachers as required	Several methods of learning can be combined, enabling all learning preferences to be met Formal teaching can be supported with informal learning	Not all learners may have access to the technology
Brainstorming	A list of suggestions or ideas regarding a particular theme, topic or problem without judgements or criticisms The list can then be refined and used as a basis for other activities, usually written on flip chart paper or a board so all learners can see	Quickly stimulates thoughts and ideas Involves everyone Builds on current knowledge and experience Can be teacher led or group led	Some learners may not contribute or might be judgemental and overpowering Ideas may be given too quickly to write down Time limits need to be set

(Continued)

Table 5.2 (Continued)

Approach/ activity	Description	Strengths	Limitations
Buzz groups	Short topics to be discussed in small groups	Can break up a more formal session Allows interaction of learners and focuses ideas Checks understanding Doesn't require formal feedback	Learners may digress Specific points could be lost Checking individual learning has taken place may be difficult
Case studies	Can be a hypothetical situation, a description of an actual event or an incomplete event, enabling learners to write how they would deal with it	Can make topics more realistic, enhancing motivation and interest Can be carried individually or in a group situation Builds on current knowledge and experience	Time limits must be set If carried out as a group activity, roles should be defined Must have clear outcomes Allow time for a de-brief to include a group discussion
Coaching	A one-to-one, or small group activity which can occur spontaneously	Ideal for on the job training Ongoing advice and guidance can be given Takes account of individual needs	Not suitable for large groups Can be time consuming Suitable environment needed
Debates	Learners or guests present a case to others, with subsequent arguments, questions and discussions	Learner centred Allows freedom of view points and demonstrates understanding	Some learners may not get involved, others may take over – teacher needs to manage this carefully Can be time consuming Learners may need to research a topic in advance Can generate inappropriate behaviour

Approach/ activity	Description	Strengths	Limitations
Demonstration	A practical way of showing how something works	Can be supported with handouts and activities to cover all learning preferences Can increase attention and confidence	Equipment may not be available or in working order Larger groups may not be able to see the demonstration or have enough resources Individuals may not pay attention or get bored
Dictation	Reading notes out loud for learners to write down	Gives emphasis to key points – should be used in moderation Can be followed up with learners carrying out research regarding what was dictated, i.e. via the internet	Learners write down what is said, but may not understand it Some learners may get behind with their writing and miss points Does not allow for clarification or questions
Discussion	Learners talk about a topic or the teacher can introduce a topic for the group to discuss	All learners can participate and share knowledge and experiences	Some learners may be shy or not want to be involved Easy to digress Teacher needs to keep the group focused and set a time limit Some learners might dominate
Distance learning or open learning	Learning which takes place away from the organisation offering the programme/ qualification Work can be posted to learners and returned for assessment	Learning can occur at a time and place to suit the learner Can be combined with other learning methods e.g. blended learning	Could be a long gap between submitting work for assessment and receiving feedback Self-discipline is needed Targets must be clearly agreed Learner may never meet teacher/assessor
Drawing	Illustrations to show how something works	Good for visual learners	Needs explaining carefully

(Continued)

Table 5.2 (Continued)

Approach/activity	Description	Strengths	Limitations
e-learning (see also online learning)	Electronic learning – learning which is supported or enhanced using information and communication technology (ICT)	Learning can take place anywhere a computer is available Learning can be flexible Ongoing support is given	Learners need access to a computer and need to be computer literate Self-discipline is needed, along with clear targets Authenticity of learner's work may need validating Technical support may be required
Essays	A formal piece of written or word-processed text, produced by the learner, for a specific topic	Useful for higher level subjects Can check a learner's English and maths skills Can confirm knowledge and understanding, along with application to practice	Not suitable for lower level learners Requires clear assessment grading criteria Marking can be time consuming Plagiarism can be an issue
Experiential/discovery	Practical tasks enabling learners to act out or experience an event	Good for group work and to put theory into practice Learners find out things for themselves	Not all learners may want to participate Some learners may lack confidence or not want to embarrass themselves in front of their peers Can be time consuming
Extension activity	A task to stretch and challenge learners	Can be used when learners finish a task earlier than others Can be used to extend a learner's thinking about a subject	Some learners might feel pressured to complete them when they are not able to, i.e. peer pressure
Flexible learning	Learning that can take place at a time and place to suit the learner and/or using different delivery approaches within a session to meet particular challenges	Suits learners who cannot attend formal sessions	Ongoing support and monitoring of achievement is required Not all learners are motivated to this style of learning

Approach/activity	Description	Strengths	Limitations
Games	A fun way of learning in pairs or groups to enable problem solving and decision making to take place	Board or card games can be designed to make learning enjoyable Assesses skills, knowledge, understanding and/or attitudes Encourages interaction and healthy competition Physical games put theory into practice Online games develop computer skills	Need to be well prepared in advance Learners need to remain focused Objectives need to be clear A *pilot* should take place first to make sure it works Careful supervision is needed Rules must be followed
Gapped handout	Blank spaces within a handout for learners to fill in missing words in sentences	Different versions for different levels of learners could be devised Useful to fill in time during a session	Some learners might find it too easy
Group work	Enables learners to carry out a specific activity, for example, problem solving Can be practical or theoretical	Allows interaction between learners Learners learn from each other's experiences and knowledge Encourages participation and variety Rotating group members enables all learners to work with each other	Careful management by the teacher is required regarding time limits, progress, and ensuring all group members are clear with the requirements Potential for personality clashes One person may dominate Learners might get left out or be too shy to contribute Ground rules might be needed to keep the group on track Time is needed for a thorough de-brief and feedback

(Continued)

Table 5.2 (Continued)

Approach/activity	Description	Strengths	Limitations
Handouts	Written information/drawings, etc. to promote and support learning	Useful for learners to refer to after a session Can incorporate questions for learners to answer as a homework activity Can be differentiated for levels of learners	Should be used in conjunction with other activities Needs to be adapted for any special learner requirements Should be produced well in advance Spelling, grammar, punctuation and syntax must be accurate
Homework	Activities carried out between sessions, for example, further reading, answering questions Learning doesn't have to stop just because the session has	Learners can complete at a time and place that suits them Maintains interest between sessions Encourages learners to stretch themselves further	Clear time limits must be set Learners might not do it Must be discussed, or marked/assessed and individual feedback given
Icebreakers/energisers team building exercises	A fun and light-hearted way of introducing learners and topics	A good way of learners getting to know each other, and for teachers to observe skills and attitudes Can revitalise a flagging session	Not all learners may want to take part Some learners may see these as insignificant – careful explanations are needed to link the experience to the topic
Instruction	Formal method of teaching learners, whereby the teacher tells or shows the learner what to do, to achieve a particular skill, the learner then performs this	If one to one, a good method of pacing learning to suit the individual Learners can hear and/or see what they should do, and try this out immediately	If to a group, some learners may get left behind or forget what to do Needs supporting with a handout or further information/activities Appropriate positioning is required, e.g. for left-handed learners of right-handed teachers
Interactive whiteboard	Teachers and learners can use various functions including linking to the internet	Good for group work and presentations	Not all learners can use it at the same time

Approach/ activity	Description	Strengths	Limitations
Journal or diary	Learners keep a record of their progress, their reflections and thoughts	Develops self-assessment skills Relates theory to practice (if learners are having work experience) Helps the teacher assess English skills	Should be specific to the learning taking place and be analytical rather than descriptive Learners need to be guided as to how to write in a particular way to meet the programme criteria Contents need to remain confidential Can be time consuming to read
Lecture	Traditional *teacher-centred* technique of delivering information	Useful for teaching theoretical subjects Key points can be prepared in advance on postcards as prompts Ideal for large groups Can be supported with visual images	Learners are passive and may not listen to what is being said Learners may not feel they can interrupt or ask questions to clarify points Learners need good listening and note taking skills Good voice projection and clarity of speech required
Mentoring	One-to-one guidance and support by someone other than the teacher, who is usually experienced in the subject	Expertise and knowledge can be passed on through ongoing support Times can be arranged to suit both parties	Can be time consuming Mentor and mentee might not get along
Micro-teaching	A simulated teaching session taught by the learner, usually in front of their peer group	Enables learners to practice in a safe environment Can be recorded to aid self-evaluation Peer feedback can be given by the other learners	Not all learners enjoy the experience Recording equipment, if used, can be difficult to manage while observing learners Some learners might not give constructive feedback

(Continued)

Table 5.2 (Continued)

Approach/activity	Description	Strengths	Limitations
Mind maps/spidergrams	A visual way of organising information and making plans, learners draw a circle with a key point and branch from this with subheadings to explore and develop points further	Learners are active Topics can be explored in a fun and meaningful way Links between ideas are easy to see New information can easily be added	Not all learners may want to contribute or understand what to do One learner may dominate Needs careful supervision Large paper or a board and marker pens required
Mnemonics	Remembering things by associating the first letters of words with something else, e.g. Richard of York Gave Battle In Vain (RYGBIV) is Red, Orange, Yellow, Green, Blue, Indigo, Violet for the colours of the rainbow	A quick way of remembering facts	Demonstrates knowledge but not understanding Some learners might get the letters mixed up
Models	Useful where the real object cannot be seen Life models, for example, in art classes or machinery models in engineering	Learners have a chance to see how something looks and/or works, and ask questions	Must be clearly explained and demonstrated May be an additional cost Needs careful planning and preparation Should be supported with a handout
Online learning (see also e-learning)	Learning that takes place in a virtual learning environment (VLE) via a computer connected to an intranet or the internet Asynchronous learning does not need to be accessed at fixed times Synchronous learning takes place in an environment where the teacher and learner are simultaneously present, perhaps at different locations, but communicating with	Learning can take place anywhere a computer with internet access is available Learning can be flexible Ongoing support is given	Learners need access to a computer with internet access Learners need to be computer literate Self-discipline is needed, along with clear targets Authenticity of learner's work may need validating Technical support may be required Reliable internet connection needed

Approach/activity	Description	Strengths	Limitations
Paired work	Enables learners to carry out a specific activity with their peer, for example, problem solving Can be practical or theoretical	Allows interaction between learners Learners learn from each other Encourages participation and variety Pairs can then link up as fours and so on to share experiences and knowledge	Careful management by the teacher is required regarding time limits, progress, and ensuring each pair is clear with the requirements Potential for personality clashes Difficult to assess individual contributions Time is needed for feedback from each pair
Peer learning Peer assessment Peer feedback	Learners gaining skills and/or knowledge from their peers	Enables learners to work together in an informal way to learn from each other's experiences and knowledge Learners support each other throughout the session or programme Learners give feedback to each other	There may be personality clashes resulting in subjective feedback Not all information given may be correct
Podcast	A digital, audio or video file of the session uploaded to the internet	Useful if learners cannot attend a session Can listen or watch the session again	Some learners might not be able to access them May encourage non-attendance
Pose, pause, pick questioning	Ask a question, then pause for a few seconds so that all learners are thinking about a response. Then pick a learner to answer the question, stating their name as you look at them	Enables all learners to consider the answer rather than thinking they might be asked	Chosen learner might not know the answer

(Continued)

Table 5.2 (Continued)

Approach/ activity	Description	Strengths	Limitations
Practical work	A task that individuals can carry out, while the teacher observes progress, usually follows a demonstration or presentation	Actively involves the learners Help and advice can be given as needed	Some learners may not respond well to practical activities Can be time consuming
Presentations	Similar to a lecture, with greater use of audio-visual aids	Interaction can take place between the teacher and learners Visual and aural learning preferences can be reached Effective use of media can make presentations stimulating, motivating and inspiring A good activity can be for learners to carry out research and then present their findings to others	Kinaesthetic learning preferences might not be included Some learners may not pay attention Too many slides can switch off learners' attention
Projects	A longer-term activity enabling learners to provide evidence of, or consolidate their learning and experiences	Can be interesting and motivating Can be individual or group led Learners could choose a relevant topic to cover the learning outcomes, leading to autonomous learning	Clear outcomes must be set, along with a time limit, must be relevant, realistic and achievable Progress should be checked regularly If a group is carrying out the project, be aware of each individual's input Thorough feedback should be given
Questions	A key technique for checking understanding and stimulating thinking	Can be written or oral Enables the learner to think about what they are learning Can challenge a learner's potential An effective way of testing knowledge when open questions are used	Closed questions only give a yes or no response which doesn't demonstrate knowledge Questions must be unambiguous Learners might struggle to answer oral questions in front of their peers Written questions might be misinterpreted Time constraints might be necessary

Approach/ activity	Description	Strengths	Limitations
Quizzes	Fun activities to test knowledge, skills and/or attitudes by the use of crosswords, panel games, online activities, etc.	Learners are actively involved Useful backup activity if spare time available	Can seem trivial to mature learners Dominant learners might take over Shy learners might not get involved
Reading	Learners work from relevant texts/ books/journals, etc.	Good for read/write learning preferences Encourages further learning	Reading and note taking skills required Learners can get bored or easily distracted May need to have differentiated texts to account for a range of levels in the group
Repetition or rote learning	Learners repeat aspects such as the times tables (1×6 is 6, 2×6 is 12, etc.)	A good way of remembering useful facts	Only demonstrates the learner can remember and repeat, doesn't demonstrate understanding
Reports	Learners produce a document to inform, recommend and/or make suggestions based on a given topic	Useful for higher level learners Encourages the use of research techniques	Good writing skills and the use of referencing might be required Learners need to interpret and evaluate their reading to demonstrate their understanding
Research	An in-depth way of finding out answers or more information regarding a topic	Learners can use the internet, texts, journals, etc. in their own time	Learners need to know how to research Learners might not know how to apply their research to real situations
Rhyme and Rap	Repeating phrases or songs to aid memory, for example, 30 days have September, April, June and November	Learners can create their own phrases or songs Can be fun	Can seem trivial to mature learners Does not test knowledge and understanding, only the ability to recite or recall

(Continued)

Table 5.2 (Continued)

Approach/ activity	Description	Strengths	Limitations
Role plays	A practical activity to demonstrate skills, knowledge and understanding of a particular topic Acting out a hypothetical situation or scenario	Can see learners' behaviour and actions Encourages participation in a safe environment A fun method of learning Can lead to debates Links theory to practice Gives learners the opportunity to demonstrate communication skills Learners can observe and give peer feedback	Can be time consuming Clear roles must be defined Not all learners may want, or be able to participate Time limit should be set Some learners may get too dramatic Time is needed for a thorough de-brief Some learners might be excluded
Self-assessment	Learners decide how they have met the assessment criteria, or are progressing at a given time	Promotes ownership, learner involvement and personal autonomy Encourages learners to check their own work before handing in Encourages reflection Learners need to be specific about what they have achieved and what they need to do to complete any gaps Promotes individual thinking regarding progress and achievements	Some learners may feel they are doing better or more worse than they actually are Assessor needs to discuss progress and achievements with each learner to confirm their decisions Learners need to be specific about what they have achieved and what they need to do to complete any gaps Difficult to be objective when making a decision
Seminars	A presentation of ideas, followed by questions and a discussion – usually by the learners	Allows learners to research topics and gain confidence at speaking to a group Can lead to worthwhile discussions	Agree topics well in advance along with a running order of who will present first Learners need specific objectives and a time limit Other learners may not pay attention

Approach/ activity	Description	Strengths	Limitations
Simulation	An imitation activity carried out when the real activity would be too dangerous. For example, the evacuation of a building when the fire alarm goes off, there's no need to set fire to the building for a simulated evacuation	Enables learners to demonstrate skills Learners may realise things about themselves they were not aware of	Careful planning is needed Can be time consuming Specialist equipment may be needed Ground rules must be agreed Not all learners may be able to participate fully May not be taken seriously Thorough de-brief needed
Starter activity (welcome activity)	A short activity at the beginning of a session to settle learners and focus their attention towards learning It could be a quiz to test knowledge gained so far, a discussion to open up thinking about the current subject, or an energiser activity focusing upon the session topic	If a learners arrives late, they only miss the starter activity not the introduction to the session	Some learner might feel it's trivial or wasting time
Surveys	Learners ascertain information regarding a particular topic, from others	Active task, learners can work individually, in pairs or groups Learners can meet other people enhancing their experience	Permission may be required Ethics and confidentiality required Quality of question content is important Confidentiality should be maintained Time consuming to analyse
Teaching/ training/ tutoring	Educating learners in a subject, furthering their skills, knowledge, understanding and/or attitudes using formal and informal approaches	A variety of approaches can be used depending upon the subject If planned well, can reach all learning preferences, motivate learners and encourage development and progression	Some learners do not respond well to formal teaching Not all learning preferences reached all of the time

(Continued)

Table 5.2 (Continued)

Approach/activity	Description	Strengths	Limitations
Team teaching or co-training	Facilitating a session with a colleague	Enables learners to see different styles of delivery	Staff involved need to plan carefully who is doing what and when
Technology-based learning	Using relevant equipment and materials, for example, videos/CDROMs/DVDs/the internet, etc.	Generates discussions and leads to further learning and questions Brings *real* events to learners	Can be time consuming Learners need to pay attention Learners should not be left unsupervised
Tests	Written questions (open, closed, multiple choice) to test knowledge and understanding Practical activities to assess skills	Learners are active Can be used to fill in time towards the end of a session or to extend learning Useful for individual learners who like to be challenged further	Needs to be carried out in supervised conditions Time limits required Can be stressful to learners Feedback may not be immediate If set by an Awarding Organisation, ensure all aspects of the syllabus have been taught before issuing the test
Tutorial reviews	A one-to-one or group discussion between the teacher and the learner/s, with an agreed purpose, for example, discussing progress so far	A good way of informally assessing a learner's progress and/or giving feedback An opportunity for learners to discuss issues or for informal tuition to take place	Needs to be in a comfortable, safe and quiet environment as confidential issues may be discussed Time may overrun Records should be maintained and action points followed up

Approach/ activity	Description	Strengths	Limitations
Undoing	Learners can *undo* or *take apart* an object, to learn how it was put together. An example is taking a plug apart to see how it was originally wired	Great for kinaesthetic learners and for developing practical skills Needs to be demonstrated by the teacher first Useful in practical sessions, needs to be supported with a handout, further information and careful guidance	Not so good for theoretical learners Objects/resources need to be available for all learners
Video/ TV/DVD and online recordings	Watching a recording or a live programme via various media including the internet	Good for visual learners Promotes discussions	Not interactive Doesn't suit all learning preferences
Virtual learning environment (VLE)	An online platform for teachers to upload learning materials and interact with learners	Enables learners to access materials outside the sessions Can be used for online learning instead of attending sessions Allows online interaction between other learners and the teacher Assignments can be accessed by learners and uploaded once complete, teachers can give feedback via the VLE and records are automatically maintained	Not all learners might be computer literate Not all learners have internet access
Visiting speakers	An expert in the subject area speaks to the group	Can give variety and expertise to a topic, with a different perspective	Must be arranged well in advance Some speakers may charge a fee Allow time for questions and discussions

(Continued)

Table 5.2 (Continued)

Approach/ activity	Description	Strengths	Limitations
Visits/field trips	Learners visit a venue relevant to the programme or qualification	Fact finding, active, interesting and stimulating Makes the subject real Puts theory into practice Can be discussed in subsequent sessions Can link with projects and assignments	Needs careful planning, organisational and health and safety procedures must be followed Needs finance Group needs to be well briefed and prepared, ground rules must be set Supervision usually required De-brief needed
Webcast	Videos and information uploaded to the internet Similar to podcasts	A useful way of distributing additional information to support current teaching	No interaction between learners Not all learners have internet access
Worksheets	Handouts to read and complete to check knowledge and understanding (can also be electronic) Blank spaces can be used for learners to complete sentences Words can be circled, phrases completed, lists put in order	Fun informal activity can be done individually, in pairs or groups Useful for lower level learners or homework Can be created at different degrees of difficulty to address differentiation	Mature learners may consider them inappropriate Too many worksheets can be boring, learners might not be challenged enough
Workshops	An opportunity to share practice, use activities and develop knowledge and understanding in a real or simulated environment (RWE)	Enables learners to work at their own pace Learners can support each other and learn from each other's experiences	Individual support is required Suitable workpacks need producing or resource packs need purchasing to enable learners to progress at their own pace

Communication, behaviour and respect

Communication is an essential skill of a teacher, whether it's used verbally, non-verbally or in written form. Used effectively, it will enable you to share knowledge and skills with your learners. This can involve using interpersonal skills, which not only includes how you communicate and interact with others, but also reflects your confidence and ability to listen and respond. Interpersonal skills can also include problem solving, decision making and other skills such as time management. The way you communicate with your learners will convey a powerful message. It should lead to good behaviour, respect for others and facilitate the learning process.

Communication

Communication is not only a means of passing on information from one person to another, it is also a manner of expression: for example, your body language, voice and the gestures you make. The first time you meet your learners they will probably make a subconscious judgement about you, and you will probably make one about them. These judgements often turn out to be wrong; therefore it is important not to make any assumptions about your learners.

Body language includes facial expressions, eye contact, gestures, posture, non-verbal signals and appearance. Your personality will show through when you are teaching; however, there are some aspects you might not be able to control, such as facial flushing, blinking or clearing your throat. Some you should be able to control, such as winking, giving a thumbs-up sign or laughing. You need to be aware not only of your own body language, but that of your learners. You need to sense what they are not saying as well as what they are saying.

Communication is the key to encouraging learner motivation and respect, managing behaviour and disruption, and becoming a successful teacher or trainer. It should always be appropriate and effective, and to the level of your learners. If you need to write on a board or flipchart while speaking to your learners, don't do both at the same time. If you face the board, they may not hear you speak and you might miss something happening in the room.

Activity

What communication methods, besides speaking, will you use with your learners and why? How can you incorporate the use of information and communication technology for communication either during or outside of your sessions?

Successful communication includes:

- oral communication, i.e. the way you speak when explaining, describing, summarising, questioning and giving feedback – be aware of your voice projection and when to use pauses to gain attention or allow thinking time

- written communication, i.e. presentations, handouts, worksheets, written feedback and progress reports – always check your spelling, grammar, punctuation and sentence construction

5 FACILITATING LEARNING

- non-verbal communication, i.e. the way you act, your body language, appearance, facial expressions, eye contact, gestures, posture and non-verbal signals

- questioning, i.e. oral or written should include all learners and preferably use open questions

- listening skills, i.e. eye contact, not interrupting, not being judgemental

- other qualities you can convey such as empathy and sympathy

The language you use should reflect equality and inclusiveness, be relevant to the subject, not offend anyone in any way and be at the right level for your learners. You may have to practise with your voice projection, but don't shout, just speak a little louder and slower than normal and ask if learners can hear you. Sometimes nerves might make you speak faster. Don't expect your learners to remember everything first time; they don't know what you know. You should repeat or rephrase key points regularly. You might even get frustrated if asked questions regarding points you have already explained. Try not to say things like *I just told you that* or *Can't you remember what I just said?* Repeating key points will help your learners remember them. Don't embarrass a learner in front of their peer group; they may feel they can't ask you anything again. Learning occurs best in an active, not a passive, environment where communication is a two-way process. Always watch for signals from your learners to check they are learning.

Example

Olga was explaining a complex topic and noticed one of her learners, Josh, was making a strange expression, furrowing his brow as if he didn't understand. As Olga regularly uses eye contact with her learners, she quickly spotted this and asked Josh if he would like her to explain the topic in a different way. She rephrased what she had just explained and could see from his smiling and nodding face that he now understood. To double-check his understanding, she asked an open question which required an answer other than 'Yes' or 'No'.

You could use the following checklist to help you improve your verbal, non-verbal and written communication.

Verbal

☐ speak clearly and a little louder and slower than normal, emphasising new or unusual words and limit the use of jargon and acronyms

☐ be conscious of your dialect, pitch, accent and tone

☐ be aware of your posture, gestures and body language, even if you are you are not in face-to-face contact, as these can help with how you express yourself

☐ ensure you have the required subject knowledge, introducing and conveying this confidently, convincingly, passionately and enthusiastically

☐ introduce points in a logical and progressive order, avoiding ambiguity

126

- ☐ back up explanations with handouts and/or visuals
- ☐ emphasise key words and summarise key points regularly
- ☐ allow time for questions (by you and from your learners) but don't get too sidetracked by these
- ☐ use learners' names
- ☐ watch and listen to your learners for their reactions
- ☐ recognise group dynamics, encourage shy learners and manage over-confident ones
- ☐ use active listening skills
- ☐ try not to say *erm, yeah, okay, you know,* or *does that make sense* (the latter may only gain a *yes* response as learners feel that is what you want to hear, ask open questions instead)
- ☐ give constructive and positive feedback

Non-verbal

- ☐ dress appropriately, act professionally and confidently
- ☐ be aware of your posture, gestures and body language
- ☐ use eye contact
- ☐ position yourself so all your learners can see you
- ☐ don't fiddle or fidget with things
- ☐ don't fold your arms or keep your hands in your pockets
- ☐ observe your learners' reactions and their body language, and react to this

Written

- ☐ keep sentences short and to the point
- ☐ don't include too many facts or dates
- ☐ use visuals if possible
- ☐ keep your text logical and progressive
- ☐ use subject headings, underlining, bullets or bold to emphasise points
- ☐ avoid slang words, abbreviations, symbols, too much jargon or acronyms
- ☐ don't cut out vowels
- ☐ proof read your work for spelling, grammar, punctuation and sentence construction
- ☐ check to see if anything could be misinterpreted – remember that the tone of how you write it might not be the same as how your learner reads it
- ☐ ensure your text covers equality, differentiation and inclusiveness
- ☐ express numbers as words when the number is less than 10, or begins a sentence (e.g. Five days later...). The number 10, or anything greater than 10, should be written as a figure (e.g. ...there were 15 in the group.)

- [ ] don't raise any questions which are left unanswered

- [ ] use correct referencing if you are including quotations

- [ ] issue a reading list, website list and/or guide learners where they can obtain further information

Try to minimise any barriers to communication; for example, background noise, seating positions or the way you explain a topic. If a learner asks a question, repeat this when you answer it so that everyone can hear what was asked. The same applies if a learner answers a question, repeat their answer as not everyone might have heard it. Encourage your learners to ask you questions, no matter how silly they think they are; probably another learner is thinking the same but daren't ask. To save your learners any embarrassment of asking questions in front of their peers, you could ask them to write their question down on a small piece of paper or sticky note. You could then periodically collect these in and answer them all to the group. This way, no one knows who asked the question. If you are asked something you don't know the answer to, say you will find out later and then make sure you do.

If your subject includes the use of acronyms or jargon, you could encourage your learners to create a glossary. They can add to it throughout the duration of the programme when they come across new terms. This way they will have a complete glossary when they leave, that they have produced. If your organisation has a VLE, there is often a glossary function that can be used to enable all learners to add to it at any time.

Behaviour and respect

Behaviour is all about how you and your learners interact with each other in an acceptable way. Respect is about accepting others, not being rude to them or lowering their confidence and self-esteem in any way. Depending upon the age group of your learners, the subject and environment, you might encounter issues which you will need to deal with promptly.

It would be wonderful if you could get through a session without any issues arising relating to behaviour and respect. Usually, changes in behaviour or disruptions occur because a learner doesn't follow the ground rules; for example, their mobile phone rings or they do something other than that which you have asked them to do. If this is the case, politely ask them to stop, remind them of the ground rules and how they are also disrupting their peers' learning. Other occurrences happen because people are bored, they don't understand what you are saying, their attention span is different to the others, or you are not stretching them enough. You could give an alternative activity to extend their learning, get them involved with other learners in an activity, or have a quick one-to-one chat to find out why they are behaving that way.

You may find it useful to maintain a record of the behaviour of your learners during your sessions to help you prepare for future incidents. For example, do some learners become disruptive after a certain time period has elapsed; when seated in particular combinations with others, when asked to carry out a theory task, or when practical activities are taking place? This information can be useful when planning future sessions: for example, the timing of breaks, the use of energiser activities or planning group work.

Behaviour patterns could highlight the need for additional support as disruption could be away of asking for help.

You should lead by example and always be polite, show respect and say *please* and *thank you* to help encourage this behaviour in your learners.

Ways to demonstrate respect include:

- don't be overly judgemental
- encourage trust, honesty, politeness and consideration towards others
- listen to others' points of view
- value others' opinions and don't impose your own upon them
- treat everyone as an individual

Whatever the disruption may be, you need to handle it professionally to minimise any effect it may have on teaching and learning. Don't just ignore the behaviour, address it immediately. However, with experience you will realise that some things can be ignored providing this does not affect the safety of your learners.

Example

Philip was giving a presentation to a group of 15 learners during a Monday morning session. Three learners in the group began talking among themselves about what they did at the weekend. Rather than reprimand them, Philip decided to stop speaking altogether and use eye contact with them. They soon realised he was no longer speaking to the group, but looking at them. Because he was silent, they stopped talking and paid attention again.

Your learners might not be attending voluntarily, or they may be there for social reasons rather than having an interest in achieving something. They may therefore not be as keen as you would like them to be and you will need to keep them continuously interested and motivated. Try and relate your subject to their interests and/or their personal or working life.

Example

Sahib was having problems with a group of 14 learners in the computer suite. Some would talk over him, access the internet and use their mobile phones. He decided to spend a few minutes at the beginning of the next session asking each learner in turn (in front of the rest of the group) to state a reason for using a computer, that they could relate to their personal or working life. He also asked the group to agree some ground rules which included switching off their mobile phones. This helped the learners see the relevance of having various computer skills, enabling them to be more focused during the sessions.

You can help maintain motivation and good behaviour by including all learners during discussions and activities, keeping your sessions active wherever possible and teaching your subject in an interesting and challenging way. Ultimately, you need to find your own way of dealing with situations based upon your experiences. Don't show favouritism, lose your temper, make threats or touch learners inappropriately. Try to have a positive approach, praise performance and good behaviour and be consistent and fair to everyone. Most learners respond positively to a well-organised programme taught by an enthusiastic person who has a genuine interest in them and the subject.

Please see the theory section at the end of the chapter for relevant text books and websites regarding behaviour.

Extension Activity

What situations might arise with your learners which could lead to issues with behaviour and respect? How could you effectively deal with the situations?

Working with groups and individuals

Whether you work with groups, or individuals on a one-to-one basis will influence the teaching, learning and assessment approaches you choose to use. You might be teaching a broad spectrum of ages from 14 upwards, either by age group, for example, 14–16 year olds, 16–19 year olds, or a mixture of younger and older learners. Never assume or underestimate your learners' knowledge or experience and try to draw on this during your sessions, relating new learning whenever possible to their current and future aspirations. Whether you teach groups or train individuals, you always need to manage any risks that might occur, monitor learner progress and achievement, establish routines and aim to overcome any barriers to learning.

Groups are usually in environments that are fit for the purpose, such as a classroom, conference room or seminar room. Individuals are usually in their own normal working environment, or a room suitable for one-to-one teaching or training. However, you might have a group of learners, but at some point during the session work with an individual on a one-to-one basis. This could be if they needed some extra support to understand a topic.

Groups

When teaching a group, accept that this is a collection of individuals, all with different needs and wants, and it's up to you to address these while keeping focused on the subject or topic of learning. Make sure you include everyone, either during activities or when asking questions. Your learners will probably be from different backgrounds and different age groups, have different skills, knowledge and experiences, but will all expect to learn something from you. Having some prior knowledge, gained from initial assessment, or by talking to your learners, is a good foundation on which to start.

Individuals often behave differently in a group situation from when they are with other individuals. Group dynamics can change; for example, when new learners commence, when the venue or seating arrangements alter or if there are personality clashes. You will need to make new learners welcome, perhaps buddying them with another learner, or challenging behaviour and changing seating positions if disruption occurs.

Activity

Imagine you are due to facilitate a six-hour one-day training event with 30 learners whom you have never met before. All the event materials have been designed for you, and there are four different group activities of 30 minutes each to be carried out. How would you manage the process of grouping the learners and keeping them on task? All you know is their names.

Ideally, you need to find out a little about your learners in advance, perhaps their prior knowledge and experience, to enable you to relate the activities to their interests and/or job roles. If you can't obtain this information in advance, ask the learners at the beginning of the event.

When facilitating group activities, make sure you give very clear instructions and a time limit. If the activity is to be carried out in small groups, knowledge of your learners will help you decide if they have the maturity to team up themselves or whether you need to group them. Consider which learners will work together in case learners with strong personalities dominate and change the group dynamics. Equally, make sure quiet learners don't get left out and are able to participate. You might like to decide who will work with whom, or decide by their learning preferences, levels of ability/experience, random names, or pairs. If you are carrying out several activities, you could mix your learners to give them the opportunity to work with everyone over time.

Don't be afraid of trying something different; for example, giving your learners responsibility for part of a session. Always remain in control and consider what you will be doing while your learners are working; for example, going around each group, listening, giving advice and encouragement, and reminding them of the time left for completion of the activity.

Individual personalities and the roles learners take on when part of a group, may impede the success of the achievement of the task. Make sure you supervise group work carefully to keep all individuals focused.

Some issues which might occur with groups includes:

- higher level learners not being stretched and challenged enough
- interruptions and behaviour issues
- learners finishing activities before others

- learners being excluded by others during group activities

- lower level learners falling behind

- peer pressure

- personality clashes

It takes practice to control a group and deal with any situations which might occur. You might like to arrange to observe an experienced teacher or trainer to see how they manage their group.

Belbin's (1981) team roles

Belbin (1981) defined team roles as: *A tendency to behave, contribute and interrelate with others in a particular way.* Belbin's research identified nine clusters of behaviour, each of which is termed a *team-role*. Each team-role has a combination of strengths they contribute to the team, and allowable weaknesses. It's important to accept that people have weaknesses, therefore if you can focus on their strengths you will be able to help manage their weaknesses.

The team-roles are grouped into *action, people* and *cerebral* roles:

- **action-oriented roles:** Shaper, Implementer, and Completer Finisher

- **people-oriented roles**: Co-ordinator, Team worker and Resource Investigator

- **cerebral roles:** Plant, Monitor Evaluator and Specialist

See Table 5.3 Team Role Summary Descriptions for the contributions and allowable weaknesses of each team role. Sometimes groups or teams become problematic, not because their members don't know their subject, but because they have problems accepting, adjusting and communicating with each other as they take on different roles. Knowing that individuals within teams take on these different roles will help you manage group work more effectively, for example, by grouping a mixture of the *action, people* and *cerebral* roles within each group.

Coverdale's (1977) task, team and individual needs

Coverdale (1977) states the essence of team working is that individuals have their own preferred ways of achieving a task, but that in a team, they need to decide on one way of achieving this. In a team, three overlapping and interacting circles of needs have to be focused upon at all times. The *task needs,* the *team needs* and the *individual needs.*

When setting tasks or activities for learners to carry out in groups, consider the following:

To achieve the task ensure:

- a SMART objective or target is stated

- responsibilities are defined

- working conditions are suitable

- supervision is available

Table 5.3 Team Role Summary Descriptions

BELBIN®

Team Role Summary Descriptions

Team Role	Contribution	Allowable Weaknesses
Plant	Creative, imaginative, free-thinking. Generates ideas and solves difficult problems.	Ignores incidentals. Too preoccupied to communicate effectively.
Resource Investigator	Outgoing, enthusiastic, communicative. Explores opportunities and develops contacts.	Over-optimistic. Loses interest once initial enthusiasm has passed.
Co-ordinator	Mature, confident, identifies talent. Clarifies goals. Delegates effectively.	Can be seen as manipulative. Offloads own share of the work.
Shaper	Challenging, dynamic, thrives on pressure. Has the drive and courage to overcome obstacles.	Prone to provocation. Offends people's feelings.
Monitor Evaluator	Sober, strategic and discerning. Sees all options and judges accurately.	Lacks drive and ability to inspire others. Can be overly critical.
Teamworker	Co-operative, perceptive and diplomatic. Listens and averts friction.	Indecisive in crunch situations. Avoids confrontation.
Implementer	Practical, reliable, efficient. Turns ideas into actions and organises work that needs to be done.	Somewhat inflexible. Slow to respond to new possibilities.
Completer Finisher	Painstaking, conscientious, anxious. Searches out errors. Polishes and perfects.	Inclined to worry unduly. Reluctant to delegate.
Specialist	Single-minded, self-starting, dedicated. Provides knowledge and skills in rare supply.	Contributes only on a narrow front. Dwells on technicalities.

© BELBIN® 2012   'BELBIN' is a registered trademark of BELBIN UK.   www.belbin.com

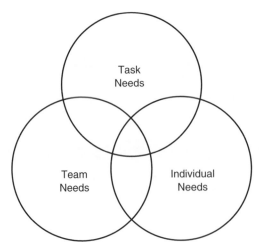

Figure 5.2 Task, team and individual needs

To build and maintain the team ensure:

- the size of the team is suitable for the task
- health and safety factors are considered
- consultation takes place
- discipline and order are maintained

To develop the individual ensure:

- responsibilities are defined
- grievances are dealt with
- praise is given
- learners feel safe and secure

Tuckman's (1965 and 1975) group formation theory
When working with groups, you could consider Tuckman's (1965 and 1975) group formation theory of forming, storming, norming, performing and adjourning. This relates to how a group bonds and works on a task, either short term or long term.

- **Forming** This is the *getting to know you* and *what shall we do?* stage. Individuals may be anxious and need to know the boundaries and code of conduct within which to work.
- **Storming** This is the *it can't be done* stage. It's where conflict can arise, rebellion against the leader can happen and disagreements may take place.
- **Norming** This is the *it can be done* stage. This is where group cohesion takes place and the norms are established. Mutual support is offered, views are exchanged and the group co-operates.
- **Performing** This is the *we are doing it* stage. Individuals feel safe enough to express opinions and there is energy and enthusiasm towards completing the task.
- **Adjourning** This is the *we will do it again* stage. The task is complete and the group separates. Members often leave the group with the desire to meet again or keep in touch.

Individuals

Working with an individual on a one-to-one basis may sound like the ideal approach, but if your learner is not committed to their learning you will need to motivate them and ensure your time with them is interesting and stimulating. You still need to set clear aims, objectives and targets, and you must remain professional at all times and not get personally involved. It could be that you are training a staff member in a workshop or working environment, therefore you are carrying out your own job role as well as supporting their learning. They may feel they can come to you at inappropriate times and you would need to set clear boundaries of what you expect from each other.

Example

Dawn is employed full time in a call centre which has just recruited 10 new members of staff. She has been promoted to supervisor and as such is expected to train the new staff, yet still continue with her own duties. She hasn't been given any formal training herself regarding how to train others, nor has she been allocated time to do this. As a result, her own job role and targets suffer as she is spending most of her time with the new staff. She soon realises she must have a meeting with her manager to discuss her new duties, the time allocated to them, and how to become trained herself to train others.

Individuals often act differently depending upon the situation and the other people they are with at the time. How you act towards your learner might also be different depending upon the context, environment or circumstances you are in. Different issues will arise when teaching or training an individual, as opposed to groups. It takes practice to remain focused upon the topic while giving the individual an appropriate amount of attention and not feeling you want to do things for them. It's still useful to agree ground rules with an individual to ensure the learning process remains professional.

Usually, individual learners have the opportunity to work at their own pace and have their training geared towards particular outcomes. For example, learning a new skill to support their job role, or gaining new knowledge to pass a test. You still need a plan of what you want to achieve, often referred to as an individual learning plan or action plan. These are very similar to a session plan, but are geared towards one person rather than groups. You can easily adapt your teaching or training approaches to fit in with your learner's requirements, change dates and times to suit, and address any barriers or challenges to learning.

One-to-one teaching or training can also occur as part of the coaching and mentoring process. It could be that you are responsible for coaching and/or mentoring a staff member as opposed to formally training them. It's important you find out what your role involves, and the time you can allocate to it, otherwise your own job role might begin to suffer as a result.

Other one-to-one training, coaching and mentoring opportunities might occur during:

- appraisals

- meetings

- online learning programs

- tutorial reviews

- workplace discussions

Whichever approach you take with individuals, remember to remain professional throughout and resist the temptation to get too personal. You will be spending quite a lot of time with the individual and although this will enable you both to get to know each other well, you mustn't blur the boundaries of your role.

EDIP

EDIP is an acronym for **E**xplain, **D**emonstrate, **I**mitate and **P**ractice. Allen's (1919) four-step training method was originally devised for training shipyard workers in the United States. It is now widely used by the British and American forces and is a useful method when teaching a practical subject. It can be used when training groups or individuals; however, it isn't very flexible as it was designed to get people performing a task quite quickly.

- **E**xplain clearly to your learners in words they can understand, all the main points of the task you are about to demonstrate, and why. Keep the points brief and simple.

- **D**emonstrate the task slowly so that your learners can see exactly what you have just explained. Make sure everyone can see what you are doing.

- **I**mitate. Demonstrate the task again and this time ask your learners to mirror and copy what you have just done. Watch them and reiterate the main points as they do it.

- **P**ractice. Ask your learners to carry out the task on their own. Correct any errors and answer any questions they might have.

With EDIP, learners might be able to learn and perform a task quickly, but not really understand why they are doing it. If you are delivering a practical training session to an individual, make sure you have a clear aim of what you want them to do, and objectives of how they will achieve it. You can then go through a logical process to demonstrate the activity, followed by both doing it together, and then your learner doing it on their own. Think of this as *I do it, we do it, you do it.* EDIP is quite a formal method of demonstrating a task, whereas the following checklist should help you do this more informally by involving your learner and checking that understanding is taking place.

Checklist for demonstrating a task

☐ Position yourself so that your learner can see what you are doing, check if they are left- or right-handed

☐ State the aim and objectives, set it in context, i.e. why the learner is doing it

☐ If possible, show an example of the finished item that you expect your learner to achieve

☐ Help make your learner feel at ease, by talking to them and asking if they have ever done anything like this before. If they have, you can discuss and build on their knowledge – go from the *known* to the *unknown*

☐ Demonstrate the task, explaining as you go along

☐ Encourage your learner to ask questions

☐ Carry out the task alongside your learner, let them make a mistake if it's safe to do so. You could have a handout or pictures and text for your learner to refer to

☐ Ask questions to check they know why they are doing it

☐ Ask your learner to demonstrate the task on their own, ask questions as they are doing it, and let them learn from their mistakes if it's safe to do so. Don't be tempted to do anything for them

☐ Ask your learner how they think they have done, this can promote self-assessment and help them realise what they might have done wrong

☐ Make a decision and give feedback

☐ Agree on any development points

☐ Relate the task to the next activity or job role

Extension Activity

Create an activity that you could use with a group of learners or something you could demonstrate to an individual learner for your specialist subject. Ensure you have a clear aim, objectives and a time limit. If possible, carry out the activity to see how effective it was. If you used a group activity, see how far your learners progressed through Tuckman's stages and why this was. If you demonstrated a task to an individual learner, how did the process go and what would you do differently?

Maintaining a safe and supportive learning environment

These are important aspects which form part of your responsibility as a teacher. You have a duty of care to ensure your learners are able to learn and achieve in a safe and supportive environment.

Safeguarding

Safeguarding is a term used to refer to the duties and responsibilities that those providing a health, social or education service have to carry out/perform to protect individuals and vulnerable people from harm. Following the publication of the Safeguarding Vulnerable Groups Act in 2006, a vetting and barring scheme was established in autumn 2008. This Act created an Independent Barring Board to take all discretionary decisions on whether individuals should be barred from working with children and/or vulnerable adults. In 2006, the Department for Education and Skills (DfES) produced a document called *Safeguarding Children and Safer Recruitment in Education*. This guidance was aimed at local authorities, schools and further education colleges in England who are responsible for promoting the welfare of children and young people, up to the age of 18 (age 25 for those with learning difficulties and/or disabilities). Following this, the document *Safer Practice, Safer Learning* (NIACE, 2007) was produced to provide guidance in relation to adults in further education. It recommends that safeguarding duties extend to whole-organisation policies, values and ethos, and include all staff and learners. It is everyone's duty to promote the concepts of the safe learner.

The Department of Health (DoH) (2000) document *No Secrets* specifies a definition of vulnerable adults.

> *A vulnerable adult is defined as a person 'who is or may be in need of community care services by reason of mental or other disability, age or illness; and who is or may be unable to take care of him or herself, or unable to protect him or herself against significant harm or exploitation'*

(Department of Health, 2000)

A vulnerable adult can be put at risk of harm through a variety of actions, inadequate policies and procedures, and failures of people to act. There are six types of abuse defined by the Department of Health:

- physical
- sexual
- psychological/emotional
- financial or material
- neglect and acts of omission
- discriminatory

A young person or adult could potentially be the victim of abuse, it is therefore your duty to ensure that you take proper steps to safeguard your learners. If a young person or vulnerable adult discloses abuse to you, take the disclosure seriously and never dismiss any allegation. An allegation of abuse or neglect may lead to a criminal investigation and asking leading questions or attempting to investigate the allegations yourself may cause problems for any subsequent court proceedings.

Don't make promises regarding confidentiality or offer to give support yourself. Explain to your learner at the outset that you will need to report the disclosure and share the information with your organisation's Safeguarding Officer (if there is one) or person responsible for this (you need to find out who this is). They will, where possible, respect the wishes of the individual; however, information will be shared with external agencies, such as the Local Safeguarding Children Boards (LSCB), where it is judged that a person is at risk of suffering significant harm.

Activity

Find out what the policies are regarding Safeguarding at your organisation and who you would need to go to should you have any concerns.

Hopefully, the environment you and your learners are in is safe; however, there could be circumstances where abuse, threatening behaviour, stealing or bullying might occur. Learners need to know where they can feel safe and there are a number of ways in which they could be involved in identifying safe areas.

Example

During a group tutorial session regarding safety with Warwick's Sport and Leisure learners, he decided to:

- *discuss potential issues and concerns, and what learners could do if any of these occurred*

- *identify wellbeing, personal safety and security issues, and how these might be resolved*

- *take digital photographs of safe and unsafe areas around the learning environment to discuss with his learners*

- *encourage his learners to create a display of the results*

- *create a wider consultation involving other learners and staff*

Your learners need to know that their safety is of paramount importance to you and your organisation and that everyone has a responsibility for this. This information can be communicated to your learners in various ways, i.e., through staff and learner handbooks, marketing materials, induction procedures, learner contracts, tutorials, reviews, online and learner focus/involvement groups.

Extension Activity

What issues might learners encounter regarding their safety in the learning environment? How can you maintain a safe and supportive environment for your learners? What can you do if something occurs which is outside of your control?

Summary

In this chapter you have learnt about:

- *induction, icebreakers and ground rules*
- *teaching and learning approaches*
- *communication, behaviour and respect*
- *working with groups and individuals*
- *maintaining a safe and supportive learning environment*

Cross-referencing grid

This chapter contributes towards the following assessment criteria of the units which form the Award in Education and Training, along with aspects of the Professional Teaching Standards. Full details of the learning outcomes and assessment criteria of each unit can be found in the appendices.

Award units	Assessment criteria
Roles, responsibilities and relationships in education and training	1.1, 1.4 2.1
Understanding and using inclusive approaches in education and training	1.1, 1.2 2.1, 2.2, 2.3, 2.4 4.2
Understanding assessment in education and training	1.2, 1.3
Learning and Development units	*Assessment criteria*
Facilitate learning and development for individuals	1.1, 1.2, 1.3, 1.4, 1.5, 1.6, 1.7 2.1, 2.2, 2.3 3.1, 3.2 4.1, 4.2, 4.3
Facilitate learning and development in groups	1.1, 1.2, 1.3, 1.4, 1.5, 1.6, 1.7 2.1, 2.2, 2.3 3.1, 3.2 4.1, 4.2, 4.3
Understanding the principles and practices of assessment	1.1, 1.2

Domain	Professional Teaching Standards
A	ASI, AS2, AS3, AS6, AK2.1, AK2.2, AK3.1, AK5.1, AK6.1, AK6.2, AP1.1, AP2.1, AP2.2, AP6.1, AP6.2
B	BSI, BS2, BS3, BS5, BK1.1, BK1.2, BK1.3, BK2.1, BK2.2, BK2.3, BK2.4, BK2.5, BK2.7, BK3.1, BK3.2, BK3.3, BK3.4, BP1.1, BP1.2, BP1.3, BP2.1, BP2.2, BP2.3, BP2.4, BP2.5, BP3.1, BP3.2, BP3.3, BP3.4, BP3.5, BP5.1
C	CS2, CS3, CS4, CK2.1, CK3.1, CK3.2, CP1.2, CP2.1, CP3.1, CP3.5, CP4.2
D	DSI, DK1.1, DK1.2, DK2.1, DP1.1, DP1.2
E	
F	FK3.1, FPU, FP1.2, FP3.1, FP4.1, FP4.2

Theory focus

References and further information

Allen, CR (1919) *The Instructor: The man and the job: A hand book for instructors of industrial and vocational subjects.* USA: J B Lippincott Company.

Appleyard, N and Appleyard, K (2010) *Communicating with Learners in the Lifelong Learning Sector.* Exeter: Learning Matters.

Belbin, M (1993, 1996, 2010) *Team Roles At Work.* Oxford: Elsevier Science & Technology.

Coverdale, R (1977) *Risk Thinking.* Bradford: The Coverdale Organisation.

Dale, E (1969) *Audio Visual Methods in Teaching.* Texas: Holt Rinehart and Winston.

Dennick, R and Exley, K (2004) *Small Group Teaching: Tutorials, Seminars and Beyond.* Routledge: Abingdon.

Department for Education and Skills (DfES) (2006) *Safeguarding Children and Safer Recruitment in Education.* London: DfES.

Department of Health (DoH) (2000) *No Secrets.* London: The Stationery Office.

Department of Health, Home Office and Department for Education and Employment (DfEE) (1999) *Working Together to Safeguard Children.* London: The Stationery Office.

Gravells, A (2013) *Passing Assessments for the Award in Education and Training.* London: Learning Matters.

Hill, C (2008) *Teaching with e-learning in the Lifelong Learning Sector* (2nd Edn). Exeter: Learning Matters.

Knowles, M, Elwood, FH and Swanson, A (2011) *The Adult Learner* (7th Edn). Oxford: Butterworth-Heinemann.

Lucas, B, Spencer, E and Claxton, G (2012) *How to Teach Vocational Education: A theory of vocational pedagogy.* City & Guilds Centre for Skills Development. Available at www.skillsdevelopment.org/PDF/How-to-teach-vocational-education.pdf

National Institute of Adult and Continuing Education (2007) *Safer Practice, Safer Learning.* Ashford: NIACE.

Vizard D (2012) *How to Manage Behaviour in Further Education.* London: SAGE Publications Ltd.

Wallace, S (2007) *Managing Behaviour in the Lifelong Learning Sector* (2nd Edn). Exeter: Learning Matters.

Websites

Behaviour tips – www.pivotaleducation.com

Belbin team roles – www.belbin.com

Classroom management free videos – www.bestyearever.net/videos/?goback=.gmr_27003.gde_27003_member_196422762

Coaching and mentoring – www.coachingnetwork.org.uk/resourcecentre/whatarecoachingandmentoring.htm

Dealing with behaviour – http://newteachers.tes.co.uk/content/dealing-behaviour-issues-%E2%80%93-guide-new-teachers

Games to download for activities – www.npted.org/schools/sandfieldsComp/games/Pages/default.aspx

Icebreakers – http://adulted.about.com/od/icebreakerstp/toptenicebreakers.htm and www.mwls.co.uk/icebreakers/

Local Safeguarding Children Boards (LSCB) – www.education.gov.uk/childrenandyoungpeople/safeguardingchildren/protection/b00219380/lscb

Motivation – http://serc.carleton.edu/NAGTWorkshops/affective/motivation.html

Pedagogy and andragogy – http://archive.excellencegateway.org.uk/page.aspx?o=135534

Safeguarding – http://www.education.gov.uk/search/results?q=safeguarding

Safeguarding Vulnerable Groups Act – www.opsi.gov.uk/Acts/acts2006/pdf/ukpga_20060047_en.pdf

Teacher Tube videos – http://teachertube.com/

Teaching groups – www.faculty.londondeanery.ac.uk/e-learning/small-group-teaching

Team roles – www.belbin.com

Tuckman – www.infed.org/thinkers/tuckman.htm

6 ASSESSING LEARNING

In this chapter you will learn about:

- assessment in education and training
- assessment types and methods
- involving learners and others, peer and self assessment
- making decisions and giving feedback
- assessment records

There are activities and examples to help you reflect on the above which will assist your understanding of how to assess learning in education and training contexts. At the end of each section within the chapter are extension activities to stretch and challenge your learning should you wish to carry them out. A list of useful references, further information and website links can be found at the end in case you would like to research the topics further.

At the end of the chapter is a cross-referencing grid showing how the chapter's contents relate towards the units of the Award in Education and Training and the Professional Teaching Standards.

If you are taking the Award in Education and Training, it is possible to take one of the units from the Learning and Development qualification: *Understanding the principles and practices of assessment* instead of the Award unit: *Understanding assessment in education and training*. This chapter therefore covers the content of both units, but might not all apply to your current role as a teacher, trainer and/or assessor.

Assessment in education and training

Assessment is a way of finding out if learning has taken place. It enables you to ascertain if your learner has gained the required skills, knowledge, understanding and/or attitudes needed at a given point in time, towards their programme of learning. It also provides your learners with an opportunity to demonstrate what progress they have made and what they have learnt so far. If you don't plan for and carry out any assessment with your learners, you will not know how well, or what they have learnt.

Assessment should not be in isolation from the teaching and learning process. You can assess that learning is taking place each time you are with your learners. This can simply be by watching what they are doing and/or asking questions. If your learners are taking a qualification, there will be formal methods of assessment you will need to use such as an assignment, or a workplace observation. However, you can devise informal methods to use with your learners to check their progress at any time such as quizzes. There are some assessors who do not teach or train, but will just assess, make decisions and give feedback. For example, where competent staff are demonstrating their skills, knowledge and understanding towards their job role, or an aspect of a qualification in the workplace.

Assessment should focus on improving and reinforcing learning as well as measuring achievements. It should help your learners realise how they are progressing and what they need to do to improve and/or develop further. Assessment should be a regular and continual process; it might not always be formalised, but you will be watching what your learners are doing, asking them questions, and reviewing their progress whenever you are in contact with them. If you also teach or train, your learners will be demonstrating their skills, knowledge and understanding regularly, for example, through tasks, discussions and regular working activities. It's good practice to give your learners feedback when assessing them informally to help them see what progress they are making. If they haven't reached a certain standard, you should still give feedback on what they have done well so far, and how they can improve.

You are therefore constantly making judgements and should also be aware of the impact that your comments and grades can have on your learners' confidence when you give feedback. Comments which specifically focus on the activity or work produced, rather than the individual, will be more helpful and motivating to your learners. Assessment should not become a personal subjective judgement, but should be objective and relate to the activity or criteria being assessed.

Assessment activities can take place in different environments depending upon what is being assessed and why.

Example

- *classroom – group activities, tests, discussions, role-plays, projects, presentations*

- *lecture theatre or hall – examinations*

- *library – assignments, research and reading*

- *outside environment – practical activities*

- *work environment – observations and questions*

- *workshop – practical tests and simulations*

Assessment can help your learners by:

- acknowledging what progress has been made

- addressing issues where there are gaps in learning

- ascertaining areas for development

- confirming achievements

- diagnosing any areas of concern to enable support to be arranged

- encouraging discussions and questions

- ensuring they are on the right programme at the right level

- identifying what is yet to be learnt and achieved

- maintaining motivation

- seeing any mistakes they have made; for example, spelling errors in a written task or mistakes during a practical task

Assessment is not another term for evaluation; assessment is *of the learners* whereas evaluation is *of the programme*. Assessment is specific towards a learner's progress and achievement and how they can improve and develop. Evaluation includes feedback from your learners and others to help you improve your own practice and the overall learner experience.

Assessments are usually:

- internally set – produced by you, or your organisation: for example, questions or projects, which will also be marked by you

- externally set – usually produced by an awarding organisation: for example, an assignment or an examination

Activity

Are there any assessment materials provided for your subject, or do you have to devise your own? If none are available, consider how you will assess that learning has taken place. If you are assessing towards a qualification, obtain the assessment materials so that you can familiarise yourself with them.

The assessment cycle

Depending upon the subject you are assessing, and whether it is knowledge based, performance based or a mixture of the two, you will usually follow the assessment cycle (see Figure 6.1). The cycle will continue until all aspects of the programme or qualification have hopefully been achieved by your learner, or perhaps not if they decide to leave.

The cycle will then begin again with an initial assessment regarding the next subject area or unit of the qualification. Throughout the cycle, standardisation of assessment practice between assessors should take place; this will help ensure the consistency and fairness of decisions, and that all assessors interpret the requirements in the same way. Internal quality assurance will also take place throughout as part of the quality assurance process. See Chapter 1 for further information.

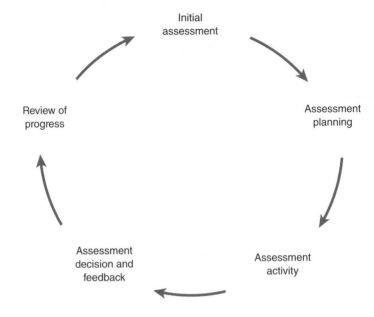

Figure 6.1 Assessment cycle

- **Initial assessment** – ascertaining if your learner has any previous knowledge and/or experience of the subject, topic or unit to be assessed. This information can be obtained through application forms and interviews to ensure they are on the right programme. The results of initial assessment activities will give you information regarding your learners: for example, any specific assessment requirements they may have, or any further training and support they may need. This process might not always be carried out by you, but the information obtained must be passed on to you.

- **Assessment planning** – agreeing suitable types and methods of assessment with learners, setting appropriate target dates, involving others as necessary (such as colleagues or supervisors) and following relevant organisational guidelines.

- **Assessment activity** – using relevant methods, approaches and activities: for example, observation, questioning, assignments, or gathering appropriate evidence of competence. Assessment can be formative (usually ongoing and informal to check progress, e.g. a discussion) and/or summative (usually at the end and formal, e.g. a test).

- **Assessment decision and feedback** – making a judgement of success or otherwise. Giving constructive feedback and agreeing any further action that may be necessary. Records of what was assessed and the decisions made should always be maintained.

- **Review of progress** – reviewing progress and achievement, discussing any other issues that may be relevant to the learning and assessment process.

Records should be maintained throughout all aspects of the assessment cycle and quality assurance activities should take place on an ongoing basis. The cycle will then begin again with an initial assessment regarding the next topic, subject, or unit of the qualification the learner is working towards.

Roles and responsibilities of an assessor

Your main role will be to carry out assessments according to the programme and/or qualification you will assess. If you don't have a job description which lists your assessment functions, following the requirements of the units which form the Assessor qualification will ensure you are performing your role adequately. It could be that you must hold a relevant Assessor qualification to be able to assess, or be working towards one, with someone countersigning your decisions in the meantime. You will need to check what the requirements are for your subject.

Your responsibilities may include:

- attending meetings, exhibitions, award ceremonies and presentation events
- completing and maintaining records
- following legal, organisational and regulatory authorities' procedures
- giving constructive and developmental feedback to learners
- identifying and dealing with any barriers to fair assessment
- implementing internal and external quality assurance action points
- liaising with others involved in the assessment process
- making judgements based on the assessment requirements
- negotiating and agreeing assessment plans with learners
- making best use of different assessment types and methods
- reviewing learner progress
- standardising practice with other assessors
- supporting learners with particular assessment requirements and dealing with sensitive issues in a supportive manner
- working towards relevant assessment qualifications

Your role as an assessor will also be to inspire and motivate your learners. If you are enthusiastic and passionate about your subject, this will help to encourage, stretch and challenge your learners. If you are unsure of any aspect of your assessor role, make sure you ask a colleague, your mentor or supervisor. You may be the only assessor for your particular subject within your organisation; therefore it is important that you liaise with your supervisor or internal quality assurer to ensure you are interpreting the requirements correctly. If you are a member of a team of assessors, you will need to ensure you all work together to give your learners equal and fair access to assessment opportunities.

Concepts and principles of assessment

Concepts are *ideas* about the assessment process, for example:

- being accountable to and following external bodies' and awarding organisations' requirements
- ensuring transparency so that everyone clearly understands what is expected and can see there is nothing untoward taking place
- using appropriate assessment methods such as assignments, observation, and questioning

- using relevant assessment types such as initial, formative and summative

Principles are *how* the assessment process is put into practice, for example, being:

- ethical by ensuring the assessment process is honest and moral, and takes into account confidentiality, integrity, safety and security

- fair by ensuring the assessment activities are fit for purpose, at the right level, differentiate for any particular needs, and that planning, decisions and feedback are justifiable

- safe by ensuring there is little chance of plagiarism, the work can be confirmed as authentic, confidentially was taken into account, learning and assessment was not compromised in any way, nor was the learner's experience or potential to achieve (safe in this context does not relate to health and safety but to the assessment types and methods used)

Two important principles are known by the acronyms VACSR and SMART. Following these will help ensure all the assessment requirements can be met by your learners, providing they have acquired the necessary skills, knowledge and understanding at the time of assessment.

VACSR

Using VACSR will help you plan and assess in a way that should meet the expected requirements.

- **V**alid – the assessment process is appropriate to the subject or qualification, assesses only what is meant to be assessed, and the learner's work is relevant to the assessment requirements

- **A**uthentic – the work has been produced solely by the learner

- **C**urrent – the work is still relevant at the time of assessment

- **S**ufficient – the work covers all the assessment requirements

- **R**eliable – the work is consistent across all learners, over time and at the required level, i.e. if the assessment was carried out again with similar learners, similar results would be achieved

SMART

Being SMART is all about being clear and precise with what you expect your learners to achieve.

- **S**pecific – the activity relates only to what is being assessed and is clearly stated

- **M**easurable – the activity can be measured against the assessment requirements, allowing any gaps to be identified

- **A**chievable – the activity can be achieved at the right level by the learner

- **R**elevant – the activity is realistic and will give consistent, valid and reliable results

- **T**ime bound – target dates and times can be achieved

Another important principle is that of ensuring you are assessing at the correct level. Please see Table 4.3 in Chapter 4 for examples of objectives that could be used at different levels.

For example, to assess your learner by asking them to *explain* something would be at level 3, whereas asking them to *analyse* would be at level 4. You also need to consider the environment in which you are assessing, i.e. that it is suitable, accessible and does not create any unnecessary barriers. Any resources you use should be relevant and effective. Always make sure you are assessing only what is necessary and relevant at the time.

Planning for assessment

Assessment planning should be a two-way process between you and your learners; you need to plan what you are going to do, and they need to know what is expected of them. Unless all your learners are taking an examination or test on the same day at the same time, assessment should be planned for and carried out on an individual basis. Failing to plan how you are going to assess your learners may result in your learners failing the assessment activity. If your learners are all working towards the same assignment, you will still need to agree target dates for completion and discuss any specific requirements your learners may have. If your learners are to be assessed in their place of work, you will need to agree how, along with target dates. You might need to complete an assessment plan or action plan with your learners to formally document what they are aiming to achieve. This record is like a written contract between you and your learner towards their achievement. However, it can be reviewed, amended and updated at any time. Your organisation should be able to provide you with the relevant documentation to use.

Minimising risks

When planning to assess your learners you need to be aware of potential risks in order to minimise them. This applies not only to those regarding the health, safety and welfare of all concerned, but the types of risks that may be involved in your own area of responsibility for your particular subject. Risks include:

- assessing at the wrong level for the learner
- expecting too much too soon
- giving too much or too little support
- learners providing too much and/or not focussing upon the requirements
- not being impartial with decisions
- not enough time to make a valid decision
- not following organisational requirements for assessment
- not giving the right support
- not noticing plagiarism or work that is not authentic
- over assessing or under assessing
- peer pressure
- putting unnecessary stress upon learners to meet targets
- using incorrect assessment approaches

Some learners might not be ready to be observed for a practical skill, or feel so pressured by target dates for a theory task that they resort to colluding or plagiarising work. If learners are under pressure, or have any issues or concerns that have not been addressed, they may perform badly or decide to leave.

There are also risks on your part as an assessor, for example, pressure to pass learners quickly due to funding implications or targets, or favouritism and bias towards some learners over others. If you are assessing in the work environment you might visit places you are not familiar with. You might therefore have to travel early or late in the dark, find locations on foot, or drive to locations you are not familiar with. If you are visiting places on your own, you will be classed as a lone worker and your organisation should have a policy for your protection. If you feel uncomfortable or unsafe at any time, you should get in touch with your supervisor. Having a mobile phone is helpful in such situations, if not, note where the nearest public phone is should you need it. You may find it useful to search the internet for the postcode you are visiting. This will give you a street map and pictures of the local area to enable you to visualise where you are going.

If you are assessing in the work environment, you might come across employers who are not supportive of their staff and may put barriers in their way. For example, someone might make it difficult for you to visit at a certain time to carry out an assessment. Careful planning and communication with everyone concerned will be necessary.

If you are assessing the work of learners you might not have met, for example, by online e-assessment, it can be very difficult to ensure the authenticity of their work. Your organisation might require each learner to attend a meeting at some point to discuss their progress and achievements. This would be an opportunity to check some form of photo identification such as a driving licence, passport or employee card.

The role of ICT in assessment

Information and communication technology (ICT) is constantly evolving and new resources are frequently becoming available. It's crucial to keep up to date with new developments and you should try to incorporate these within the assessment process when possible. It's not only about you using technology to help assess your learners, but about your learners using it to complete their assessment activities. Encouraging your learners to use technology will help increase their skills in this area. If your learners are based at different locations to you, they could send digital recordings or live transmissions of their activities. Technology can be combined with traditional methods of assessment; for example, learners can complete a written assignment by word-processing their response, and submitting it by e-mail or uploading it to a virtual learning environment (VLE). You can then give feedback via e-mail or the VLE system. Combining methods also promotes differentiation and inclusivity; for example, learners could access assessment materials via the VLE outside the normal learning environment to support their learning. See Table 6.1 for a list of advantages and limitations of using technology.

New and emerging technologies include using:

- blogs, chat rooms, social networking sites, webinars and online discussion forums to help learners communicate with each other
- computer facilities for learners to word process their assignments and save documents and pictures
- cloud storage facilities that learners and assessors can use to upload and access materials from various devices

- digital media for visual/audio recording and playback
- electronic portfolios for learners to store their work
- e-mail for electronic submission of assessments, communication and informal feedback on progress
- interactive whiteboards for learners to use for presentations and to display their work
- internet access for research to support assignments or presentations
- mobile phones and tablets for taking pictures, video and audio clips, and communicating with others
- networked systems to allow access to applications and documents from any computer linked to the system
- online and on-demand tests which can give instant results, for example, diagnostic, learning preferences and multiple-choice tests
- online discussion forums which allow asynchronous (taking place at different times) and synchronous (taking place at the same time) discussions
- scanners for copying and transferring documents to a computer
- web cameras or video conferencing if you can't be in the same place as your learners and you need to see and talk to them
- VLEs to access and upload learning materials and assessment activities

Table 6.1 Advantages and limitations of using technology

Advantages are that they are:	Limitations might be that:
• accessible and inclusive	• finance is required to purchase or upgrade
• addressing sustainability, i.e. no need for paper copies	• it can lead to plagiarism via the internet
• an efficient use of time and cost-effective	• it is time-consuming to initially set up
• auditable and reliable	• it might create barriers if learners cannot access or use technology
• available, i.e. resources and materials can be accessed at a time and place to suit	• power cuts could cause problems
• give immediate results from online tests	• some learners might be afraid of using new technology
• on demand, i.e. tests can be taken when a learner is ready	• there might not be enough resources available for all learners to use at the same time

E-learning and assessment processes are constantly advancing. Unfortunately, there isn't room in this book to explain it in great detail, therefore please refer to other appropriate texts such as those listed at the end of this chapter.

Meeting individual needs

If you have learners with any particular needs or requirements, you should consider how you can help meet these. Always check with your organisation regarding what you can and can't do as you may need approval to make any adaptations or changes. Always make sure you are following equality and diversity requirements, see Chapter 3 for further information.

Some examples of meeting your learners' needs include:

- adapting or providing resources and equipment for a learner who is partially sighted
- adapting the environment for a learner who is physically disabled
- allowing extra time for a learner with dyslexia
- arranging to use another language such as British Sign Language with a learner who is partially deaf
- changing the date and/or time for a learner who works shifts
- liaising with others who could offer advice regarding financial concerns
- providing specialist support staff to improve English and maths skills
- providing the assessment information in an alternative format such as spoken instead of written for a learner who has impaired vision
- using a different location which is more accessible to learners who have to travel far
- using different assessment activities to suit individual learning preferences
- using new and emerging technologies to help improve confidence with ICT skills
- using larger print, Braille, or other alternative support mechanisms for learners with particular needs

If you need to adapt anything, make sure you check with your awarding organisation to ensure you are following their regulations and requirements before making any changes.

Extension Activity

Design an assessment activity that you could use with your learners, preferably which incorporates the use of ICT. Make sure it is of the right level for your learners and relates to the subject being assessed. If you have learners at the moment, use it with them and then evaluate how effective it was. What changes would you make and why?

Assessment types and methods

Assessment types include initial (at the beginning), formative (ongoing) and summative (at the end). Assessment methods are the activities used to assess ongoing progress as well as achievement; for example, questions, discussions, observations, tests and assignments. All assessment methods should be suited to the level and ability of your learners. A level 1 learner might struggle to write a journal; a level 2 learner may not be mature enough to accept peer feedback; a level 3 learner may feel a puzzle is too easy, and so on.

Assessment types

Depending upon the subject you are assessing and any relevant qualification requirements, you might carry out various types of assessment with your learners which could be on a formal or informal basis. Formal assessment means the results will count towards a qualification, whereas informal assessment helps you see how your learners are progressing at a given point. Assessment types relate to the *purpose* of assessment ie the reason assessment is carried out.

Five frequently used assessment types are:

- initial
- diagnostic
- formative
- summative
- holistic

Whatever type of assessment you use with your learners, you need to ensure you are assessing only what needs to be assessed, i.e. the requirements of a unit from a qualification, aspects of a work role, or progress towards particular topics.

Initial assessment
Relevant initial assessment activities will give you information regarding your learners; for example, any specific assessment requirements or needs they may have, or any further training and support they may require. It will also ensure they are on the right programme. This should take place prior to, or when learners commence. Initial assessment can be used at the beginning of a session to ascertain current knowledge or skills. A quick question, *What experience do you have of this, if any?,* will soon give you some idea of what your learners already know. Please see Chapter 3 for further information regarding initial assessment.

Diagnostic assessment
Diagnostic assessments help identify a learner's current skills, knowledge and understanding towards a particular subject area. Learners might need to demonstrate a task or discuss their understanding of a particular topic. Checklists can be used to help assess this and the results can be used to obtain a suitable starting point. Diagnostic assessments can also identify if a learner has English, maths and ICT skills that might need supporting. Please see Chapter 3 for further information regarding diagnostic assessment.

Formative assessment
Formative assessments should take place continually throughout your learners' time with you. These are usually carried out informally to review progress, identify any support requirements and inform further development. Simply asking questions and observing actions can help you assess how your learners are progressing. You could use activities, quizzes and short tasks for them to carry out which would make the assessment process more interesting, and highlight any areas which need further development.

Assessing your learners on a formative basis will enable you to see if they are ready for a summative or final assessment.

Formative assessment is usually informal, devised by yourself, and often called assessment *for* learning as it help prepare learners for formal assessment.

Summative assessment

Summative assessments usually occur at the end of a session, programme, topic, unit or full qualification. They are a measure of achievement towards set requirements or criteria rather than focussing on progress. This type of assessment can often be quite stressful to learners and sometimes lead to a fail result even though the learner is quite capable under other circumstances. If you are assessing a programme where the activities are provided for you, for example, examinations or tests, there is often a tendency to teach purely what is required to achieve a pass. Teaching to pass examinations or tests does not maximise a learner's ability and potential. They might be able to answer the questions just by relying on their memory. This doesn't help them in life and work, as they might not be able to put theory into practice afterwards, or even understand what they have learnt.

Summative assessment is usually formal, devised by the awarding organisation that accredits the qualification, and often called assessment *of* learning as it counts towards the achievement of something.

Holistic assessment

This is a method of assessing several aspects of a qualification, unit, programme or job specification at the same time. It should be a more efficient and quicker system as one piece of good quality evidence or a carefully planned observation could cover several areas. Holistic assessment enables learners to integrate knowledge and performance, for example, as part of an apprenticeship programme. It should be planned to enable the learner to know what they need to demonstrate and/or produce by a certain date. Assessment of a learner's skills, knowledge and understanding can be much more efficient and cost effective if planned correctly, for both the assessor and learner. Demonstration of a skill often implies the knowledge required to perform that skill, however, the use of questions will confirm understanding.

The methods you use will depend upon your subject, the requirements of the qualification programme or job specification, and any particular learner needs.

Assessment methods

All assessment methods should be suited to the level and ability of your learners. Assessment methods will be either formal or informal. You will need to know what formal assessments your learners must do to achieve the programme or qualification, as well as what informal assessments you can use to check ongoing progress and performance. Table 6.3 lists the strengths and limitations of a variety of assessment methods, approaches and activities.

Formal assessment

Formal assessment activities usually count towards your learners' achievement of their qualification; for example, successful completion of an assignment, examination or test. The criteria for these will be stated in the qualification handbook and will probably be known as assessment criteria and linked to the learning outcomes of the qualification. Formal assessments are usually completed with certain constraints such as a time limit or the amount of resources that can be used by learners. Table 6.2 lists a few formal and informal assessment methods; however, some can occur in both depending upon the situation, for example, a case study could be used informally during a session, but formally at the end of a unit of learning.

Assessment should be a regular process; it might not always be formalised, but you should be observing what your learners are doing, asking questions and reviewing their progress throughout their time with you. Even if you are not assessing towards a qualification, for example, you are training and assessing a colleague regarding a new working procedure on the job, you should assess their ongoing progress and achievement.

Informal assessment
Informal assessment activities can take place at any time you are in contact with your learners; for example, oral questions during a tutorial review, or a quiz or discussion at the end of a taught session. Informal activities might not always count towards your learners' achievement of their qualification, but will inform you how much learning is taking place and what progress is being made.

Example

Cameron has taught a maths programme according to the qualification requirements, over three months. At the end of each month, his learners take an externally-set formal test provided by the awarding organisation. Prior to this he gives them an internally devised test to check their progress and ensure they are ready. He had also been asking questions throughout the months to check their knowledge and understanding. This informal assessment ensured that his learners were ready for the formal assessment.

Table 6.2 Formal and informal assessment methods
(note – some can occur in both depending upon the situation)

Formal	Informal
• assignments • case studies • essays • examinations • multiple-choice questions • observations • professional discussions and questions • projects • tests • witness testimonies	• crosswords • discussions • gapped handouts (sentences with missing words) • journals/diaries • peer and self-assessment • puzzles and crosswords • practical activities • questions: oral, written, multiple choice • quizzes • role plays • worksheets

Activity

Design a formative assessment activity that you could use with your learners. You could create a crossword, a quiz, a role play or something else which is relevant to their level and ability. If possible, carry out the activity with your learners and evaluate how successful it was. Then consider what changes would you make and why.

Questioning techniques

Questions are often the best way to assess knowledge and understanding. If you are asking questions verbally to a group of learners, ensure you include all learners. Don't just let the keen learners answer first as this gives the ones who don't know the answers the chance to stay quiet. Pose a question, pause for a second and then state the name of a learner you would like to answer. This way, all learners are thinking about the answer as soon as you have posed the question, and are ready to speak if their name is asked. This technique is often referred to as *pose, pause, pick* (PPP). To ensure you include everyone throughout your session with a question, you could have a list of their names handy and tick each one after you have asked them a question. If a learner doesn't know the answer or gets it wrong, state it was a good attempt and then ask another learner.

When questioning:

- allow enough time for your questions and your learners' responses
- ask open questions, i.e. those beginning with *who, what, when, where, why* and *how*
- avoid trick or complex questions
- be aware of your posture, gestures and body language
- be conscious of your dialect, accent, pitch and tone
- don't ask more than one question in the same sentence
- make sure you don't use closed questions to illicit a *yes* response, learners may feel that is what you want to hear but it doesn't confirm understanding
- use active listening skills
- try not to say *erm, yeah, okay, you know,* or *does that make sense?*
- use eye contact
- use learners' names
- watch your learners' reactions

When asking questions, use only one question in a sentence, as more than one may confuse your learners. Try not to ask *Does anyone have any questions?*, as often only those who are keen or confident will ask, and this doesn't tell you what has been learnt. Try not to use questions such as *Does that make sense?* or *Do you understand?*, as your learners will often say *Yes* as they feel that's what you expect to hear but does not inform you what they know or understand.

Try to use *open questions* which require an answer to demonstrate knowledge and understanding. For example, *How many days are there in September?* This ensures your learner has to think about their answer. Using a closed question such as *Are there 30 days in September?* would only give a *yes/no* answer which doesn't show you if your learner has the required knowledge.

If you are having a conversation with your learner, you can ask probing questions to ascertain more information. These can begin with: *Why was that?* You can prompt your learner to say more by asking *What about...?* You can also clarify what your learner is saying by asking *Can you go over that again?*

If you have to write your own questions for learners, think how you will do this, i.e. short questions, essay-style questions, open, closed or multiple choice. If you are giving grades, e.g. A, B, C, or pass/merit/distinction, you need clear grading criteria to ensure your decisions are justified, otherwise your learners may challenge your decisions. You may need to rephrase some questions if your learners are struggling with an answer, as poor answers are often the result of poor questions. For essay and short-answer tests you should create sample answers to have something to compare with. Be careful with the use of jargon – just because you understand doesn't mean your learners will.

You need to be aware of plagiarism, particularly now that so much information is available via the internet. Learners should take responsibility for referencing any sources of all work submitted, and may be required to sign an authenticity statement. If you suspect plagiarism, you could type a few of their words into an internet search engine or specialist program and see what appears. You would then have to challenge your learner as to whether it was intentional or not, and follow your organisation's plagiarism procedure.

If you are using the same questions for different learners at different times, be careful as they may collude and share their answers with each other. Therefore, you will need to satisfy yourself that the work is that of each learner.

Multiple-choice questions
Multiple-choice questions should have a clear question and three or four possible answers. The question is known as the *stem*, the answer is called the *key* and the wrong answers are called *distracters*. Answers should always be similar in length and complexity. Answers should not be confusing, and there should be only one definite key.

Example

The acronym VARK relates to which one of the following:

A assessment types
B learning preferences
C delivery techniques
D evaluation methods

You will see that all the answers contain words of a similar length. None of the answers contains a clue from the question. A, C and D are the distracters and B is the correct answer (the key).

Observation
Observation is a good way to assess skills and attitudes. Observing your learners enables you to see just how well they are doing. Let your learner make a mistake (if it is safe) rather than interrupt them as they should learn from this. You can then ask them afterwards to see if they realised. You can also observe group work and presentations; this can encourage learners to give peer feedback. You would need to make a decision as to the contribution of each learner if their work was part of a group activity. Observations are useful in the workplace to assess your learners' skills, knowledge and attitudes. You can always follow an observation with questions to check understanding.

Extension Activity

List six different assessment methods you could use for your subject and compare the strengths and limitations of each. How can the activities you have chosen meet any particular learner needs if necessary? Look at Table 6.3 for some ideas.

Table 6.3 Assessment methods and activities: strengths and limitations

Method/activity	Description	Strengths	Limitations
Activities – group or individual	Different tasks carried out by learners to demonstrate their skills, knowledge, understanding and/or attitudes	Can be individual, paired or group tasks Ideal as a formative assessment approach to establish progress at a given point during a session, or as a summative approach for workplace tasks	If paired or grouped, assessor must establish achievement of individuals Can be time consuming for the assessor to devise
Assignments	Can be practical or theoretical tasks which can assess various aspects of a subject or qualification over a period of time	Consolidates learning Several aspects of a qualification can be assessed Some assignments are set by the Awarding organisation who will give clear marking criteria Learners might be able to add to their work if they don't meet all the requirements first time	Everything must have been taught beforehand or known by the learner Questions can be misinterpreted Can be time consuming for learners to complete Must be individually assessed and written feedback given Assessor might be biased when marking
Blended assessments	Using more than one method of assessment, usually including technology	Several methods of assessment can be combined, enabling all learning preferences to be reached	Not all learners may have access to the technology
Buzz groups	Short topics to be discussed in small groups	Allows learner interaction and focuses ideas Checks understanding Doesn't require formal feedback	Learners may digress Specific points could be lost Checking individual learning may be difficult

activity	Description	Strengths	Limitations
Case studies/ scenarios	Can be a hypothetical situation, a description of an actual event or an incomplete event, enabling learners to explore the situation	Can make topics more realistic, enhancing motivation and interest Can be carried out individually or in a group situation Builds on current knowledge and experience	If carried out as a group activity, roles should be defined and individual contributions assessed Time should be allowed for a de-brief Must have clear outcomes Can be time consuming to prepare and assess
Checklists	A list of criteria which must be met to confirm competence or achievement	Can form part of an ongoing record of achievement or job profile Assessment can take place when a learner is ready Ensures all criteria are documented	Learners may lose their copy and not remember what they have achieved
Controlled assessment	An activity or test which occurs in a number of stages with varying levels of control to ensure realiability Usually timed	Can be formative to assess progress or summative to assess achievement Can be used for knowledge and/or performance Is flexible and modification is possible. Ensures the same conditions for everyone Makes assessment activities manageable	Can be stressful to learners Learners might study just to pass the requirements
Discussions with learners *also known as a professional discussion*	A one–to-one conversation between the assessor and learner based around the assessment criteria	Ideal way to assess aspects which are more difficult to observe, are rare occurrences, or take place in restricted or confidential settings Useful to support observations to check knowledge Learners can describe how they carry out various activities	A record must be kept of the discussion, for example, audio/digital/visual along with notes Needs careful planning as it's a discussion not a question and answer session Learners need time to prepare Assessor needs to be experienced at questioning and listening skills Assessor needs to be experienced at using open and probing questions, and listening carefully to the responses

(Continued)

Table 6.3 (Continued)

Method/ activity	Description	Strengths	Limitations
Discussions/ debates	Learners talk about a relevant topic either in groups or pairs	All learners can participate Allows freedom of view points, questions and discussions Can contribute to meeting assessment criteria	Easy to digress Assessor needs to keep the group focused and set a time limit Some learners may not get involved, others may dominate Assessor needs to manage the contributions of individuals and know what has been achieved by each learner Can be time consuming Learners may need to research a topic in advance Can lead to arguments
e-assessments/ online assessments	*Electronic assessment* – assessment using information and communication technology (ICT) *Synchronous* – assessor and learner are simultaneously present, communicating in real time *Asynchronous* – assessor and learner are interacting at different times	Teaching, learning and assessment can take place in a virtual learning environment (VLE) Assessment can take place at a time to suit learners Participation is widened Results and feedback can be instantly generated Ensures reliability Less paperwork for the assessor Improves computer skills Can be blended with other assessment methods Groups, blogs, forums and chat rooms can be set up to improve	Learners need access to a computer and need to be computer literate Reliable internet connection needed Self-discipline is needed Clear targets must be set Authenticity of learner's work may need validating Technical support may be required

Method/ activity	Description	Strengths	Limitations
Essays	A formal piece of written text, produced by a learner, for a specific topic	Useful for academic subjects Can check a learner's English skills at specific levels Enhances a learner's knowledge by using research and reading	Not suitable for lower level learners Marking can be time consuming Plagiarism can be an issue Doesn't usually have a right or wrong answer therefore difficult to grade Learners need good writing skills
Examinations	A formal test which must be carried out in certain conditions	Can be *open book*, or *open notes*, enabling learners to have books and notes with them Some learners like the challenge of a formal examination and cope well	Invigilation required Security arrangements to be in place prior to, and afterwards for exam papers Learners may have been taught purely to pass expected questions by using past papers, therefore they may forget everything afterwards Some learners may be anxious Can be closed book, or closed notes not allowing learners to have books and notes with them Results might take a while to be processed If a learner fails, they may have to wait a period of time before a re-take
Group work	Enables learners to carry out a specific activity, for example, problem solving Can be practical or theoretical	Allows interaction between learners Encourages participation and variety Rotating group members enables all learners to work with each other	Careful management by the assessor is required regarding time limits, progress, and ensuring all group members are clear about the requirements

(Continued)

Table 6.3 (Continued)

Method/ activity	Description	Strengths	Limitations
Group work cont.			Could be personality problems with team members or large groups One person may dominate Difficult to assess individual contributions Time is needed for a thorough de-brief
Holistic	Enables learners to demonstrate several aspects of a programme or qualification at the same time	Similar criteria from different units can be assessed at the same time Makes evidence collection and demonstration of achievement and competence much more efficient	Could confuse the learner if aspects were assessed which were not planned for
Homework	Activities carried out between sessions, for example, answering questions to check knowledge	Learners can complete at a time and place that suits them Maintains interest between sessions Encourages learners to stretch themselves further Consolidates learning so far	Clear time limits must be set Learners might not do it, or get someone else to do it for them Must be marked/assessed and individual feedback given
Interviews	A one-to-one discussion, usually before a learner commences a programme, or part way through to discuss progress	Enables the assessor to see how much a learner knows Enables the assessor to get to know each learner, and discuss any issues	Not all learners may react well when interviewed Needs careful planning, and consistency of questions between learners
Learner statements	Learners write how they have met the assessment criteria	Enables learners to take ownership of their achievements	Learners might misinterpret the assessment criteria and/or write too much or too little Another assessment method should be used in addition to confirm practical skills

Method/activity	Description	Strengths	Limitations
Learning journal/diary	Learners keep a record of their progress, their reflections and thoughts, and reference these to the assessment criteria	Helps assess English skills Useful for higher level programmes	Should be specific to the learning taking place and be analytical rather than descriptive Contents need to remain confidential Can be time consuming and/or difficult to read
Observations	Watching learners perform a skill	Enables skills to be seen in action Learners can make a mistake (if it is safe) enabling them to realise their errors Learners can be observed again if they didn't fully achieve the requirements Can assess several aspects of a qualification at the same time (holistic assessment)	Timing must be arranged to suit each learner Communication needs to take place with others (if applicable) No permanent record unless visually recorded Questions must be asked to confirm knowledge and understanding Assessor might not be objective with decision Learner might put on an act for the assessor which isn't how they normally perform
Peer assessments	Learners give feedback to their peers after an activity	Promotes learner and peer interaction and involvement Learners may accept comments from peers better than those from the assessor Enables learners to assess each other Activities can often correct misunderstandings and consolidate learning without intervention by the assessor	Everyone needs to understand the assessment criteria and requirements Needs to be carefully managed to ensure no personality conflicts or unjustified comments Assessor needs to confirm progress and achievements as it might differ Some peers may be anxious about giving feedback Should be supported with other assessment methods Needs careful management and training in how to give feedback

(Continued)

Table 6.3 (Continued)

Method/ activity	Description	Strengths	Limitations
Portfolios of evidence	A formal record of evidence (manual or electronic) produced by learners towards a qualification	Ideal for learners who don't like formal exams Can be compiled over a period of time Learner centred therefore promotes autonomy Evidence can be left in its natural location to be viewed by the assessor	Authenticity and currency to be checked Computer access required to assess electronic portfolios Tendency for learners to produce a large quantity of evidence All evidence must be cross-referenced to the relevant criteria Can be time consuming to assess Confidentiality of documents within the portfolio must be maintained
Practical activities/tasks	Assesses a learner's skills in action	Actively involves learners Can meet all learning preferences if carefully set	Some learners may not respond well to practical activities Can be time consuming to create Questions must be asked to ascertain knowledge and understanding
Presentations	Learners deliver a topic, often using information and communication technology	Can be individual or in a group Can assess skills, knowledge, understanding and attitudes	If a group presentation, individual contributions must be assessed Some learners may be nervous or anxious in front of others
Products	Evidence produced by a learner to prove competence, for example, paintings, models, video, audio, photos, documents	Assessor can see the final outcome Learners feel a sense of achievement, for example, by displaying their work in an exhibition	Authenticity needs to be checked if the work has not been seen being produced

Method/ activity	Description	Strengths	Limitations
Projects	A longer-term activity enabling learners to provide evidence which meets the assessment criteria	Can be interesting and motivating Can be individual or group led Can meet all learning preferences Encourages research skills Learners could choose their own topics and devise tasks	Clear outcomes must be set, along with a time limit, must be relevant, realistic and achievable Progress should be checked regularly If a group is carrying out the project, ensure each individual's input is assessed Assessor might be biased when marking
Puzzles, quizzes, word searches, crosswords, etc.	A fun way of assessing learning in an informal way	Fun activities to test skills, knowledge and/or understanding Useful backup activity if learners finish an activity earlier than planned Useful way to assess progress of lower level learners Good for assessing retention of facts	Can seem trivial to mature learners Does not assess a learner's level of understanding or ability to apply their knowledge to situations Can be time consuming to create and assess
Questions	A key technique for assessing understanding and stimulating thinking, can be informal or formal Questions can be closed, hypothetical, leading, open, probing, multiple choice	Can be short answer or long essay style Can challenge and promote a learner's potential A question bank can be devised which could be used again and again for all learners Can test critical arguments or thinking and reasoning skills Oral questions suit some learners more than others, e.g. a learner who is dyslexic might prefer to talk through their responses	Closed questions only give a yes or no response which doesn't demonstrate knowledge or understanding Questions must be written carefully, i.e. be unambiguous, and can be time consuming to prepare If the same questions are used with other learners, they could share their answers Written responses might be the work of others, i.e. copied or plagiarised Expected responses or grading criteria need to be produced beforehand to ensure consistency and validity of marking May need to re-phrase some questions if learners are struggling with an answer

(Continued)

Table 6.3 (Continued)

Method/ activity	Description	Strengths	Limitations
Recognition of prior learning (RPL)	Assessing what has previously been learnt, experienced and achieved to find a suitable starting point, or to claim equivalent or exemption units on the Qualifications and Credit Framework (QCF)	Ideal for learners who have achieved aspects of the programme prior to commencement No need for learners to duplicate work, or be reassessed Values previous learning, experiences and achievements	Checking the authenticity and currency of the evidence provided is crucial Previous learning, experiences and achievements might not be relevant in relation to current requirements Can be time consuming for both learner to prove, and the assessor to assess
Reports, research and dissertations	Learners produce a document to inform, recommend and/or make suggestions based on the assessment criteria	Useful for higher level learners Encourages the use of research techniques	Learners need research and academic writing skills Time consuming to mark Plagiarism and authenticity can be an issue
Role plays	Learners act out a hypothetical situation	Enables the assessor to observe learners' behaviour Encourages participation Can lead to debates Links theory to practice	Can be time consuming Clear roles must be defined Not all learners may want, or be able to participate Some learners may get too dramatic Individual contributions must be assessed Time needed for a thorough de-brief

Method/ activity	Description	Strengths	Limitations
Self-assessment	Learners decide how they have met the assessment criteria, or how they are progressing at a given time	Promotes learner involvement and personal autonomy Encourages learners to check their own work Encourages reflection	Learners may feel they are doing better or worse than they actually are Assessor needs to discuss progress and achievements with each learner to confirm their decisions Learners need to be specific about what they have achieved and what they need to do to complete any gaps Difficult for the learner to be objective when making a decision
Skills tests	Designed to find out the level of skill or previous experience/ knowledge towards a particular subject or vocation	Could be online or computer based to enable a quick assessment, for example, English Results can be used as starting point for learning or progression	Learners might be apprehensive of formal tests Feedback might not be immediate
Simulation	Imitation or acting out of an event or situation	Useful when it is not possible to carry out a task for real, for example, to assess whether learners can successfully evacuate a building in the event of a fire	Only enables an assessment of a hypothetical situation, learners may act very differently in a real situation Not usually accepted as demonstration of competence
Team building exercises/ energisers	A fun and light hearted way of re-energising learners after a break Can be used to informally assess skills, knowledge and attitudes	A good way of learners getting to work with each other Can revitalise a flagging session	Not all learners may want to take part Some learners may see them as insignificant and time wasting Careful explanations are needed to link the experience to the topic being assessed

(Continued)

Table 6.3 (Continued)

Method/ activity	Description	Strengths	Limitations
Tests	A formal assessment situation	Cost effective method as the same test can be used with large numbers of learners Some test responses can be scanned into a computer for marking and analysis Other tests can be taken at a computer or online which give immediate results	Needs to be carried out in supervised conditions or via a secure website Time limits usually required Can be stressful to learners Does not take into account any formative progress Feedback might not be immediate Learners in other groups might find out the content of the tests from others Identity of learners needs confirming
Tutorials	A one-to-one, or group discussion between the assessor and learner, with an agreed purpose, for example, assessing progress so far	A good way of informally assessing a learner's progress and/or giving feedback An opportunity for learners to discuss issues or for informal tuition to take place	Needs to be in a comfortable, safe and quiet environment as confidential issues may be discussed Time may overrun Records should be maintained and action points followed up
Video/audio	Recorded evidence of actual achievements	Direct proof of what was achieved by a learner Can be reviewed by the assessor and internal quality assurer after the event	Can prove expensive to purchase equipment and storage media Can be time consuming to set up and use Technical support may be required Storage facilities are required

Method/ activity	Description	Strengths	Limitations
Walk and talk	A spoken and visual way of assessing a learner's competence	Enables a learner to *walk and talk* through their product evidence within their work environment Gives an audit trail of the evidence relating to the assessment criteria Saves time producing a full portfolio of evidence, the walk and talk can be recorded as evidence of the discussion Useful where sensitive and confidential information is dealt with	Can be time consuming Difficult for quality assurers to sample the evidence
Witness statements/ testimonies	A statement from a person who is familiar with the learner (they could also be an expert in the standards being assessed and the occupation of the learner in the work environment)	The witness can confirm competence or achievements for situations which might not regularly occur, or when the assessor cannot be present	The assessor must confirm the suitability of the witness and check the authenticity of any statements Learners could write the statement and the witness might sign it not understanding the content
Worksheets and gapped handouts	Interactive handouts to check knowledge (can also be electronic) Blank spaces can be used for learners to fill in the missing words	Informal assessment activity which can be done individually, in pairs or groups Useful for lower level learners Can be created at different degrees of difficulty to address differentiation	Mature learners may consider them inappropriate Too many worksheets can be boring Learners might not be challenged enough

Involving learners and others, peer and self-assessment

It could be that you are not the only person involved with your learner's progress. There could be others such as their supervisor at work, or different trainers and assessors. It's important that you communicate with all concerned to ensure the learning and assessment process is effective. You should also ensure that aspects are not unnecessarily duplicated or assessed more than necessary. You can also involve the learner in their own assessment of progress, and the assessment of their peers as necessary.

Involving learners

Learners should be involved in the assessment process from commencement to completion. Initial assessment involves the learner in discussions. The results can be used as a foundation on which to agree a suitable individual learning plan (ILP) or assessment plan. This information will also help you plan an appropriate course of action should any support be necessary. Involving your learners gives them the opportunity to inform you of anything which might affect their progress and/or achievement. It also helps them take ownership of their development and progress if they have a copy of what is to be assessed.

It might be that one of your learners has already achieved a unit or part of the programme requirements elsewhere. You could ascertain if they have any evidence of this, i.e. proof of their achievement, to enable you to instigate the process of recognition of prior learning (RPL). If your learner wasn't involved at this stage, they could unnecessarily repeat certain aspects.

If you are teaching or training as well as assessing, you can involve your learners at the commencement of a session by asking them what they already know. In this way, you can draw and build upon their experiences throughout the session. At the end of the session you could involve your learners by asking them what they feel they have learnt, and how they can apply it to other situations.

If you are assessing in the workplace you should involve your learners by discussing what will be assessed, how and when. This would enable a two-way conversation to take place leading to an appropriate plan of action for further training and/or formal assessments to take place. You could also ask your learners to complete a SWOT (strengths, weaknesses, opportunities and threats) analysis. This would give them the opportunity to consider their current skills and knowledge and how it relates to their development and progression.

Depending upon the topic you are assessing, there are different ways of involving your learner with questions. If you are assessing informally, for example, asking questions during a session, you could start with an open question and then move on to a hypothetical question if you are not getting the response you expected. If you are formally assessing a learner for a practical skill, you could ask them some open questions to check their knowledge and understanding. If you are asking questions to a group, make sure you give everyone the chance to answer, not just those who are keen to answer first. If possible, ask a question to everyone in the group, this enables all individuals to be included and involved.

You could regularly ask your learners how they feel they are progressing, hopefully they will identify any issues before you need to tell them. Sometimes, learners are unsure of what they have achieved and what they need to do to progress further. Asking them to reflect upon their progress can be a useful way of linking it towards the programme or qualification they are aiming to achieve.

Involving others

At some point, you might need to liaise with other people who are involved in the assessment process of your learners, for example, to inform others of any particular learner requirements to ensure consistency of support. You might have a learner who would benefit from a different assessment method i.e. oral questions instead of written questions. You might therefore need to liaise with the awarding organisation to ensure this is acceptable. You could have a learner who would prefer to be assessed bilingually, and you would therefore need to contact another member of staff who could help. Table 6.4 lists some of the people you may need to liaise with who are internal or external to your organisation.

If you are liasing with external contacts, you should remain professional at all times as you are representing your organisation. People might not always remember your name; however, you will be known as *that person from XYZ organisation*. You therefore need to create a good and lasting impression of yourself and your organisation. You should also remember aspects of confidentiality and data protection, and keep notes of all activities in case you need to refer to them again.

Table 6.4 People you may need to liaise with

Internal to the organisation	External to the organisation
• administrators	• careers advisers
• assessors	• employers
• colleagues	• external quality assurers
• exam officers	• inspectors and regulators
• internal quality assurers	• parents, guardians or carers
• invigilators	• probation officers
• managers	• social workers
• mentors	• supervisors
• teachers	• staff from other organisations and agencies
• trainers	• witnesses and others involved in the assessment of your learners
• support staff	

Sources of information

You will need to know what sources of information can be available to help support the assessment process for your learners and others who are involved. For example, information such as the standards or units to be assessed, assessment plans and feedback records, and resources such as text books, internet websites and journals that will prove useful. Workplace supervisors, mentors and witnesses will need details of your learner's progress and achievements. Support staff will need relevant information regarding your learner to provide any necessary help and guidance. Communicating regularly will ensure everyone who is involved with your learner knows their progress and achievement.

Activity

Why do you think it's important to involve your learners and others in the assessment process? Find out who you need to liaise with, either internally or externally, regarding the subject you will assess. Make a note of their contact details for future reference. What information should you make available to your learner and others and why?

Peer and self-assessment

Peer assessment involves a learner assessing another learner's progress. Self-assessment involves a learner assessing their own progress. Both methods encourage learners to make decisions about what has been learnt so far, take responsibility for their learning and become involved with the assessment process. Your learners will need to fully understand what needs to be assessed, and how to be fair and objective with their decisions and any feedback given to others. Throughout the process of peer and self-assessment, learners can develop skills such as listening, observing and questioning. However, the results of peer and self-assessment are usually not counted towards meeting the requirements of a qualification as you should make the final decision regarding achievement. In the workplace, peer assessment might be counted as proof the learner has met the requirements of a job role, for example, if the peer is their supervisor or manager.

Peer assessment
Peer assessment involves a learner assessing another learner's progress. This would actively involve your learners; however, you would need to ensure everyone was aware of the criteria to be assessed, how to reach a decision and how to give constructive feedback.

Peer assessment can also be useful to develop and motivate learners. However, this should be managed carefully, as you may have some learners who do not get along and might use the opportunity to demoralise one another. You would need to give advice to your learners as to how to give feedback effectively. If learner feedback is given skilfully, other learners may think more about what their peers have said than about what you have said. If you consider peer assessment has a valuable contribution to make to the assessment process, ensure you plan for it to enable your learners to become accustomed and more proficient at giving it. The final decision as to the achievement of your learner will lie with you. Table 6.5 lists a few advantages and limitations of peer assessment.

Examples of peer assessment activities include:

- assessing each other's work anonymously and giving written or verbal feedback
- giving grades and/or written or verbal feedback regarding peer presentations

- holding group discussions before collectively agreeing a grade and giving feedback, perhaps for a presentation

- suggesting improvements to their peers' work

- writing a written statement of how their peers could improve

Table 6.5 Advantages and limitations of peer assessment

Peer assessment advantages are that:	Peer assessment limitations include:
• helps develop communicating skills	• all peers should be involved, therefore planning needs to take place as to who will give feedback and to whom
• leads to discussions which everyone can benefit from	• appropriate conditions and environment are needed
• learners are focused upon the assessment requirements or can use a checklist	• assessor needs to confirm each learner's progress and achievements as it might be different from their peers' judgements
• learners may accept comments from peers more readily than those from the assessor	• everyone needs to understand the assessment requirements
• peers might notice something the teacher hasn't	• learners might be subjective and friendly rather than objective with their decisions
• promotes attention as learners have to focus on what is happening	• needs to be carefully managed to ensure no personality conflicts or unjustified comments
• they increase attention for activities such as peer presentations if feedback has to be given	• should be supported with other assessment methods
• they promote learner and peer interaction and involvement	• some peers may be anxious, nervous or lack confidence to give feedback

Self-assessment

Self-assessment involves a learner assessing their own progress, which can lead to them setting their own goals. It can give responsibility and ownership of their progress and achievements. However, learners might feel they have achieved more than they actually have, therefore, you will still need to confirm their achievements or otherwise. Table 6.6 lists a few advantages and limitations of self-assessment.

Examples of self-assessment activities include:

- awarding a grade for their presentation

- suggesting improvements regarding their skills and knowledge

- compiling a written statement of how they could improve their work

Table 6.6 Advantages and limitations of self-assessment

Self-assessment advantages are that:	Self-assessment limitations include:
• it encourages learners to check their own progress • it encourages reflection • mistakes can be seen as opportunities • it promotes learner involvement and personal responsibility • learners are focused upon the assessment requirements • learners identify when they are ready for a formal assessment • learners take ownership of the process ie identifying areas for improvement	• assessor needs to discuss and confirm progress and achievement • difficult to be objective when making a decision • learners may feel they have achieved more than they actually have • learners must fully understand the assessment requirements • learners need to be specific about what they have achieved and what they need to do to complete any gaps • some learners may lack confidence in their ability to make decisions about their own progress

Extension Activity

How can you use peer and self-assessment activities with your learners? List the strengths and limitations of each in relation to the subject or qualification you will assess.

Making decisions and giving constructive feedback

Making decisions

The decisions you make regarding your learners' progress can affect them both personally and professionally. It's important to remain factual about what you have assessed and to be *objective* with your judgements. You should not be *subjective* and let other aspects influence or compromise your decision. For example, passing a learner just because you like them, feel they have worked hard or are under pressure to meet certain targets. When making a decision, refer to the principles of VACSR and SMART as stated in the first section of this chapter. You should always inform your learners when they can expect to receive any feedback or formal recognition of their achievements.

You will need to complete relevant records to prove that assessment took place. Usually, you will keep the original document and give your learner a copy. This is because it is more difficult to forge a copy than an original document.

Reviewing progress

It's useful to review your learners' progress regularly, as this gives you the opportunity to discuss on a one-to-one basis how they are progressing, what they may need to improve and what they have achieved. Often, this can be carried out during a tutorial session and should be formally documented and signed by both parties so that records of the discussion are maintained.

Reviews are a good opportunity to carry out formative assessments in an informal way. They also give your learner the chance to ask questions they might have been embarrassed about asking in a group situation.

Giving constructive feedback

Feedback is a way of helping reassure, boost confidence, encourage and motivate your learners. All learners need to know how they are progressing, and what they have achieved, giving feedback will help them realise this. Feedback can be given formally, i.e. in writing, or informally, i.e. verbally, and should be given at a level which is appropriate for each learner. Feedback can be direct, i.e. to an individual, or indirect, i.e. to a group. It should be more thorough than just a quick comment such as *well done*. It should be given in a constructive way and include specific facts which relate to progress, achievement or otherwise in order to help your learners develop.

If you are giving verbal feedback you could always ask your learners first how they think they have done. For example, if you have just observed them perform a task and they made a mistake, it gives them the opportunity to say so before you need to, providing they realised it.

Activity

Think back to the last time you received feedback from someone for something you did. Was this feedback constructive? Did it leave you feeling motivated and good about what you had done? Or did it leave you feeling demotivated and not willing to continue? How could you use this experience to make sure you give feedback which will not demoralise?

If possible, feedback should be a two-way process, allowing a discussion to take place to clarify any points. If you are giving verbal feedback, be aware of your body language, facial expressions and tone of voice. Don't use confrontational words or phrases likely to cause offence such as racist or stereotypical remarks. Take into account any non-verbal signals from your learners; you may need to adapt your feedback if you see they are becoming uncomfortable. If you are giving written or electronic feedback consider that how your learner reads it may not be how you intended it.

Feedback should never just be an evaluative statement like *Well done*, or *That's great, you've passed*. This doesn't tell your learner what was done well, or was great about it. Your learner will be pleased to know they have passed; however, they won't have anything to build upon for the future.

Descriptive feedback lets you describe what your learner has done, how they have met the requirements and what they can do to progress further. It enables you to provide opportunities for your learner to make any adjustments or improvements to reach a particular standard.

Most people need encouragement, to be told when they are doing something well and why. When giving feedback it can really help your learner to hear first what they have done well, followed by what they need to improve, and then end on a positive note to keep them motivated. This is known as the *praise sandwich*. Often, the word *but* is used to link these points; replacing this with the word *however* can make it much easier for your learner to accept.

Example

Start with something positive, e.g. 'George, I really liked the way you delivered your presentation, you came across as very confident.'

Link with 'however' to anything that needs improving, e.g.'... however, I feel if you had faced the group a bit more rather than looking at the screen I could have heard your voice better.'

End on a positive note, e.g. 'It was a very interesting topic and I feel I've learnt something new.'

Using your learner's name makes the feedback more personal, and making the feedback specific enables your learner to know what they have achieved and what they need to do to improve and/or progress further. You will need to find out from your organisation how they require you to give feedback: for example, writing in the first, second or third person. You also need to know whether it should be given verbally and/or written; formally or informally; how much detail should be given; what forms must be completed; and what records must be maintained.

The advantages of giving constructive feedback are that it:

- creates opportunities for clarification and discussion

- emphasises progress rather than failure

- enables the learner to know what they have achieved

- helps improve confidence and motivation

- identifies further learning opportunities or any action required

Extension Activity

What might influence your decision when assessing learners? How can you remain objective and not become subjective with your judgements?

Assessment records

Assessment records must be maintained to satisfy your organisation's internal quality-assurance systems, and external regulators such as Ofsted, along with the awarding organisation's requirements. Assessment records must show an audit trail of your learners' progress from commencement to completion and are usually kept at your organisation for three years. If a learner loses their work, without any assessment records you have nothing to show what was assessed. Table 6.7 lists assessment records you might be required to maintain in alphabetical order. However, you will need to check with your organisation which are relevant and why, as you probably won't need to maintain them all.

If you are teaching a programme which does not lead to a formal qualification acredited by an awarding organisation, i.e. non-accredited, you will still need to record learner progress. This is known as recognising and recording progress and achievement (RARPA).

Records must be up to date, accurate, factual and legible, whether they are stored manually or electronically. If you are saving to a computer, always ensure you have a backup copy in case any data is lost. You must always maintain confidentiality and follow relevant legislation such as the Data Protection Act (1998), which is mandatory for all organisations that hold or process personal data. Keeping full and accurate factual records is also necessary in case one of your learners appeals against an assessment decision or a dispute occurs.

Table 6.7 Assessment records

Assessment records	
• achievement dates and grades	• initial assessment records
• action plans	• learning preference results
• appeals records	• observation checklists
• application forms	• observation reports
• assessment plan and review records	• performance and knowledge records
• assessment tracking sheet showing progression through a qualification for all learners	• professional discussion records
	• progress reports
• authentication declarations/statements	• receipts for submitted work
• checklists	• records of achievement
• copies of certificates	• records of oral questions and responses
• diagnostic test results	• retention and achievement records
• enrolment forms	• standardisation records
• formative and summative records	• tutorial reviews
• feedback records	• witness testimonies

Extension Activity

Make a list of all the assessment records you would use for your subject and state why you would need to keep them. What organisational or regulatory requirements must you follow regarding assessment records and why?

Summary

In this chapter you have learnt about:

- *planning for assessment*
- *assessment types and methods*
- *involving learners and others, peer and self-assessment*
- *making decisions and giving feedback*
- *assessment records*

Cross-referencing grid

This chapter contributes towards the following assessment criteria of the units which form the Award in Education and Training, along with aspects of the Professional Teaching Standards. Full details of the learning outcomes and assessment criteria of each unit can be found in the appendices.

Award units	Assessment criteria
Roles, responsibilities and relationships in education and training	1.1, 1.4 3.1, 3.3
Understanding and using inclusive approaches in education and training	1.3 2.2 3.2 4.1, 4.2, 4.3
Understanding assessment in education and training	1.1, 1.2, 1.3, 1.4 2.1, 2.2, 2.3 3.1, 3.2, 3.3 4.1, 4.2
Learning and Development units	Assessment criteria
Facilitate learning and development for individuals	1.4, 1.6 2.3 3.1, 3.2 4.1

Learning and Development units	Assessment criteria
Facilitate learning and development in groups	1.4, 1.6 2.3 3.1, 3.2 4.1
Understanding the principles and practices of assessment	1.1, 1.2, 1.3, 1.4 2.1 3.1, 3.2, 3.3, 3.4, 3.5 4.1, 4.2, 4.3, 4.4 5.1, 5.2 6.1, 6.2, 6.3 7.1, 7.2 8.1, 8.2, 8.3
Domain	Professional Teaching Standards
A	ASI, AS5, AS7, AK6.1, AK6.2, AK7.1, API.1, AP2.1, AP7.1
B	BS3, BS4, BK2.5, BK3.2, BK3.4, BK5.1, BP2.1, BP2.3, BP2.5, BP3.2, BP4.1
C	CS2,CS3,CK3.2,CP3.2
D	DS2, DK1.1, DK2.1, DK2.2, DP2.2
E	ESI, ES2, ES3, ES4, ES5, EK1.1, EK1.2, EK1.3, EK2.1, EK2.2, EK2.3, EK2.4, EK3.1, EK3.2, EK4.1, EK4.2, EK5.1, EK5.2, EK5.3, EP1.1, EP1.2, EP1.3, EP2.1, EP2.2, EP2.3, EP2.4, EP3.1, EP3.2, EP4.1, EP4.2, EP5.1, EP5.2, EP5.5
F	

Theory focus

References and further information

Gravells, A (2012) *Achieving your TAQA Assessor and Internal Quality Assurer Award.* London: Learning Matters.

Gravells, A (2013) *Passing Assessments for the Award in Education and Training.* London: Learning Matters.

Ofqual (2009) *Authenticity – A Guide for Teachers.* Coventry: Ofqual.

Read, H (2011) *The Best Assessor's Guide.* Bideford: Read On Publications Ltd.

Tummons, T (2011) *Assessing Learning in the Lifelong Learning Sector* (3rd Edn). Exeter: Learning Matters.

Wilson, LA (2012) *Practical Teaching: A guide to assessment and quality assurance.* Andover: Cengage Learning.

Websites

Assessment methods in higher education – www.brookes.ac.uk/services/ocsld/resources/methods.html

Assessment tools (literacy, numeracy, ESOL, dyslexia) – www.excellencegateway.org.uk/toolslibrary

Developing Assessment Feedback – http://escalate.ac.uk/4147

Plagiarism – www.plagiarism.org and www.plagiarismadvice.org

SWOT analysis – www.mindtools.com/pages/article/newTMC_05.htm

7 EVALUATING LEARNING

In this chapter you will learn about:

- evaluation in education and training
- obtaining and responding to feedback
- reviewing own progress and using learning journals
- continuing professional development
- using a checklist for teaching, learning and assessment

There are activities and examples to help you reflect on the above which will assist your understanding of how to evaluate yourself and the programmes you have taught. At the end of each section within the chapter are extension activities to stretch and challenge your learning should you wish to carry them out. A list of useful references, further information and website links can be found at the end in case you would like to research the topics further.

At the end of the chapter is a cross-referencing grid showing how the chapter's contents relate towards the units of the Award in Education and Training and the Professional Teaching Standards.

Evaluation in education and training

Whichever type of programme or qualification you deliver, short- or long-term, no matter when or where, it is important to evaluate everything you have been involved with, to help you make improvements for yourself, your current and future learners.

Evaluation is not another term for assessment; evaluation is *of the programme* whereas assessment is *of the learners*. Evaluation includes feedback from your learners and others to help you improve your own practice and the overall learner experience. Assessment is specific towards learners' achievements and how they can improve and develop.

Evaluation is a quality assurance tool for a *product* or *service*. If you are delivering a qualification or programme, then that is the *product*. The facilities of the organisation and the support your learners receive relate to the *service*. Your learners should have the opportunity to evaluate the product and service at some point, perhaps by completing a survey to give feedback. Other people will also be able to give you feedback, such as your mentor, line manager or supervisor. You might also have an external inspector or external quality assurer observe you teaching, training and/or assessing at some point. As a result, you will receive feedback to help you develop as a person, as well as feedback which will help improve the product and the service your learners receive. External quality assurers will often write a report which might include action points that will need addressing regarding a particular qualification.

If you are having a meeting with a manger, or are going to be observed, you will need to prepare yourself beforehand. You should be notified of the date and time, and it's important to have all your records available, i.e. teaching and learning plans, learner details, assessment results and records of attendance. Your manager or observer might also talk to your learners about their progress and how you support the learning process.

Evaluation should be an ongoing process throughout all aspects of the teaching, learning and assessment cycle. It can be informal by talking to others, or formal by using a survey. Either way, the process should help you realise how effective things were, and what you could change or improve. It will also help you identify any problem areas, enabling you to do things differently next time. Using feedback from others, information and data is key to evaluation, never assume everything is going well just because you think it is.

Example

Jim is a new training manager in the workplace and he has been asked by his director to devise a way of evaluating all the in-house training which takes place. He has decided to create an online survey which each learner can complete anonymously, at three key points in their development. He will devise the questions then e-mail the survey weblink to them at the appropriate times. The survey he uses will automatically analyse the data for him. This will give him valuable feedback on which to act both during and after the training has taken place. He will carry out a staff appraisal and an observation with each trainer twice a year, which will lead to a development plan if necessary. Jim will also carry out a standardisation activity at the monthly trainer meetings to help ensure all trainers are being consistent with the way they train and assess their learners. In this way, Jim is being proactive and seeking information while learning is taking place, rather than being reactive to a situation after the event.

Evaluation can take many forms; for example, self-evaluation can include completing a journal or keeping a diary of incidents, how you dealt with them and what you would do differently next time. Peer evaluation can take the form of observations; for example, your mentor watching one of your sessions. Employer evaluation includes appraisals and reviews of progress. You will probably participate in an appraisal or performance review system at some point in your organisation. This is a valuable opportunity to discuss your learning, development and any training or support you may need. It is also a chance to reflect upon your achievements and successes. Having the support of your organisation will help you decide what is relevant to your development as a teacher or trainer, your job role and your specialist subject. You could share your ideas with colleagues if it's something everyone could benefit from.

Extension Activity

Make a list of different methods that could be used to help you evaluate:
1) your own performance as a teacher or trainer; and 2) the programme you have
delivered and assessed.

Obtaining and responding to feedback

Obtaining feedback from learners and others will help you to respond to it, in the hope of improving the product and service, as well as your own professional development. You could obtain information and statistics to help you evaluate your programme such as retention, achievement, destination and progression data. This information might be compiled by another department within your organisation or it might be a record you have maintained yourself. If you start a programme with 15 learners and only 9 achieve at the end, then you need to respond to this to find out why. It could be that the learners' needs were not met, they were on the wrong programme, or they left by personal choice. Keeping records and audit trails should help you identify situations and respond to them. For example, it could be that the learners were not capable of achieving, therefore the interview and initial assessment process will need reviewing for future applicants.

If your organisation is inspected by Ofsted, they are keen on the *learner voice*. This is the involvement of learners and potential learners in shaping the learning opportunities that are available to them. It means involving and supporting them to act as partners with policy makers, providers, practitioners and other agencies. Learner voice initiatives seek to include the learner by enabling them to express their concerns, needs and views, in a safe way. This could be by the use of anonymous questionnaires or online surveys. Organisations should respond appropriately to the issues that are raised and give feedback as to developments and changes as a result. This places the learner at the centre of policy and practice.

Talking to your learners informally will help you realise how successful the learning process has been. This can be done during tutorial reviews, at break times, or before or after your sessions. Your learners are the best judges of whether they are getting what they feel they need. If given the opportunity, they may give you more feedback in an informal situation.

You could give your learners a questionnaire at the end of the programme or event. Always build in time to your session for this to take place, otherwise your learners might take away the questionnaire and forget to return it. Alternatively, you could create an online survey with an agreed completion date.

It could contain closed questions such as:

Were the teaching, learning and assessment approaches suitable? Yes/No

or open questions such as:

How did you find the teaching, learning and assessment approaches?

The latter is best as you should gain more information. If you are delivering a longer-term programme, it's best to gain feedback early on so that you can act upon it if necessary while the learners are still with you.

When issuing questionnaires or using online surveys, decide whether you want the responses to be anonymous, as you might gain more feedback if learners know they can't be identified. Always give a date for return, otherwise people will take their time and then might forget. The response rate is not usually high when people are left to complete them in their own time. Therefore, if you can allow time during a session for your learners to complete them, you should receive a higher response rate.

You might decide to use a mixture of open and closed questions. Open questions always require a full response and give you *qualitative* data to work with, i.e. quality feedback. Closed questions obtain only a yes or no answer and give you *quantitative* data, i.e. you can add up the quantity (number) of responses. If you use a closed question, follow this up with an open question to enable you to obtain further quality information. It might take longer for you to read and analyse, but you will have something more substantial to help with the evaluation process.

Example

1. **Did the programme fulfil your expectations? Yes/No**

   How did/didn't it achieve this?

2. **Were the delivery approaches and resources appropriate? Yes/No**

   Why was this?

3. **Was the venue suitable? Yes/No**

   What did/didn't you like about it?

4. **Did you enjoy your learning experience? Yes/No**

   What did/didn't you like?

There are many ways of writing questions to gain different types of responses. A closed question could be followed by a response scale of 1-5 for learners to circle.

(1 being no or low, 5 being yes or high); for example:

Did the programme fulfil your expectations?   1   2   3   4   5

The tendency might be to choose number 3 as it is in the middle. Removing one number makes the response more definitive one way or the other; for example:

Did the programme fulfil your expectations?   1   2   3   4

Instead of numbers, you could use smiley faces for learners to circle. For example:

Did the programme fulfil your expectations?   ☹   ☺   ☺

Having fewer options should help to gain a more realistic response. Whatever you decide to ask, make sure you keep your questions simple: don't ask two questions in one sentence or use complicated jargon, allow space for written responses and thank your learners for their contributions. Always analyse the responses and inform your learners how their contributions have led to changes and improvements.

Evaluation and feedback can contribute to your organisation's quality assurance cycle by helping improve the service given to learners and the product they hope to achieve.

Extension Activity

Design a short questionnaire or online survey that you could use with your own learners. Consider what information you would like to know and why, and then devise your questions carefully. You could use a free online program such as Survey Monkey® at www.surveymonkey.com

If possible, use it with your learners, analyse the responses and write a short report as to what changes you would make as a result. If possible, implement the changes.

Reviewing own progress and using learning journals

Reviewing your progress will help you learn about yourself and what you could improve. For example, how you react to different situations or learners, how patient you are and what skills you may need to develop. You might also decide you need further training to improve your subject knowledge and/or English and maths skills.

Self-evaluation should take place after each session you deliver, or any significant incident that occurs, to enable you to consider what went well and what could be improved. For example, you could ask yourself if you used eye contact with each learner and addressed everyone by name at some point during the session. If your answer is *no* then next time ensure that you do. Another question to ask yourself is *How do I know that learning has taken place?* If you can't answer this, you will need to make some changes to your delivery and assessment approaches.

You could use the following checklist (or adapt it to suit your own circumstances) after each session you deliver to help the self-evaluation process.

Did I?

☐ ensure I was well prepared prior to the session

☐ introduce myself and create a rapport with the learners

☐ state the topic aim and objectives of the session

☐ use equipment/resources/handouts appropriately

☐ communicate clearly (verbally and non-verbally)

☐ act confidently and professionally

☐ ask open questions to check knowledge

☐ involve and include everyone during the session

☐ demonstrate subject knowledge

☐ use a variety of teaching, learning and assessment approaches

☐ take into account: health and safety, equality and diversity, individual needs

☐ assess that learning took place

☐ summarise the session and refer to the topic aim and objectives

☐ link to the next session (if applicable)

☐ tidy the area afterwards

Reflection

Reflection is a way of reviewing your own progress, which is often just your thoughts which can be positive or negative, but can also take into account any feedback you have received. It is useful to keep a learning journal or diary to note anything important; you can then refer to this when planning your future development or preparing your sessions.

Reflection is about becoming more self-aware, which should give you increased confidence and improve the links between the theory and practice of teaching, learning and assessment.

A straightforward method of reflection is to have the *experience*, then *describe* it, *analyse* it and *revise* it (EDAR). This method incorporates the *who, what, when, where, why* and *how* approach (WWWWWH) and should help you consider ways of changing and/or improving.

Experience ⟶ Describe ⟶ Analyse ⟶ Revise

EDAR

- *Experience* – a significant event or incident you would like to change or improve
- *Describe* – aspects such as *who* was involved, *what* happened, *when* it happened and *where* it happened
- *Analyse* – consider the experience deeper and ask yourself *how* it happened and *why* it happened
- *Revise* – think about how you would do it differently if it happened again and then try this out if you have the opportunity

See Table 7.1 for an example of a completed learning journal based on EDAR.

Table 7.1 Example completed learning journal

Learning Journal	
Name: Devra Cohen	Date: 20th October
Experience significant event or incident	Last night was the first session with a new group and I felt it didn't go well. I focused too much on what I wanted to do and too little on how and what the group wanted to learn. Some of the learners stayed behind to ask a lot of questions that I thought I had addressed in the session, a few said they were confused and thought the programme would not meet their expectations.
Describe who, what, when, where	There were 16 learners aged 29 to 65 attending an evening class (Accountancy for Beginners) from 6–9 p.m. The session took place in a classroom with a broken data projector, windows that wouldn't open and not enough chairs.
Analyse why, how (i.e. the impact on learning)	I should have arrived earlier to check that the data projector was working properly, as this delayed the session by 10 minutes. I had to move some chairs from the room across the corridor and leave the door wedged open to let fresh air in. Had I sorted this out prior to the learners arriving, they would not have known of the problems. The class would then have started promptly and I would not have been flustered. I had too much administrative work to get through, the learners had to fill in an enrolment form, I needed to carry out an initial assessment of their prior learning, and ascertain if anyone had any particular needs. I also wanted them to complete a learning preference questionnaire but there wasn't enough time. I had a list of things I wanted to get through, including agreeing the ground rules but I forgot to do these as I was rushing things. As a result I felt I looked very unprofessional. The icebreaker went well but was a bit hurried due to the late start. I had an induction checklist which kept me focused, but it was 7.30 p.m. before I realised the learners needed a break. By this time, some of them were not paying attention to me but talking to others. I felt not a lot of learning took place as I was focusing too much on the administration and programme requirements.
Revise changes and/or improvements required	I have realised the first session is not about me and the paperwork I need to complete, but about what the learners want to know and learn about the subject. I will arrive earlier to ensure there are enough chairs and that the data projector is working. I will apologise at the beginning of next week's session and I will ask what the learners' expectations are and explain how I can meet them. We will set the ground rules next week. In future, I will interview all learners in advance and ask them to complete the enrolment form, learning preference questionnaire and complete an initial assessment prior to the first session. This will help me ascertain all the information I need to help plan my first session, and make it go more smoothly. It will also ensure the learners are on the right programme. I have reported the windows to the caretaker. I will allow extra time in my session plan to account for questions and answers, and ensure the focus is upon their learning rather than my teaching.

Self-reflection should become a part of your everyday activities, enabling you to ana-lyse and focus on things in greater detail. All reflection should lead to an improvement in practice; however, there may be events you would not want to change or improve as you felt they went well. If this is the case, reflect as to why they went well and use these methods in future sessions. If you are not able to write a reflective learning jour-nal, mentally run through the EDAR points in your head when you have time. As you become more experienced at reflective practice, you will see how you can improve and develop further.

There are various theories regarding reflection. Schön (1983) suggests two methods:

- reflection in action

- reflection on action

Reflection in action happens at the time of the incident, is often unconscious, is proactive and allows immediate changes to take place.

Example

Sangita was teaching a group of adults attending college as part of a day-release Business Studies programme. She had underestimated how fast they would learn as they were getting through the day's activities much more quickly than she had originally planned. At break time, she obtained some extra, more challenging activities, which she then used with the group. This enabled her to reflect immediately, ensuring the session was effective and meeting the learners' needs. Sangita therefore carried out reflection in action.

Reflection on action takes place after the incident, is a more conscious process and is reactive. This allows you time to think about the incident, consider a different approach, or to talk to others about it before making changes. However, it might not allow you to deal with a situation as it occurs.

Brookfield (1995) identified the importance of being critical when reflecting. He advocated four points of view when looking at your practice which he called *critical lenses*. These lenses are from the point of view of: the teacher, the learner, colleagues, theories and literature.

Using these points makes the reflection critical, by first looking at it from your own point of view; second, how your learner perceived your actions and what they liked and disliked; third, the view from colleagues, for example, your mentor is taken into consideration. This enables you to have a critical conversation about your actions which might highlight things you hadn't considered. Fourth, you should link your reflections to theories and literature, comparing your own ideas with others.

The process of self-reflection and your own further development should help improve the quality of your delivery to your learners.

Reflect upon the next session you either attend or deliver. Evaluate how the session went, what was good about it, and how you reacted to situations. If you have delivered a session, use the EDAR points to help you evaluate what went well, and what didn't. Identify areas for improvement and/or development.

Continuing professional development

Continuing professional development (CPD) can be anything that you do that helps you improve your practice. It shows you are a committed professional and it should help improve your skills, knowledge and understanding. CPD should relate to your job role as well as your specialist subject. You should reflect on the activities you carry out so that they have a positive impact upon your development and role. There are constant changes in education; therefore it is crucial to keep up to date and embrace them. Examples include changes to the qualifications you will deliver, changes to policies and practices within your organisation, regulatory requirements and government initiatives.

Your organisation might have a strategy for CPD which will prioritise activities they consider are important to improving standards, and may or may not provide any funding for them. However, you can partake in lots of activities outside of your organisation, which cost very little, such as researching websites, reading journals and text books. CPD can be informal or formal, planned well in advance or be opportunistic, but should have a real impact upon your teaching role, leading to an improvement in practice.

The Institute for Learning (IfL), the professional body for teachers, trainers and tutors in the Educational and Skills Sector states:

> *CPD, in relation to a teacher, means continuing professional development, which is any activity undertaken for the purposes of updating knowledge of the subject taught and developing teaching skills.*

(IfL, 2007, page 2)

Opportunities for professional development include:

- attending events and training programmes
- attending meetings
- e-learning and online activities
- evaluating feedback from peers, learners and others
- formally reflecting on experiences and documenting how it has improved practice
- improving own skills such as English and maths
- researching developments or changes to your subject and/or relevant legislation
- secondments
- self-reflection
- shadowing colleagues
- standardisation activities
- studying for relevant qualifications
- subscribing to and reading relevant journals and websites

- membership of professional associations or committees
- observing colleagues
- reading text books
- visiting other organisations
- voluntary work
- work experience placements
- writing or reviewing books and articles

To help you improve and develop, all CPD activities should be reflected upon and documented in some way. This can be via your organisation's systems, or your own manual or electronic records. Using a document such as that in Table 7.2 would be a helpful way of documenting your CPD activities. You can give each activity a reference number to link it to any supporting information. The amount of detail you need to write will differ depending upon your organisation's requirements. Maintaining your CPD will ensure you are not only competent at your job role, but also up to date with the latest developments regarding your specialist subject and teaching, learning and assessment approaches.

Table 7.2 Example CPD record

Continuing professional development record					
Name: Marie Brown			Organisation: Excellence Training Centre		
Date	Activity & venue	Duration	Justification towards role and subject specialism	Further training needs	Ref no
11 May	Attendance at standardisation event. We discussed how we interpreted the requirements of unit 301, how we each delivered and assessed it and then we re-assessed each other's decisions.	3 hrs	Standardised training and assessment practice to ensure I am assessing unit 301 in the same way as the other assessors.	Unit 302 to be reviewed at the next meeting	1
23 June	Attendance at a First Aid training day at the local community hall.	6 hrs	To ensure I am current with First Aid in case someone has an accident.	-	2
20 July	Attendance at staff training event. We were able to get together and discuss the documents and records we use as these have recently been updated. We were also given updates regarding policies and procedures.	3 hrs	This ensured I am up to date with documents and procedures regarding my practice.	-	3

The following websites are useful to gain up-to-date information regarding developments in the Further Education and Skills Sector. Most of them allow you to register for electronic updates.

- Department for Business, Innovation and Skills – www.bis.gov.uk

- Department for Education – www.education.gov.uk

- Equality and Diversity Forum – www.edf.org.uk

- Government updates: Education and Learning – www.direct.gov.uk/en/EducationAnd Learning/index.htm

- Institute for Learning – www.ifl.ac.uk

- National Institute of Adult Continuing Education – www.niace.org.uk

- Ofqual – www.ofqual.gov.uk

- Ofsted – www.ofsted.gov.uk

- Post Compulsory Education and Training – www.pcet.net

- Times Educational Supplement Online – www.tes.co.uk

You could join free social network sites such as *LinkedIn,* which is a professional networking site, at www.linkedin.co.uk. Here you will find groups you can join specifically aimed at your specialist subject. You can post questions and answers and join in regular topics which are discussed.

Extension Activity

Thinking about the subject you wish to deliver, what do you need to do to ensure you are up to date and current with your skills, knowledge and understanding? Access the websites listed above and subscribe to any electronic updates. Search for other appropriate information such as that available on the awarding organisation's website if you are assessing a qualification.

Using a checklist for teaching, learning and assessment

To help you review your practice and evaluate your role, you could use the following checklist which is based on the teaching, learning and assessment cycle. The checklist is very comprehensive to take into account all the different roles you might perform, and the different environments within which you might teach or train. If you wish, you could devise a shortened version based upon your own requirements. Don't forget that quality assurance should take place throughout.

Identifying needs

Do I…?

☐ Know who I will be teaching, i.e. details of all learners and any specific requirements or needs

☐ Know anything about the learners that might affect my teaching or their learning

☐ Need to carry out an initial or diagnostic assessment with learners

☐ Need to use a learning preference questionnaire with learners

☐ Need to agree an action plan or individual learning plan with learners

☐ Need to learn anything myself before I can teach the subject

☐ Know the organisational policies such as health and safety, equality and diversity, safeguarding

☐ Need to carry out any risk assessments or necessary equipment checks

Planning learning

Do I…?

☐ Need to obtain the qualification handbook

☐ Have an induction checklist of points to discuss with learners

☐ Need to create a scheme of work which shows a logical progression of learning

☐ Need to create a session plan

☐ Have a clear topic aim and SMART objectives

☐ Know when and where I will be teaching, to how many and for how long

☐ Need to prepare the learning environment

☐ Need a clock or watch to keep track of time

☐ Need to reserve or obtain any specialist equipment or resources

☐ Have the opportunity to use technology within the session, for teaching, learning and assessment

☐ Need to know any organisational procedures such as accidents, appeals

☐ Need to find out where facilities are such as refreshment venues, toilets, smoking areas, fire assembly points

☐ Need to arrange refreshments, transport or parking

☐ Need to send out any pre-programme information and/or inform reception staff where to direct learners

☐ Need to devise suitable learning activities, resources and assessments and get these photocopied or uploaded to an online site for electronic access

☐ Need to check spelling, grammar and punctuation of presentations and handouts

☐ Have a contingency plan in case anything goes wrong

☐ Have extra activities if learners and/or the session finishes earlier than planned

Facilitating learning

Can I…?

☐ Ensure the environment is suitable, e.g. heating, lighting, ventilation, seating arrangements and access

☐ Arrive early to set up and check equipment, obtain resources, etc.

☐ Complete any necessary administrative requirements, e.g. register/record of attendance

☐ Introduce the session aim and objectives

☐ Recap the previous session (if applicable)

☐ Use an icebreaker, energiser or starter activity

☐ Negotiate ground rules

☐ Stipulate the times of breaks

☐ Check the prior skills, knowledge and understanding of learners regarding the current topic

☐ Use a variety of teaching and learning approaches, activities and resources to include, involve and differentiate for all learners, taking into account equality and diversity

☐ Manage behaviour and disruption as it occurs

☐ Manage situations which might impact on learning, such as noise

☐ Keep learners interested and suitably challenged and motivated

☐ Take any additional learner needs into consideration and support learners as necessary

☐ Remember to use learners' names

☐ Recap points regularly

☐ Link topics to the topic aim as well as to practical situations (i.e. theory to practice)

☐ Integrate appropriate use of information and communication technology

☐ Use formative assessment activities and give constructive feedback

☐ Ask open questions (ones beginning with *who, what, when, where, why* and *how*)

☐ Use an extension activity for learners who finish tasks earlier than others, or need stretching and challenging further

☐ Allow time for learners' questions

☐ Summarise the session and recap the topic aims and objectives

☐ Link to the next session (if applicable)

☐ Leave the venue tidy

☐ Maintain all relevant records

Assessing learning

Can I...?

☐ Devise formative assessment activities to take place during sessions

☐ Obtain summative assessment activities from the awarding organisation (if applicable)

☐ Ensure the validity and reliability of all assessment activities and decisions

☐ Ask open questions

☐ Assess learners on an individual basis

☐ Differentiate assessment activities to meet any particular learner needs

☐ Give feedback to learners on an individual basis in a constructive manner

☐ Review learner progress, e.g. through tutorial reviews and discussions

☐ Keep records of individual progress and feedback given

☐ Track progress of all assessment grades and dates of achievement

☐ Communicate with others, e.g. the internal quality assurer (if required)

Evaluating learning

Did I...?

☐ Deliver a beginning, middle and end to the session

☐ Follow the timings on the session plan, if not, what would I change and why

☐ Have a structured and logical approach

☐ Establish and maintain a rapport, putting learners at ease

☐ Engage and motivate learners

☐ Project energy, enthusiasm and passion for the subject

☐ Remain in control and deal with any difficult or unexpected situations appropriately

☐ Appear confident and professional with a positive and helpful attitude

☐ Speak clearly and confidently

☐ Leave personal problems behind and act professionally at all times

☐ Use eye contact with all learners

☐ Fidget or fiddle with anything, if so, how can I stop

☐ Listen actively

☐ Dress and act appropriately

☐ Answer questions

☐ Recap key points regularly

☐ Use appropriate body language and non-verbal communication

☐ Limit the use of jargon or acronyms

☐ Use a variety of teaching, learning and assessment approaches

☐ Differentiate for different learners' needs and abilities

☐ Achieve the planned topic aim, enabling the learners to achieve their objectives

☐ Provide opportunities for learner feedback

☐ Enjoy the session, if not, why not

☐ Follow all regulations and codes of practice

☐ Reflect on the session content, along with the teaching, learning and assessment process to make improvements for the future

Summary

In this chapter you have learnt about:

- *evaluation in education and training*

- *obtaining and responding to feedback*

- *reviewing own progress and using learning journals*

- *continuing professional development*

- *using a checklist for teaching, learning and assessment*

Cross-referencing grid

This chapter contributes towards the following assessment criteria of the units which form the Award in Education and Training, along with aspects of the Professional Teaching Standards. Full details of the learning outcomes and assessment criteria of each unit can be found in the appendices.

Award units	Assessment criteria
Roles, responsibilities and relationships in education and training	
Understanding and using inclusive approaches in education and training	3.2 5.1, 5.2
Understanding assessment in education and training	

(Continued)

(Continued)

Learning and Development units	Assessment criteria
Facilitate learning and development for individuals	4.1
Facilitate learning and development in groups	4.1
Understanding the principles and practices of assessment	7.2 8.4
Domain	**Professional Teaching Standards**
A	AS4, AS7, AK4.2, AK4.3, AK7.3, AP4.2, AP4.3, AP7.3
B	BS2, BK2.6, BP2.6, BP2.7
C	CSI, CS3, CS4, CK1.1, CK3.4, CK4.1, CPU, CP3.3, CP3.4, CP4.1
D	DS3, DK3.1, DK3.2, DP2.1, DP3.2
E	ES4, EK4.2, EK5.1.EP4.2.EP5.1
F	FS3, FP3.1

Theory focus

References and further information

Brookfield, SD (1995) *Becoming a Critically Reflective Teacher.* San Francisco, CA: Jossey Bass.

Gravells, A (2013) *Passing Assessments for the Award in Education and Training.* London: Learning Matters.

Institute for Learning (2007) *Guidelines for your Continuing Professional Development (CPD).* London: IfL.

Roffey-Barentsen, J and Malthouse, R (2013) *Reflective Practice in Education and Training* (2nd Edn). London: Learning Matters.

Scales, P, Pickering, J, Senior, L, Headley, K, Garner, P and Boulton, H (2011) *Continuing Professional Development in the Lifelong Learning Sector.* Maidenhead: Open University Press.

Schön, D (1983) *The Reflective Practitioner.* London: Temple Smith.

Wood, J and Dickinson, J (2011) *Quality Assurance and Evaluation in the Lifelong Learning Sector.* Exeter: Learning Matters.

Websites

English and Maths online learning – www.move-on.org.uk

Institute for Learning (IfL) – www.ifl.ac.uk

Institute for Learning: CPD – www.ifl.ac.uk/cpd

LinkedIn – www.linkedin.co.uk

Online free survey program – www.surveymonkey.com

In this chapter you will learn about:

- the micro-teach session
- planning to deliver your session
- facilitating your session
- assessing learning
- evaluating your session

This chapter will assist you in preparation for your micro-teach session. At the end of each chapter section is an activity to help you to put theory into practice. Guidance is given for pre-service and in-service sessions. A more detailed version of this chapter, which includes a sample session plan and a micro-teaching checklist, appears in Gravells (2013) *Passing Assessments for the Award in Education and Training*.

A list of useful references, further information and website links can be found at the end in case you would like to research the topics further.

At the end of the chapter is a cross-referencing grid showing how the chapter's contents relate towards the units of the Award in Education and Training and the Professional Teaching Standards.

The micro-teach session

To achieve the Award you need to demonstrate your skills, knowledge and understanding as a teacher or trainer. You are therefore required to facilitate a short session with learners, known as a micro-teach session and then evaluate your practice. This might be either to your peers if you are pre-service or to your current learners if you are in-service. This gives you the opportunity to put theory into practice, and will usually be for a minimum of 15 or 30 minutes delivery. You will also need to partake in your peers' micro-teach sessions by being one of their learners and/or observing how they facilitate their session. The date, time and place will be agreed in advance and you will be assessed by an observer who will make notes and/or use an observation checklist. You may find it useful to see the checklist in advance as it will help you know what they are looking for. Your observer might make a visual recording of your session which you can view afterwards to help you evaluate how you performed. This will enable you to see things you were not aware of: for example, saying *erm,* using a lot of hand gestures, or not using enough eye contact with your learners. You should be told in advance if you are going to be visually recorded; try not to be put off by it, but embrace it as a way of developing yourself further.

The micro-teach session is a learning experience for you and a chance to put all your new found knowledge into practice. You may feel nervous which is quite normal. However, try to imagine you are acting a role and this should help boost your confidence and calm your nerves. You are the teacher in this situation; you need to be in control and not let any personal issues affect you. If you are organised and have checked the room and equipment in advance, hopefully you won't encounter any problems. Try to relax, but stay focused and above all enjoy yourself. As you will have prepared your session carefully, your delivery should follow logically through the introduction, development and summary stages.

Deciding what to deliver

You might be required to deliver the subject you wish to teach; or, you might be able to deliver anything you wish such as a hobby or something that interests you. It might be an academic topic such as identifying key dates in history, a vocational topic such as creating a hairstyle, or something else such as folding napkins, icing cup cakes, or creating a hanging basket. Whatever subject you choose to deliver, you will need to carefully plan what you will be doing, what your learners will be doing and how long the activities will take. You will also need to assess that learning has taken place.

If you are unsure about what to deliver, have a chat in advance with your observer. They might be able to help you with some ideas to get you thinking about a suitable subject. Table 8.1 lists some topics that people have used for their micro-teach session in the past. Looking at the list might give you some ideas.

Table 8.1 Some topics used in the past for micro-teach sessions

Aromatherapy	Creating a hanging basket	Interpreting road signs
Astrology	Creative writing	Kite making
Astronomy	Dog grooming	Manual handling
Backgammon	Drawing a portrait	Map reading
Ballroom dancing	Fire prevention	Origami
Bandaging	First aid	Poetry
Basic dance moves	Folding napkins	Reflexology
Basket weaving	Food hygiene	Salsa dancing
Bird watching	Hand massage	Using a digital camera
Calligraphy	Historical key dates	Using search engines
Control and restraint	How to eat healthily	Wine tasting
Creating a hairstyle	Icing cup cakes	Zumba dancing

To help you prepare for your session, you might find it useful to ask your observer the following questions:

- How long will my session be?

- When and where will it take place?

- Who will observe me and will they make a visual recording?

- Will you need to see my session plan in advance?

- What if I change my mind about what I'm going to deliver?

- How should I dress?

- What equipment and resources are available to me?

- How many people will I be delivering to?

- Do I need to know their learning preferences or any individual needs?

- Can I find out in advance what prior knowledge and/or experience my learners have of my subject?

- Can I show a video clip? If so, how long can it be?

- What will I need to bring with me, e.g. board markers, clock, paper?

- Can I arrive early to set up the area, e.g. move tables, check resources and equipment?

- Will I have internet access?

- If I use a presentation, should I e-mail it to you or bring it on a memory stick?

- Is there somewhere I can get handouts photocopied in advance?

- Should I start with an icebreaker and ground rules?

- What kind of assessment activity should I use?

- How will I receive feedback afterwards?

Pre-service micro-teach session

As a pre-service teacher or trainer you will usually be delivering to a group of your peers who will become your learners for the micro-teach session. This might be the first time you have taught a group of people and your peers will probably be very encouraging and supportive. If you have chosen to deliver a subject you know well, your knowledge should help your confidence. You will probably be in the same environment you have been learning in, or a central meeting point if you have been studying through a distance learning programme. Hopefully you will have met your peers previously and feel comfortable with them; if not, it would be useful to talk to them beforehand to help everyone relax. If you are due to deliver after someone else, you will probably be thinking about your own micro-teach session rather than focusing upon theirs. Try not to do this as it may make you more nervous. Being well prepared and having self-confidence and knowledge of your subject should help alleviate any worries.

In-service teaching session

If you are currently employed as a teacher or trainer, you will be classed as in-service, and might be able to deliver a session to your own learners in your usual environment.

As you already have some experience of teaching or training, delivering a session to your own learners should be fairly straightforward. Your session might last longer than the time your observer will be present; they might therefore miss the beginning or ending and arrive part way through. You should try to plan the session to allow time to talk to your observer either before or after. This will enable you to discuss your delivery, justify any aspects they have missed and to receive feedback. You may want to introduce the observer to your learners and state they are observing you, not them. Having a stranger in the room might lead to some behaviour issues. If so, you must deal with these as soon as they arise and act professionally at all times.

If you are in-service, it is possible to take one of the units from the Learning and Development qualification:

- Facilitate learning and development for individuals OR

- Facilitate learning and development in groups

instead of the Award in Education and Training unit which relates to micro-teaching called *Understanding and using inclusive approaches in education and training*. Therefore, if you are taking either of the above two units, you must be observed with your own learners and meet all the assessment criteria of the unit.

Activity

Think of a suitable topic you would like to deliver for your micro-teach session. Ensure it is something that also enables you to assess that learning has taken place. Look at the previous bulleted list and ask your observer any of the questions that are relevant to you, or any other questions you think of.

Planning to deliver your session

Once you know which subject you will deliver, you will need to create a plan which should have a clear *aim* (what you want your learners to achieve), which is then broken down into *objectives* (how your learners will achieve your aim). Your plan should show what you expect your learners to achieve expressed in a way that will enable you to determine that learning has taken place. For example, your learners might *explain*, and/or *demonstrate* something. Your observer will probably want to see your plan well in advance to give you advice and support. See Chapter 4 for guidance regarding planning sessions and examples of objectives you could use. Knowing whether you are delivering a practical session, i.e. skills, or a theory session, i.e. knowledge and understanding, will help you choose appropriate objectives at the right level for your learners.

Your session should have a beginning (the introduction), a middle section (the development) and an ending (the summary/conclusion) which should show a logical progression of learning and assessment. Timings should be allocated to each of the teaching, learning and assessment activities you plan to use in each section. You should not be speaking for the majority of the session. Your learners should be active not passive.

Once you have your plan, you will need to prepare all the activities, handouts, resources, presentations and assessment activities you intend to use. You may need to learn how to use something in advance; for example, if you wish to use a computerised presentation during your session or link to the internet via an interactive whiteboard. You should check all presentations and handouts for spelling, grammar and punctuation errors, and ensure text and pictures positively represent all aspects of equality and diversity. If you are delivering a 30-minute session and you plan to show a video for 10 minutes, this will not demonstrate how teaching and learning is taking place. Videos are good for visual learners but, if used, keep them short or you may lose the attention of other learners.

Carry out a trial run with friends or family to check your timings. You might find that what you planned to cover in 30 minutes takes only 20. Time will go quickly during your micro-teach session, particularly if you are asked lots of questions. Make sure you have all the necessary equipment, resources and stationery. A clock or a watch in a visible place will help you keep track of time. Try to have a contingency plan in case anything goes wrong; for example, a hard copy of an electronic presentation.

If possible, check in advance and/or arrive early to see that everything is available and working in the room you will be in. You may want to rearrange the area beforehand to suit your subject and to enable everyone to see and hear you. You might find your peers are willing to help with this. Time for setting up and clearing away afterwards should be outside of your observed time. You may need two copies of your plan, one for yourself and one for your observer.

Activity

Obtain the document you are required to use for your micro-teach session – often called a session plan or teaching and learning plan. Complete it with the relevant information and allocate timings to each of the activities, for example, two minutes for the introduction, five minutes for a group activity. This will help ensure you can cover everything within the allocated time. It's useful to have an additional activity you can use if you have spare time, or know what you can cut down on or remove if you run out of time.

Facilitating your session

You should be able to facilitate your session logically through the introduction, development and summary/conclusion sections.

Introduction

Before you speak, take a few deep breaths, smile at your learners and use eye contact with everyone; this should help you to relax. You can then introduce yourself by saying *Hello, my name is ...,* followed by your topic aim and objectives. You might like to keep these on display throughout your session, perhaps on a piece of flipchart paper on the wall or as a handout. Don't tell your learners if you are nervous as it probably won't show. Be aware of your posture, speak a little more loudly and slowly than normal as being anxious or nervous may make you speak softly or quickly. If you feel you are shaking, it is highly likely no one will notice. If your mind suddenly goes blank, take a couple of deep breaths for a few seconds and look at your plan to help you refocus; it might seem a long time to you but it won't to your learners. You will need to establish a rapport with your learners and engage and interact with them from the start. Asking the question *What experience, if any, do you have?* is a good way of involving your learners in your subject from the start and helps you check any prior learning. Make sure you communicate effectively with everyone and ensure you can meet any individual needs.

Keep your plan handy as a prompt. If you feel you might forget something, use a highlight pen beforehand to mark key words which you can quickly look at. Standing rather than sitting might help your confidence and voice projection. Keep things simple, don't complicate things or try to deliver too much too quickly. Conversely, don't expect too much from your learners, as your subject may be very new to them. If this is the first time you have met your learners, you might want to carry out a short icebreaker with them or ask them to introduce themselves to you if you have time. If your peer group know each other, they will be familiar with each other, the ground rules and other requirements such as fire drills. You might like to encourage your learners to ask questions if they need to clarify any points at any time.

Development

You should develop your session by using a variety of teaching and learning approaches to reach all learning preferences and to keep your learners motivated. Summarise and recap regularly to reinforce your points. Assessment should take place at key points, for example, ask open questions to check knowledge (ones that begin with *who, what, when, where, why* and *how*). Try to use names when talking to your learners and if possible address everyone in the group; don't just focus on a particular learner who you know can give you the correct answers. Having your learners' names written down in advance will help. Try to use the PPP (Pose, Pause, Pick) method when asking questions. If you have a small group, you could plan to ask one open question to each learner.

The timing of activities needs to be followed carefully; if you are only delivering a 15-minute session you may not have time for group activities. If you do set activities, think what you will be doing while your learners are working, i.e. moving around them and observing or asking questions shows you are in control. Longer sessions benefit from a mixture of teaching and learning approaches and different assessment activities. If you have delivered a practical task, you will need to observe that your learners have the skill to demonstrate what you have taught, and have the required understanding to explain why they are doing it that way.

Summary/conclusion

You need to summarise or conclude your session in a succinct way and relate it back to your topic aim and objectives. If you have time, you can summarise learning with a short quiz or multiple-choice test which is a good way to check knowledge and understanding. You might like to ask your learners if they have any questions. However, you may be met with silence, or they might have lots of questions which will then impact upon your time. If you find you have covered everything and have spare time, you could ask each member of the group to state one significant thing they feel they have learnt from the session. This is a good way of filling in spare time if necessary, and shows you what each individual learner has learnt. You could issue a handout which summarises your session and which could be given out at the end. If you issue it during the session your learners may look at it and not focus on you.

If you are unsure of how to end your session, simply say *Thank you, I've enjoyed my session with you today* this will indicate to your group you have finished. Make sure you tidy the area afterwards.

Activity

Rehearse your micro-teach session to a few trusted people. Make sure you have your plan and all relevant resources to hand. Although this is a role-play activity, treat it seriously and work through all your planned teaching, learning and assessment activities. Afterwards, ask for feedback as to what you could do differently. You might have to revise your timings or redesign some resources as a result.

Assessing learning

At some point during your micro-teach session, you will need to assess that learning has taken place by each learner. You will probably not be using formal assessment activities, as your learners might not be taking a qualification (unless you are an in-service teacher with your own learners). You therefore need to use informal assessment activities to ensure learning has been successful. The following are some informal assessment activities you could use with your learners depending upon the level of learning:

- completing gapped handouts or word searches
- discussions in pairs or groups
- group tasks
- questions – written or oral
- multiple-choice questions
- observation of a practical task
- puzzles
- quizzes
- role plays

You might assess as you progress through your session by asking questions, for example using the PPP technique. If you are using this technique, make sure you have a different question for everyone in the group. If you have demonstrated a practical topic, make sure everyone has the opportunity to have a go and that you can observe them doing it. You could use a gapped handout and issue this at an appropriate time. A gapped handout is a page of text with missing words which the learners have to complete. Quizzes, puzzles and word searches can be fun and be completed individually, in pairs or groups. However, you need to assess what each individual has achieved.

Once you have assessed that learning has taken place, you need to give feedback to your learners in a constructive way. If you don't, they won't know if they have been successful or not. Don't forget that assessment should not be in isolation from teaching and learning.

Please see Chapter 6 for more information regarding assessing learning and giving feedback.

Activity

Design an activity that you could use to assess your learners during your micro-teach session; for example, a quiz, a multiple-choice test, a task learners are to demonstrate, or some open questions.

Evaluating your session

Evaluating your delivery is an important aspect of your own learning and development and you may need to complete a self-evaluation form to formalise this. You might think you have done really well, but you might have received some helpful advice during the feedback process which could help you improve further.

After your session you may find that your observer will ask you how you felt it went before giving you feedback. This will enable you to consider what went well and what you could have done differently. You should receive oral feedback along with written feedback such as a completed observation checklist. You should also receive constructive feedback from your peers, which can be used to inform your self-evaluation process. Once you have finished your micro-teach session, you might be so relieved or busy packing away that you don't fully take on board what is being said to you. Listen carefully and ask questions to clarify any points you are unsure of. Try not to interrupt or become defensive when receiving feedback and don't take anything personally as the feedback will be given to help you improve. When evaluating yourself, consider your strengths, areas for development and any action and improvements required from a teaching and training perspective as well as a subject perspective.

Hopefully, you enjoyed your micro-teach session and it has confirmed you do want to have a career as a teacher or trainer. However, the experience might have made you think that it just isn't for you at this point in time. Conversely, it might make you more determined to improve and develop further.

Activity

After you have delivered your role-play micro-teach and received feedback, identify areas for improvement. Did you achieve your aim effectively? Did your learners achieve the objectives? Consider what you would change or modify for your actual micro-teach session.

Summary

In this chapter you have learnt about:

- *deciding what to deliver*
- *planning to deliver your session*
- *facilitating your session*
- *assessing learning*
- *evaluating your session*

Cross-referencing grid

This chapter contributes towards the following assessment criteria of the units which form the Award in Education and Training, along with aspects of the Professional Teaching Standards. Full details of the learning outcomes and assessment criteria of each unit can be found in the appendices.

Award units	Assessment criteria
Roles, responsibilities and relationships in education and training	1.3, 1.4 2.1, 2.2
Understanding and using inclusive learning approaches in education and training	1.1, 1.2, 1.3 2.1, 2.2, 2.3, 2.4 3.1, 3.2 4.1, 4.2, 4.3 5.1. 5.2
Understanding assessment in education and training	1.2, 1.4 2.1, 2.2 3.1, 3.2, 3.3
Learning and Development units	**Assessment criteria**
Facilitate learning and development for individuals	2.1, 2.2 3.1, 3.2
Facilitate learning and development in groups	2.1, 2.2 3.1, 3.2
Understanding the principles and practices of assessment	7.2 8.4
Domain	**Professional Teaching Standards**
A	ASI, AS4, AS7, AK7.3, API.1, AP4.1, AP4.2, AP6.2, AP7.3
B	BSI, BS2, BS3, BS5, BK2.6, BK3.1, BK3.2, BK3.3, BPI.1, BPI.2, BPI.3, BP2.1, BP2.2, BP2.3, BP2.4, BP2.6, BP3.1, BP3.2, BP3.3, BP3.4, BP5.1, BP5.2

(Continued)

(Continued)

Domain	Professional Teaching Standards
C	CS2, CS4, CK1.1, CK2.1, CP2.1, CP3.1
D	DS1, DS3, DK1.1, DK1.2, DK1.3, DK2.1, DK3.1, DP1.1, DP1.2, DP1.3, DP2.1, DP3.1
E	ES1, ES2, ES4, EK1.1, EK1.2, EK1.3, EK2.3, EK4.2, EP1.1, EP1.2, EP1.3, EP2.1, EP2.2, EP2.3, EP4.1, EP4.2
F	

Theory focus

References and further information

Duckworth, V, Wood, J, Bostock, J and Dickinson, J (2010) *Successful Teaching Practice in the Lifelong Learning Sector.* Exeter: Learning Matters.

Gravells, A (2013) *Passing Assessments for the Award in Education and Training.* London: Learning Matters.

Websites

Assessment resources – www.excellencegateway.org.uk

Learning preferences questionnaire – www.vark-learn.com

Oxford Learning Institute – Giving and receiving feedback – http://tinyurl.com/688tfev

Unit title: Understanding roles, responsibilities and relationships in education and training (Award unit)
Level 3 (3 credits)

Learning outcomes The learner will:	Assessment criteria The learner can:	
1. Understand the teaching role and responsibilities in education and training	1.1	Explain own role and responsibilities in education and training
	1.2	Summarise key aspects of legislation, regulatory requirements and codes of practice relating to own role and responsibilities
	1.3	Explain ways to promote equality and value diversity
	1.4	Explain why it is important to identify and meet individual learner needs
2. Understand ways to maintain a safe and supportive learning environment	2.1	Explain ways to maintain a safe and supportive learning environment
	2.2	Explain why it is important to promote appropriate behaviour and respect for others
3. Understand the relationships between teachers and other professionals in education and training	3.1	Explain how the teaching role involves working with other professionals
	3.2	Explain the boundaries between the teaching role and other professional roles
	3.3	Describe points of referral to meet the individual needs of learners

APPENDIX 2

Unit title: Understanding and using inclusive approaches in education and training (Award unit)
Level 3 (6 credits)

Learning outcomes The learner will:	Assessment criteria The learner can:	
1. Understand inclusive teaching and learning approaches in education and training	1.1	Describe features of inclusive teaching and learning
	1.2	Compare the strengths and limitations of teaching and learning approaches used in own area of specialism in relation to meeting individual learner needs
	1.3	Explain why it is important to provide opportunities for learners to develop their English, mathematics, ICT and wider skills
2. Understand ways to create an inclusive teaching and learning environment	2.1	Explain why it is important to create an inclusive teaching and learning environment
	2.2	Explain why it is important to select teaching and learning approaches, resources and assessment methods to meet individual learner needs
	2.3	Explain ways to engage and motivate learners
	2.4	Summarise ways to establish ground rules with learners
3. Be able to plan inclusive teaching and learning	3.1	Devise an inclusive teaching and learning plan
	3.2	Justify own selection of teaching and learning approaches, resources and assessment methods in relation to meeting individual learner needs
4. Be able to deliver inclusive teaching and learning	4.1	Use teaching and learning approaches, resources and assessment methods to meet individual learner needs
	4.2	Communicate with learners in ways that meet their individual needs
	4.3	Provide constructive feedback to learners to meet their individual needs
5. Be able to evaluate the delivery of inclusive teaching and learning	5.1	Review the effectiveness of own delivery of inclusive teaching and learning
	5.2	Identify areas for improvement in own delivery of inclusive teaching and learning

Unit title: Understanding assessment in education and training (Award unit)
Level 3 (3 credits)

Learning outcomes The learner will:	Assessment criteria The learner can:	
1. Understand types and methods of assessment used in education and training	1.1	Explain the purpose of types of assessment used in education and training
	1.2	Describe characteristics of different methods of assessment in education and training
	1.3	Compare the strengths and limitations of different assessment methods in relation to meeting individual learner needs
	1.4	Explain how different assessment methods can be adapted to meet individual learner needs
2. Understand how to involve learners and others in the assessment process	2.1	Explain why it is important to involve learners and others in the assessment process
	2.2	Explain the role and use of peer and self-assessment in the assessment process
	2.3	Identify sources of information that should be made available to learners and others involved in the assessment process
3. Understand the role and use of constructive feedback in the assessment process	3.1	Describe key features of constructive feedback
	3.2	Explain how constructive feedback contributes to the assessment process
	3.3	Explain ways to give constructive feedback to learners
4. Understand requirements for keeping records of assessment in education and training	4.1	Explain the need to keep records of assessment of learning
	4.2	Summarise the requirements for keeping records of assessment in an organisation

Unit title: Facilitate learning and development for individuals (Learning and Development unit)
Level 3 (6 credits)

Learning outcomes The learner will:	Assessment criteria The learner can:	
1. Understand principles and practices of one to one learning and development	1.1	Explain purposes of one to one learning and development
	1.2	Explain factors to be considered when facilitating learning and development to meet individual needs
	1.3	Evaluate methods for facilitating learning and development to meet the needs of individuals
	1.4	Explain how to manage risks and safeguard individuals when facilitating one to one learning and development
	1.5	Explain how to overcome individual barriers to learning
	1.6	Explain how to monitor individual learner progress
	1.7	Explain how to adapt delivery to meet individual learner needs
2. Be able to facilitate one to one learning and development	2.1	Clarify facilitation methods with individuals to meet their learning and/or development objectives
	2.2	Implement activities to meet learning and/or development objectives
	2.3	Manage risks and safeguard learners participating in one to one learning and/or development
3. Be able assist individual learners in applying new knowledge and skills in practical contexts	3.1	Develop opportunities for individuals to apply their new knowledge and learning in practical contexts
	3.2	Explain benefits to individuals of applying new knowledge and skills
4. Be able to assist individual learners in reflecting on their learning and/or development	4.1	Explain benefits of self-evaluation to individuals
	4.2	Review individual responses to one to one learning and/or development
	4.3	Assist individual learners to identify their future learning and/or development needs

APPENDIX 5

Unit title: Facilitate learning and development in groups (Learning and Development unit)
Level 3 (6 credits)

Learning outcomes The learner will:	Assessment criteria The learner can:
1. Understand the principles and practices of learning and development in groups	1.1 Explain purposes of group learning and development 1.2 Explain why delivery of learning and development must reflect group dynamics 1.3 Evaluate methods for facilitating learning and development to meet the needs of groups 1.4 Explain how to manage risks and safeguard individuals when facilitating learning and development in groups 1.5 Explain how to overcome barriers to learning in groups 1.6 Explain how to monitor individual learner progress within group learning and development activities 1.7 Explain how to adapt delivery based on feedback from learners in groups
2. Be able to facilitate learning and development in groups	2.1 Clarify facilitation methods with group members to meet group and individual learning objectives 2.2 Implement learning and development activities to meet learning objectives 2.3 Manage risks to group and individual learning and development
3. Be able to assist groups to apply new knowledge and skills in practical contexts	3.1 Develop opportunities for individuals to apply new knowledge and skills in practical contexts 3.2 Provide feedback to improve the application of learning
4. Be able to assist learners to reflect on their learning and development undertaken in groups	4.1 Support self-evaluation by learners 4.2 Review individual responses to learning and development in groups 4.3 Assist learners to identify their future learning and development needs

**Unit title: Understanding the principles and practices of assessment
(Learning and Development unit)
Level 3 (3 credits)**

Learning outcomes: The learner will:	Assessment criteria: The learner can:
1. Understand the principles and requirements of assessment	1.1 Explain the function of assessment in learning and development 1.2 Define the key concepts and principles of assessment 1.3 Explain the responsibilities of the assessor 1.4 Identify the regulations and requirements relevant to the assessment in own area of practice
2. Understand different types of assessment method	2.1 Compare the strengths and limitations of a range of assessment methods with reference to the needs of individual learners
3. Understand how to plan assessment	3.1 Summarise key factors to consider when planning assessment 3.2 Evaluate the benefits of using a holistic approach to assessment 3.3 Explain how to plan a holistic approach to assessment 3.4 Summarise the types of risks that may be involved in assessment in own area of responsibility 3.5 Explain how to minimise risks through the planning process
4. Understand how to involve learners and others in assessment	4.1 Explain the importance of involving the learner and others in the assessment process 4.2 Summarise types of information that should be made available to learners and others involved in the assessment process 4.3 Explain how peer and self-assessment can be used effectively to promote learner involvement and personal responsibility in the assessment of learning 4.4 Explain how assessment arrangements can be adapted to meet the needs of individual learners

Learning outcomes: The learner will:	Assessment criteria: The learner can:
5. Understand how to make assessment decisions	5.1 Explain how to judge whether evidence is: • sufficient • authentic • current 5.2 Explain how to ensure that assessment decisions are: • made against specified criteria • valid • reliable • fair
6. Understand quality assurance of the assessment process	6.1 Evaluate the importance of quality assurance in the assessment process 6.2 Summarise quality assurance and standardisation procedures in own area of practice 6.3 Summarise the procedures to follow when there are disputes concerning assessment in own area of practice
7. Understand how to manage information relating to assessment	7.1 Explain the importance of following procedures for the management of information relating to assessment 7.2 Explain how feedback and questioning contribute to the assessment process
8. Understand the legal and good practice requirements in relation to assessment	8.1 Explain legal issues, policies and procedures relevant to assessment, including those for confidentiality, health, safety and welfare 8.2 Explain the contribution that technology can make to the assessment process 8.3 Evaluate requirements for equality and diversity and, where appropriate, bilingualism in relation to assessment 8.4 Explain the value of reflective practice and continuing professional development in the assessment process

Qualification structure for the Level 3 Award in Education and Training (12 credits)

The Award is made up of the following three units (which total 12 credits):

- Understanding, roles, responsibilities and relationships in education and training (3 credits)
- Understanding and using inclusive approaches in education and training (6 credits)
- Understanding assessment in education and training (3 credits)

However, it is possible to achieve part of the Award by taking units from the Learning and Development qualification (see the table below). These units are known as *accepted equivalents*, but they are only for those who are currently in a teaching and assessing role with learners of their own:

- Facilitate learning and development for individuals (6 credits) OR
- Facilitate learning and development in groups (6 credits)
- Understanding the principles and practices of assessment (3 credits)

If you wish to substitute any units, you will need to discuss this with the organisation you are taking the Award with, as they might only offer the three main units of the Award and not the Learning and Development units.

Group A This 3-credit unit is mandatory	**Understanding roles, responsibilities and relationships in education and training** *(3 credits Education and Training unit)*		
Group B One unit (6 credits) must be achieved from this group	**Understanding and using inclusive teaching and learning approaches in education and training** *(6 credits Education and Training unit)*	**Facilitate learning and development for individuals** *(6 credits Learning and Development unit)*	**Facilitate learning and development in groups** *(6 credits Learning and Development unit)*
Group C One unit (3 credits) must be achieved from this group	**Understanding assessment in education and training** *(3 credits Education and Training unit)*		**Understanding the principles and practices of assessment** *(3 credits Learning and Development unit)*

INDEX

A

abuse, disclosure of 138
abbreviations and acronyms xix
activist learners 41
affective learning domain 47, 48
age ranges 33–6
  14–16 year olds 34–5
  16–19 year olds 35
  adult learners 36
aims and objectives 69, 71–2
andragogy 103
arrival time 4, 28
assessing learning 3, 194
assessment 143–78
  concepts and principles of 147–9
  cycle 145–6
  decision making 174
  feedback 175–6
  formal/informal 154–5
  involving learners 170–1
  involving others 171–2
  internal/external 171
  meeting individual needs 151–2
  methods 154–69
  minimising risks 149–50
  peer 172–3
  planning for 149
  questioning techniques 155–7
  records 176–8
  reviewing progress 174–5
  role of ICT in 150–1
  roles and responsibilities of assessor 147
  self 173–4
  strengths and limitations of methods and activities
     158–69
  types 152–4
assessment criteria see learning outcomes and
     assessment criteria
assessor, roles and responsibilities of 147
asynchronous learning 37, 93
attention spans 31–2
Award in Education and Training xiv

B

barriers to learning 57, 90, 128, 130, 135, 149, 151
behaviour and respect 128–30
behavioural objectives 71

behaviourist theory of learning 46
Belbin's team roles 132, 133
blended learning 37
Bloom, B.S. 47
  levels of learning 73–5
body language 4, 125
boundaries 6–7
buddy approach 23

C

cabaret style (room layout) 25–6
checklists, using for teaching, learning and
     assessment 191–5
Children Act (2004) 15
closed questions 30, 156
Codes of Practice 17–18
Coffield, Professor Frank 41
cognitive learning domain 47, 48
communication 125–8
  non-verbal 127
  verbal 126–7
  written 127–8
conditions of learning 43–4
constructive feedback 175
contact time 69
Continuing Professional Development (CPD) 189–90
Control of Substances Hazardous to Health
     (COSHH) Regulations (2002) 17
Copyright Designs and Patents Act (1988) 15
Coverdale's task, team and individual needs 132, 134

D

Dale's cone of learning and experience 105
Data Protection Act (1998) 13, 16
diagnostic assessment 56, 153
differentiation 80–1
distance learners 37
diversity see equality and diversity
domains of learning 47
dyslexia 54, 91

E

EDAR 186–7
EDIP 136–7

energisers 99–100
engaging and motivating learners 106–8
English and maths skills 85–6
environment 21–9
  learning 23
  physical 22–3
  room layouts 25–7
  social 23
Equality Act (2010) 16, 62–4
equality and diversity 60–4
evaluating learning 4, 194–5
evaluation 181–95
  Continuing Professional Development
    (CPD) 189–90
  obtaining and responding to feedback 183–5
  reflection 186–9
  self 185–6
  using checklists 191–5
Every Child Matters 15
experiential learning cycle 44–5
eye contact 23

F

facilitating learning 3, 193
feedback 23, 46, 175–6
  obtaining and responding to 183–5
first impressions 2
'five Ws and one H' 69, 186
Fleming, N. 39
focused attention 31
Food Hygiene Regulations (2006) 17
formal assessment 154, 155
formative assessment 153
Freedom of Information Act (2000) 16
Further Education and Skills Sector xii

G

Gagne, R. 43
ground rules 23, 68, 90, 100–2
  ways to establish 101
  ways to maintain 102
groups 130–4
  Belbin's team roles 132, 133
  Coverdale's task, team and individual
    needs 132, 134
  Tuckman's group formation theory 134

H

handouts 82, 91–2
Health and Safety at Work etc Act (1974) 16, 29
health and safety considerations 28–9
Health and Safety (display screen equipment)
  Regulations (1992) 17
Hierarchy of Needs, Maslow's 32
holistic assessment 154

Honey, P. 41
Hull, R. 46–7
humanist theory of learning 45–6

I

icebreakers 23, 68, 98–100
identifying needs 3, 192
IfL Code of Professional Practice (2008) 18
inclusion 23
inclusive learning 58–60
individual learning plans (ILP) 68, 80, 170
individuals 135–6
induction 97–8
informal assessment 154–5
information, advice and guidance (IAG) 54
information and communication technology (ICT)
  89–94, 150–1
  advantages and limitations 151
  handouts and presentations 91–3
  online programmes 93–4
  role of in assessment 150–1
initial assessments 55, 81, 153
interactive whiteboard 90
internal quality assurance 4, 9–12
interpersonal skills 125

K

Knowles, M.S. 103
Kolb, D.A. 44–5

L

Laird, D. 42
learner needs 54–5
learner support 54
learner voice 183
learning environment 23
  examples of 24
learning journals 186, 187
learning locations 36–8
learning outcomes and assessment criteria 72–3
learning preferences 38–41
  Fleming (2005) 39
  Honey and Mumford (1992) 41
learning support 54
lecture style (room layout) 25
legislation 15–16
levels of learning (Bloom) 73–5
lone workers 149

M

mannerisms 4
Manual Handling Operation Regulations (1992) 17
Maslow's Hierarchy of Needs 32–3
maths skills see English and maths skills

mentors 7, 53
micro-teaching 197–204
  assessing learning 203–4
  deciding what to deliver 198
  evaluating the session 204
  facilitating the session 201–3
  in-service session 200
  planning delivery 200–1
  preparing for 199
  pre-service session 199
motivation 29–31 *see also* engaging
    and motivating learners
multiple-choice questions 157
Mumford, A. 41

N

names, using learners' 4, 23, 28, 99
needs, learners 54
  organisation 51
  teachers 53
nerves, dealing with 104
non-accredited programmes 52
non-behavioural objectives 71
non-contact time 69

O

objectives see aims and objectives
observation 157
offender learners 37–8
Ofqual 17
online programmes 93–4
open questions 30, 59, 156
organisational needs 51–3

P

pedagogy 103
peer assessment 172
peer support 23
personality 4
Peter, L.J. 46–7
Peter Principle 46–7
physical environment 22–3
  examples of 24
Pike, R.W. 38
plagiarism 156–7
planning learning 3, 192–3
points of referral 57
  examples of 58
policies and procedures 17–18
portable appliance tested (PAT) labels 23
pose, pause, pick (PPP) technique 59–60, 155
posters 82
potential needs of learners 56–7
  examples of 58
praise sandwich 176

pragmatist learners 41
presentations 92–3
progression xvii
Privacy and Electronic Communications
    (EC Directive) Regulations (2003) 17
process model of delivery 53
product model of delivery 52
professionals, working with other 7–9
Protection of Children Act (POCA) (1999) 16
psycho-motor learning domain 47, 48

Q

qualification handbook 52
qualifications and credit framework (QCF) xiv
qualitative/quantitative data 184
quality assurance 9–13
  standardisation of practice 12–13
quality control 9
questioning techniques 155–7

R

recognition of prior learning (RPL) 170
record keeping 13–15
referencing 156–7
referral, points of 57
reflection 186–9
reflector learners 41
Regulatory Reform (Fire Safety) Order (2005) 17
regulatory requirements 16–17
Reporting of Injuries, Diseases and Dangerous
    Occurrences (RIDDOR) Regulations
    (1995) 17
resources 81–5
  evaluating 84–5
  examples of 83
respect sees *behaviour* and respect
reviewing progress 174
Rogers, C.R. 45–6
roles, responsibilities and boundaries 1–7
  examples of 5–6
room layouts 25–7
  boardroom style 27
  horseshoe or U-shaped 26
  other layouts 27
  tables or desks in groups 25–6
  tables or desks in rows 25

S

safeguarding 137–9
*Safeguarding Children and Safer Recruitment
    in Education 138*
Safeguarding Vulnerable Groups Act (2006) 16, 138
safer Practice, Safer Children 138
scheme of work 68–71
  example of 70

self assessment 172
sensory theory of learning 42
session plan 68
    creating 76–80
Skinner, B.F. 46
SMART 72, 148
social environment 23
    examples of 24
specialist software 90
summative assessment 153–4
sustained attention 31
SWOT analysis 170
synchronous learning 37, 93

T

teacher and trainer needs 53
teaching and learning approaches 102–24
    Dale's cone of learning and experience 105
    engaging and motivating learners 106–8
    examples of 104, 109–24
teaching and learning plans 67–80
    aims and objectives 71–2
    approaches 102
    creating a scheme of work 68–71
    creating a session plan 76–80
    learning outcomes and assessment criteria 72–3
    levels of learning 73–5

teaching, learning and assessment cycle 3–6
theories of learning 42–7
    behaviourist 46
    conditions of learning 43–4
    domains of learning 47
    experiential 44–5
    humanist 45–6
    Peter Principle 46–7
    sensory 42
theorist learners 41
'toolkit' 53
Tuckman's group formation theory 134

V

VACSR 148
VARK 39–40
virtual learning environment (VLE) 37, 90, 150
vulnerable adult, definition of 138

W

websites, useful 191
well-being 15
wider skills 86–8
wireless remote control 90, 93
workplace learners 36–7